D0991726

"MAURETANIA"

THE "MAURETANIA" LEAVING THE TYNE.

THE

CUNARD TURBINE-DRIVEN QUADRUPLE-SCREW

ATLANTIC LINER

"MAURETANIA"

CONSTRUCTED BY

MESSRS. SWAN, HUNTER, AND WIGHAM RICHARDSON, LIMITED,

WALLSEND-ON-TYNE.

ENGINED BY

THE WALLSEND SLIPWAY AND ENGINEERING COMPANY, LIMITED,

WALLSEND-ON-TYNE.

Reprinted from "ENGINEERING."

Patrick Stephens
Wellingborough, Northamptonshire

For my mother

© New material in this edition 1987 Mark D. Warren

Originally published 1907
PSL edition first published 1987

2 4 6 8 10 9 7 5 3 1

All rights reserved. No part of this publication
may be reproduced, stored in a retrieval
system, or transmitted, in any form or
by any means, electronic, mechanical,
photocopying, recording or otherwise,
without prior permission in writing from
the publisher.

British Library Cataloguing in Publication Data

The Cunard turbine-driven quadruple-screw
Atlantic liner, Mauretania.
1. Mauretania (*Ship*)   2. Ocean liners
— Design and construction
I. Engineering
623.8'2432   VM383.M3

ISBN 0-85059-914-8

*Patrick Stephens Limited is part of the
Thorsons Publishing Group*

Reproduced from the original. Additional material
photoset in 8 on 8½pt Century Old Style by
Harper Phototypesetters Limited, Northants.

Printed in Great Britain by
Butler & Tanner Ltd, Frome and London

INTRODUCTION

⌇⌇

THIS book is primarily a fascimile reprint of a rare volume first published in November 1907, comprising a series of articles that had appeared in *Engineering** magazine, describing in great detail the construction, launching and outfitting of the Cunard express liner RMS *Mauretania*. This relatively unknown volume, along with the better known *Shipbuilder*† special issue on the *Mauretania*, contains the most comprehensive contemporary published account of the conception and construction of the ship, even though many important interior photographs in the *Engineering* book had not been included originally.

This reprint is published in celebration of the eightieth anniversary of the *Mauretania's* maiden voyage on 16 November 1907. It now features 41 additional photographs, 37 of which begin with Plate XXXIX, to supplement those in the original publication. For the benefit of the historian and the serious collector alike, great care has been taken to keep the original publication intact. It should be noted here, however, that the *Mauretania* photograph on page vi, the *Turbinia* photograph and text on page vii, the 'First Class Smoking Room' photograph on page viii, the 'Grand Entrance Seat' photograph on page xvi, as well as the blueprint plan following Plate XXXII are new additions, as the last three of these pages were blank in the original book. Minor discrepancies that may occur in the data given in the following text are due to inevitable variations in the sources.

If there was a single major event that triggered the idea of building the *Lusitania* and *Mauretania*, it was the third homeward voyage of the *Kaiser Wilhelm der Grosse* in November 1897, to which the British lost the prestigious Blue Riband. Both Norddeutscher Lloyd and Cunard had always recognized the value this honour had in luring passengers, and as a result of the publicity generated by the *Kaiser Wilhelm der Grosse*, in 1898, Norddeutscher Lloyd transported over 22 per cent of all transatlantic passengers arriving in New York, a total of 76,118 compared with 36,145 the year before. Throughout the ten years between 1897 and 1907, the North Atlantic passenger service was dominated by the Germans with the five fastest ships in the world: Norddeutscher Lloyd's *Kaiser Wilhelm der Grosse* (1897), *Kronprinz Wilhelm* (1901) and *Kaiser Wilhelm II* (1903), as well as Hamburg-Amerika Line's *Deutschland*, which held the Blue Riband from its maiden voyage in July 1900 to June 1906. The fifth ship, Norddeutscher Lloyd's *Kronprinzessin Cecilie*, entered service on 6 August 1907, and had the largest marine steam reciprocating engines ever built. With great speed and consistency these five ships, the world's first four-funnelled passenger liners, reaped enormous profits from the very lucrative immigrant trade as well as from the very rich, who could pay as much as £500 ($2,430) per crossing. By this time, speed had become essential for any successful steamship company, because the fastest ships were awarded the highly profitable government mail contracts, a factor of which Samuel Cunard was well aware when, in 1840, he established the first regular transatlantic service.

Germany and England had always been competing to build the fastest ships, but statistics also show that the Germans were Cunard's greatest threat in other ways. The number of people who immigrated to the United States in

1907 reached an all-time high of 1,717,864 and the Hamburg-Amerika Line was the world's largest, with 112 ships registering 714,732 gross tons. Norddeutscher Lloyd trailed with 65 ships registered at 502,656 gross tons, and even White Star Line's 29 ships at 374,130 gross tons topped Cunard's 12 ships registered at 201,160 gross tons.

While the British were losing the valuable immigrant business to the Germans, they were also losing control of many of their steamship companies to the American-sponsored shipping conglomerate, the International Mercantile Marine Company,* headed by J. P. Morgan and promoted with the assistance of Lord Pirrie. Even average citizens were alarmed when the White Star Line was purchased by the IMM on 1 December 1902, as it was evident that control over their own destiny was fading fast. The formation of the IMM, and the German superiority, were the main reasons for initiating plans to build the *Lusitania* and the *Mauretania*.

In order to stop this erosion of Britain's most valuable commercial resource, and at the same time restore the prestige of the British merchant marine and achieve supremacy on the Atlantic, a request was made to the Government by Cunard's Chairman, Lord Inverclyde, for a subsidy to build two high-speed express liners. Cunard was one of the last major independent British shipping firms, and the Admiralty was anxious to see that it remained free from foreign control. As Cunard didn't have the necessary funds to finance new building at that time, negotiations were begun with the government. After these were completed and an agreement signed on 30 July 1903 the matter was submitted to Parliament for ratification. Both Houses voted their approval on 13 August 1903, and the result was a subsidy to Cunard. Specifically, Cunard would be lent a sum of money, not to exceed £2,600,000† ($12,636,000), for twenty years, at the nominal interest rate of 2¾ per cent, to build two express steamers of unprecedented size and speed. In addition, an annual operating subsidy of £75,000 ($364,500) would be paid for the maintenance of each ship, as well as guaranteed mail contracts worth another £68,000 ($330,480).

In return, Cunard guaranteed that the company would remain under British control, be staffed exclusively by British officers, and manned by a crew three-quarters of whom would be British subjects, with a large percentage of naval reservists among them. The plans for all new vessels capable of seventeen knots or more, including the twin express steamers, were to be submitted to the Admiralty for approval, and such vessels could be taken over by the government at prescribed rates in times of war. As a result of this agreement, the two greatest liners the world had ever seen, the *Lusitania* and the *Mauretania*, came into being. This was to signal the beginning of a golden age for British commercial shipping.

Since it was agreed from the start that both ships could be converted into auxiliary cruisers in time of war, the Admiralty directed the planning and construction of the *Lusitania* and *Mauretania* so that the exact contract specifications would be met. The contract stipulated that each ship had to be capable of maintaining an average ocean speed of 24½ knots in moderate weather, something that

had never been accomplished before. Given the technology of the day, this speed requirement was extraordinary, since achieving 24½ knots was very different from maintaining 24½ knots. This minimum speed was almost 2 knots faster than the average speed of the four fastest German liners, and required 68,000 horsepower, which was a 79 per cent increase over the most powerful marine engines then known.

In addition, as was the practice with warships, both ships had to have double hulls divided into extensive watertight compartments,* and all vital machinery and steering gear, including the rudder, had to be located below the waterline as added protection against attack. Even the boiler rooms were lined on the outer sides with longitudinal coal bunkers. The plans for both ships also included reinforced decks for the possible future placement of twelve six-inch deck guns, which could be quickly installed on the Promenade and Shelter decks.

If these vessels were converted into armed auxiliary cruisers, theoretically the *Lusitania's* and *Mauretania's* deck guns would have a much greater range due to their high placement some forty to fifty feet above the waterline. Another advantage was that the cost of building a new merchant ship was less than half that of a third-class cruiser, and with the tremendous size of the permanent coal bunkers, which were capable of holding 6,354 tons, the *Lusitania* and *Mauretania* would be able to steam for six days at 25 knots — much longer than the best cruisers, which could steam at only approximately 23 knots for forty hours.

The Admiralty understood that a new source of power would have to be developed to obtain faster speeds as reciprocating engines had just about reached their maximum dimensions in size and weight by the beginning of the century. Although still in the experimental stage, turbines had already demonstrated their potential not only in the *Turbinia* of 1894, but also in the Royal Navy's first two turbine-powered destroyers of 1899, HMS *Cobra* and HMS *Viper*. The results of the trials of these two vessels astonished everyone and justified the risks taken. Speeds on the 'measured mile' exceeded 35 knots, and the *Viper* actually averaged 37.11 knots (42.71 miles per hour). However, shortly after both destroyers were handed over to the Navy, double tragedy struck. On 3 August 1901 the *Viper* ran aground on rocks, broke up, and had to be destroyed by the Navy to protect its secrets. On 18 September the *Cobra* also floundered in a storm with the loss of 57 men. At first the new turbines were thought to have been the cause, but investigations later pointed to structural weaknesses in the hull design. Nevertheless, with the Admiralty, these incidents temporarily cast a dark shadow over the future of turbines.

About the same time — in 1901 — the first commercial turbine-powered boat, the 210 ft Clyde ferry steamer *King Edward*, was launched and was so successful that a companion ferry, the *Queen Alexandra*, was launched in 1902. The competitive cross-channel steamer companies followed in June 1903 with *The Queen*, which ran between Dover and Calais, and the *Brighton* on the Newhaven-Dieppe run. The turbines of the *Queen* were the largest then in commercial service, weighing 35 tons and producing 8,000 shp.†

---

* *Engineering: An Illustrated Weekly Journal*, published in London, 14 and 21 September 1906 and 18 January, 27 September and 8 November 1907.
† *The Cunard Express Liner Mauretania — Souvenir Number of the Shipbuilder*, first published in Newcastle, November 1907, and reprinted in 1970 by Patrick Stephens Ltd in their *Ocean Liners of the Past* series, under the title: *The Cunard Express Liners* Lusitania

& Mauretania.
* IMM eventually included the American, Atlantic Transport, Dominion, Inman, Leyland, National, Red Star, Shaw Savil and Albion, White Star and 51 per cent of the Holland America Line, all of which continued to operate independently, even though their capital was controlled by Morgan.
† The actual cost of the *Mauretania* was £1,827,666 ($8,894,702).

* The *Lusitania's* and *Mauretania's* hulls were divided by twelve principal transverse bulkheads extending up to the Main Deck and, in all, incorporated some 175 watertight compartments. The bulkheads were connected with watertight doors, 38 of which could be closed simultaneously from the bridge.
† shp = shaft horsepower, the measurement of horsepower for turbine engines.

In 1903, the Allan Line began building for their Canadian service the first two turbine-powered North Atlantic passenger liners: the *Victorian*, launched on 25 August 1904, and completed on 10 March 1905, and the *Virginian*, launched on 22 December 1904, and completed on 31 March 1905. The use of turbines in these 540 ft long sister ships of approximately 10,700 tons was expected to generate at least 12,000 shp.

The initiative taken by the Allan Line provided the necessary incentive for Cunard's Chairman, Lord Inverclyde, to set up a commission of experts* in the Autumn of 1903 to determine the best type of propulsion for the proposed twin express steamers. Six months later, in March 1904, after careful consideration the commission advised Cunard's Board of Directors that the turbine principle was not only desirable but in order to achieve the power needed was without alternative. A decision was then made to confirm the committee's recommendation by experimenting with two new liners then under construction. The twin screw 678 ft long *Caronia*, which was completed in February 1905, would be fitted with two four-cylinder quadruple expansion engines as originally planned. Her sister, the triple-screw *Carmania*, which was completed in November 1905, would be fitted with three direct-drive Parsons steam turbines. From the start, the *Carmania* averaged over a half-knot faster on the trials. Once in service, it was discovered that, given the same quantity of coal, the turbines produced an extra knot of speed and therefore were more economical. Another advantage of the turbines was that, since they did not throb as reciprocating engines did, the voyage was smoother and steadier. Also, the turbine engine rooms could be smaller and lower, allowing more space for passenger accommodation, and the excessive weight of the reciprocating engines at the stern could now be avoided, distributing the weight in the hull more evenly.

Meanwhile, in 1905, the Royal Navy decided to equip its first 'all big gun' warship, HMS *Dreadnought*, as well as all subsequent naval ships, with powerful turbines. The trials of the *Dreadnought* in late 1906 demonstrated not only a significant increase in the contract speed of the ship, but also that the turbines produced some 5,000 additional horse-power over the contract requirements of 23,000 horsepower, were 1,000 tons lighter than reciprocating engines and saved an estimated £100,000 in cost.

The *Caronia* had two screws, and the *Carmania* had three, so it was originally planned that the *Lusitania* and *Mauretania* would also have triple screws, along with three funnels. In the end, however, this design was modified to four evenly spaced funnels and four screws because experts felt that the maximum amount of horsepower per shaft should not exceed 20,000, and four screws would lessen the power needed for each shaft.

Various proposals were prepared for the design of the *Mauretania* and submitted with the assistance of Cunard by the shipbuilding firms Messrs Vickers Sons & Maxim of Barrow-in-Furness and, as early as the latter part of 1901, by Swan Hunter and Wigham Richardson,† who were eventually awarded the contract.** Plans had to be frequently revised to keep up with the results of the many hull design tests and with the advancements of each new German liner German liner that appeared. The first proposal listed the ship's dimensions as 700 ft in length, by 70 ft in width, with a draught of 30 ft 6 in and an average speed of 24 knots. In 1902 a second proposal enlarged the ship to 750 ft by 75 ft, with a slightly shallower draught, a two-deck high First-Class Dining Saloon, and a speed of 25 knots. Other subsequent plans called for lengths between 750 and 760 ft, with widths varying from 76 to 82 ft. In total, there were at least nine proposals and by July 1903, when the agreement to build the ship was signed, the proposed design was for a three-funnelled vessel, 750 by 75 ft, with six decks and three sets of tandem quadruple expansion five-cylinder reciprocating engines driving three screws with over 60,000 ihp,†† which could maintain 24¾ knots.

The Admiralty had allowed hull design tests to be conducted at Haslar with a small model, but because of the unprecedented size of the proposed ship Swan Hunter was not satisfied with the results. In October 1903 they completed their own 47 ft 6 in self-propelled, electrically driven scale model measuring one-sixteenth of the actual ship's size, and conducted their own tests. For the next two years, tests exploring every possible variation of propeller, rudder, hull design and wind resistance were conducted in the Northumberland Dock on the north side of the river

Tyne, at Howden. By early 1904 the ship's final dimensions of 790 ft overall, by 87 ft 10 in, with a moulded depth of 60 ft 6 in were agreed upon as the most satisfactory, although construction did not actually start until 18 August 1904. There would now be nine decks, with six main decks, excluding the Bridge and Sun Deck, above the waterline. These six decks were reserved for passenger accommodation and public rooms. When completed, she would weigh 31,938 gross tons, which would qualify the *Mauretania* as the world's largest ship as she was 5 ft longer and 388 tons greater than the *Lusitania*. The *Mauretania* was also 83 ft longer, 15½ ft wider and over 15,575 tons greater than both the *Kaiser Wilhelm II* and the *Kronprinzessin Cecilie*, the largest German vessels.

Perhaps before the extensive description that follows one should be reminded that all ocean liners, including the *Mauretania*, are not only vehicles built to transport passengers and cargo across the seas, but ultimately develop unique 'personalities'. They incorporate the best engineering technology, and reflect the very latest tastes and fashions. Every single element, from the dimensions and shape of the hull to that of the smallest table, is pre-conceived and designed with that specific vessel in mind. The combined efforts and talents of thousands of people involved in planning and construction produce a final product with its own intrinsic beauty and character.

Almost as much thought as went into the design of the *Mauretania* also went into preparing a place for her to be built. In order to construct the ship, a special berth had to be built, covered by an open-sided steel and glass shed whose extreme inside dimensions were 682 ft long, 133 ft high and 95 ft wide. The considerable overhang of the roof at each end extended the total length to 728 ft, all of which was illuminated with arc lamps. Each of the 26 latticed steel columns that supported the roof were erected on 18 ft by 16 ft concrete bases which, in turn, were supported by eight piles driven 30 to 35 ft into the ground. Overhead, five four-ton and four three-ton revolving electric cranes moved horizontally along with trollies suspended from the longitudinal ceiling girders. When combined, these cranes were capable of lifting as much as forty tons. Adjoining the berth were all the workshop sheds for producing assorted machinery.

In order to support a hull and launching cradle that would weigh 16,800 tons, a six-foot wide, six-inch thick timber floor was built along the keel line the full length of the shed. The foundation for this floor consisted of over 16,000 thirteen inch square timbers 30 to 35 ft long, driven into the ground. It was on this centre platform that rows of blocks would be stacked, on which the keel would be laid. As the bottom took shape, rows of shores would support it.

Eight hydraulic riveting machines were employed, along with almost 4,000,000 mild-steel rivets weighing 1,013 tons,* varying in length from half an inch to some measuring eight inches and weighing 2¾ lb. The steel hull plates were more than an inch thick, 34 ft long and weighed 2½ to 3 tons. Some of the plates used at the turn of the bilge and on the sheer strakes were double-plated and as long as 40 ft, weighing four to five tons, a record at that time. In total, some 26,000 steel plates were used in the hull, decks, bulkheads and casings. The use of high-tensile steel instead of mild steel, in the strakes and bulkheads provided greater strength and reduced the weight by 200 tons, thereby increasing the capacity for carrying fuel and deadweight cargo.

A double cellular bottom five feet deep under the boiler rooms, and six feet deep under the engine rooms, extended almost the full length of the ship and well up the bilge. For 340 ft amidships the boiler rooms were flanked with longitudinal bulkheads, extending as high as the waterline, and serving as coal bunkers. The double cellular bottom and framing of the forward portion of the ship was constructed first, as the details for the propelling machinery at the stern had yet to be completed. This was followed by the construction of the coal bunkers and forward decks. When framing reached the aft end, two 24 ton and two 23½ ton cast-steel brackets needed to support the propeller shafts were put in place, along with the 54 ton cast-steel stern frame. The 63½ ton balanced rudder followed and, in all, the stern castings weighed some 222 tons.†

The tests at Hasler and Howden had given engineers valuable information regarding the design of the stern, which could now be implemented. Each of the four propellers, which were 17 ft in diameter, would be driven by 17,000 hp turbines at 180 rpm. The shape of the three bolted-on manganese-bronze blades had been slightly modified, so they were a trifle longer and narrower than the rounder blades found on the *Lusitania*. The two outer propellers were driven clockwise by two high-pressure turbines, and were

placed 9 feet further forward than those on the *Lusitania*. The two inner propellers located aft of the outer propellers, were turned counter-clockwise by two low-pressure turbines. It was at this point that the keel frame rose dramatically, as it was found that this gave water a freer flow to the inner propellers.

The launch of the *Mauretania** took place at 4.15 pm on 20 September 1906, 25 months after the laying of the keel, and was witnessed by thousands who had waited hours to see the Dowager Duchess of Roxburgh† christen the ship.

The hull was now completed and freshly painted,** with enormous wooden poppets supporting the fore and aft ends, reassuring her stability. Fourteen-and-a-half tons of tallow, over a ton of soft, black soap and 113 gallons of train oil had been applied a month earlier for lubrication. Since the ship was five feet longer than the width of the river Tyne, the *Mauretania* had to be launched at an angle, taking advantage of the bend in the river which would give her a total clearance of 1,130 feet.

In order to slow the ship's acceleration as she slid down the ways, 1,015 tons of drags consisting of five piles of heavy chains weighing 81 tons each were attached to either side of the ship by loose chains. Two additional sets of armour plate drags weighing 101 tons each at the bow waited for the trigger to release the vessel.

At first the hull seemed not to move, but within seven seconds six feet were covered, without the assistance of the powerful hydraulic rams. In seventy seconds it was all over, as the *Mauretania* came to rest after travelling her first 951 feet, her bow stem only 93 feet from the end of the ways, and her stern 222 feet from the opposite river bank.

Afterwards, a tour of the neighbouring engine builders, the Wallsend Slipway and Engineering Works, was arranged for company officials and their guests, followed by a gala luncheon, to which a catering bill of £1,475 15s 2p ($7,182) testifies.

During the next twelve months, while berthed in front of the Wallsend Shipyard in an area where the Tyne had been specially dredged to a depth of 31 ft, the process of fitting out began. At first, the nearly empty hull sat very high on the water, with only an average draught of 16 ft 6 in, but as the giant German-built floating crane, *Titan*, whose lifting capacity was 150 tons, carefully hoisted each structural element into place, the ship gradually settled lower.

The first elements to be incorporated into the hull were the 25 boilers. Twenty-three of these were double-ended, 17 ft 3 in in diameter and 22 ft long, and two were single-ended and 11 ft long. In total, they contained 192 coal-fired furnaces, with 4,068 square feet of fire grate area and a heating surface of about 159,000 square feet. The number 1 boiler room furthest forward would contain five double-ended and two single-ended boilers. Admidships, six double-ended boilers would be placed in each of boiler rooms 2, 3 and 4. It should be mentioned here that in 1906 the advantages of oil-fired boilers were known: refuelling was much faster and cleaner; the crew necessary to operate the boilers was greatly reduced; and the speed was more consistent. However, the use of oil was still a new phenomenon, with continuous supplies doubtful and expensive, and adequate storage facilities lacking. These boilers, however, were designed to be converted to oil-firing, if necessary.

By the end of 1906 all the boilers had been installed and eventually the four boiler rooms would each be capped by huge sets of exhaust uptakes, which would shoot smoke up through the four elliptical funnels, each measuring 23 ft 7 in by 16 ft 7 in. The funnels were elliptical because it had been known for years that such a shape decreased wind resistance. The height from the keel line to the tops of the funnels was 153 ft, or 120 ft above the waterline.

The next additions to follow were the very fragile turbines. The turbine rooms were located aft of the boiler rooms, and the placement of these engines required the utmost care. The outer high-pressure turbines were over 45 ft in length with a maximum internal diameter of 10 ft. Inside, fluid-pressed steel rotors which weighed 72 tons revolved at a circumferential speed of 11,000 ft per minute, with a minimum clearance of only $\frac{1}{10}$ of an inch between the delicate 2½ to 12 in long rotor blades and the cast iron casing. Both propeller shafts connected to the rotors had diameters of 22¼ in. The combined length of the astern turbine and the low-pressure turbine directly behind it was over 78 ft. The internal diameter of each of the low-pressure turbines was 16 ft 6 in and the rotor shaft inside was 48 ft long, had a maximum diameter of 11 ft 8 in, weighed 130 tons and had blades varying from eight to 22 inches in length. The propeller shafts driven by the low-pressure turbines also had

* Members of the Commission included the General Superintendent of Cunard, the Engineer-in-Chief of the Navy, the Chief Engineer Surveyor of Lloyd's, the Chief Constructor to the Admiralty, and the Honourable Charles Parsons.
† Due to heavy demand on company capital, in 1903 C. S. Swan Hunter amalgamated with Messrs Wigham Richardson of Walker-on-Tyne.
** The contract for the *Lusitania* was awarded to the Clydebank firm of John Brown & Co, Shipbuilders, near Glasgow.
†† ihp = indicated horsepower, which refers only to reciprocating steam and internal combustion engines.

* Although it is most often stated that 700 tons of rivets were used, Swan Hunter's records indicate it was actually 1,013 tons, which cost £7,669 ($37,323).
† The total cost of iron and steel was £239,771 ($1,166,893); £128,798 ($626,821) for labour; £110,973 ($540,072) for material. The total net tonnage for iron and steel was 16,581.

* As was the practice of Cunard, all vessels bore the names of ancient Roman provinces, *Mauretania* being Roman north-west Africa.
† The Duchess of Roxburgh was a sister-in-law of Lord Tweedmouth, First Lord of the Admiralty.
** The total cost of the hull amounted to £992,736 ($4,831,348), which included £605,569 ($2,947,123) for 'general work', and £30,861 ($150,191) for electric lighting.

diameters of 22¼ inches. Each set of low-pressure and astern turbine rotors weighed as estimated 186 tons, and could be adjustable to within $\frac{3}{1000}$ of an inch. In all, the *Mauretania's* six turbines contained rotor blades varying in length from two to 22 inches, with eight stages to meet the greater expanding volume of steam. The total combined weight of the propelling machinery and boilers with their accessories when originally installed was 9,402 tons. Other vital machinery such as pumps, fans and huge condensers followed. The size of the exhaust port openings alone, from the low-pressure turbine casing to the condenser, measured 11 ft by 13 ft. By May 1907 the installation of all propelling machinery had been completed, at a total cost of £834,930 ($4,063,354).

Externally, the *Mauretania* was very similar to the *Lusitania* in appearance, but there were several distinctive differences in structure. The most obvious was the 28 large, white cowl ventilators positioned on the Sun Deck and two on the Boat Deck, which provided fresh air to the engine and boiler rooms with the help of twenty large fans, ten for intake, ten for exhaust. To many the profile of these large cowls gave the impression of great power. The *Lusitania's* ventilators were of the flat-headed hinged type which, at less than half the height of the *Mauretania's*, not only accentuated the vertical profile of the funnels, but also made them look taller and gave the ship a racier profile.

Another obvious difference was the shape of the bridge front. The *Mauretania's* bowed outward further than the *Lusitania's*, as tests had shown the curved shape decreased wind resistance. The *Mauretania's* enlarged Observation Room on the Promenade Deck also provided a much larger, open curved deck space on the Boat Deck above.

Another variant feature of the *Mauretania* was the outward 20 inch extension of both sides, beyond the line of the Shelter Deck, of the Promenade and Boat Decks. This extension on the Promenade Deck added some 928 sq ft to the First-Class section and approximately 453 sq ft to the Second-Class section. On the Boat Deck the extension added 983 extra sq ft in First-Class and about 373 sq ft in Second-Class. In comparison, the sides of the *Lusitania* were flush with the hull.

Finally, the treatment of the enclosed section of the forepeak on the Promenade Deck of the *Mauretania* extended much further aft than that of the *Lusitania*. The *Mauretania* also had recessed bower anchors weighing ten tons each, and the 1,900 ft long anchor chains with adjoining shackles weighed 131½ tons, each link weighing 170 lbs and measuring 22½ in long, 13½ in wide with a 3¾ in diameter.

Although quite similar externally, the interior decors of the *Mauretania* and *Lusitania* differed completely. To design these interiors two well-known architects were chosen in 1905 by Lord Inverclyde. The young Scotsman, James Millar, who went on to work on the *Aquitania*, was picked for the *Lusitania*. Harold A. Peto, known for his work on country houses, designed the interior of the *Mauretania*. Each chose to decorate his respective ship in various historic styles that were most admired in 1905-1907. By recreating the familiar feeling of security found in sumptuous hotels and clubs, the large public rooms were designed to allay passengers' fears of ocean travel, which often was considered an inconvenient necessity. In addition, to help avoid possible boredom the rooms themselves had to be interesting enough to attract the passengers' attention. The themes reflected in these public rooms often had strong nationalistic overtones which passengers, especially Americans, could relate to in anticipation of the various countries they would soon be visiting.

Peto would be responsible for the design, and the execution of his plans would be carried out by four sub-contracting firms. W. Turner Lord & Co, of London, received the largest commission, consisting of the First-Class Grand Entrance, Smoking Room, Dining Saloon and staircases. Of the 68 Special Staterooms and *En Suite* Rooms, W. Turner Lord & Co was given the responsibility of furnishing and decorating 52, as well as the two Regal Suites. However, this order was sub-contracted to their branch firm, Messrs Morison, of Edinburgh. Messrs J. Robson, of Newcastle, was in charge of another fourteen First-Class Special State and *En Suite* Rooms, including the Sheraton, Chippendale and Adams Rooms, as well as the Children's Nursery. The shipbuilders, Swan Hunter and Wigham Richardson, also fitted out several 'En Suite' Rooms, as well as all the rooms for Second and Third-Class passengers. Messrs Ch Mellier & Co, of London, had been given the responsibility for only two rooms, the First-Class Library and Writing-Room and The Lounge, or Music Room, which are considered by many as the most magnificent on the ship.

Critics have often complained that the interiors of the *Mauretania* and *Lusitania* were 'not as luxurious as some of her contemporary competitors'. While this is debatable, it should be understood that these ships were built with restrictive government subsidies, and their goal was first speed then luxury. Nevertheless, by 1907 standards, it would be hard to deny that these ships had no rivals in speed, attention to detail and craftsmanship. Never before, and certainly very few times since, was so much time and energy devoted to the careful planning and meticulous construction of such grand and elegant spaces on board a ship. Perfection was so important that 300 woodworkers were brought over from Palestine to work nearly two years carving high-relief mouldings, columns, capitals and bulkhead walls.

For two years England and France were scoured for the enormous quantities of high-quality timber that were necessary for her fitting out. Over thirty varieties of particularily fine wood were used throughout the ship. All the bulkhead framing and deck sheathing was constructed of the best yellow pine, the wood used most extensively. Every First-Class cabin bulkhead on the Promenade and Boat Decks, as well as the First-Class Lounge and Second-Class Smoking Room, was constructed of African mahogany. The finest Austrian oak was used for the parquet floors of the First and Second-Class Smoking Rooms and the ornately carved walls and columns and parquet floors of the entire First and Second-Class Dining Saloons. One firm alone supplied four season's worth of wood — almost a quarter of a million square feet. Almost 10,000 sq ft of inlaid French walnut veneer was used in the staircases, Grand Entrances and First-Class Smoking Room. Other varieties of wood such as maple, sycamore, teak, pear, ash, birch and beech were used extensively throughout the ship.

Since the passenger accommodation included over twenty major public rooms and 664 private staterooms, a comprehensive description in this narrative is not possible. Therefore, descriptions of only five major public rooms will be included, but the 38 new photographs of various interiors will provide a more than adequate substitute.

The largest and most complicated room on board was the three-deck high First-Class Dining Saloon which was entirely clad in straw-coloured oak, and carved in high relief. The style chosen was mid-Sixteenth Century Francois I, and the major influence for its design was Château de Chambord. Numerous features such as arches, columns and their capitals, diamonds, half-circles and even crowned salamanders were copied in bas-relief on many of the bulkhead walls. The main floor of the Dining Saloon on the Upper Deck, which was the room most ornately decorated, included a large, richly carved buffet. The less ornate second floor on the Shelter Deck was often used as an *à la carte* restaurant. It has often been pointed out that one of the charms of this style is that no piece of carving is an exact reproduction of its neighbour.

Connecting both floors, and rising almost 28 feet through a third deck, was the large octagonal balustraded open well, which was crowned by an octagonal cream and gold vaulted dome. The dome, in turn, was embellished at the rib junctions with numerous medallions depicting the signs of the Zodiac. At the top of the dome was a smaller balustraded cupola which, like the base of the dome, was illuminated by indirect lighting, probably the earliest example on board a ship. The only flaw in the whole design was the communal tables and chairs. Although made smaller than their predecessors, the tables still provided little privacy. In any case, the accompanying bolted-down pink upholstered swivel chairs were rapidly becoming obsolete. Cunard, however, insisted on these, but the advent of heavy, movable chairs in the *Olympic* of 1911 signalled the end of this antiquated Nineteenth Century fixture. In addition, the smaller partitioned areas in the *Olympic's* First-Class Dining Saloon finally provided the privacy passengers had begun to expect.

On the Boat Deck, directly above the dome of the First-Class Dining Saloon, was the impressive First-Class Lounge, or Music Room, which was 79 ft 6 in long by 55 ft wide, with a ceiling 11 ft 9 in high, including the oval, gilded wrought iron and glass dome which measured 24 ft 6 in by 18 ft. This room was decorated in the lavish late Eighteenth Century French style, similiar to that found in Versailles' Petit Trianon. Here, Peto cleverly disguised unavoidable ventilators, funnel casings* and structural beams with richly carved, gilt mahogany columns and carefully selected, polished inlaid mahogany walls. Sixteen lilac-coloured Fleur de Pêche marble pilasters with ormolu capitals and bases skirted the perimeter, as well as the forward end, where there was a fireplace mantle carved of the same stone. At the other end of the room, facing the fireplace, was a grand piano, and three large Aubusson wall tapestries which accented the gracious semi-circular bays. In addition to the high glass dome, crystal chandeliers, suspended in a frozen position to counter the ship's roll, illuminated the room.

Abaft the Lounge was the late Italian Renaissance First-Class Smoking Room which was reached through bevelled glass-panelled doors. Peto used these doors for entrance into every First-Class public room on the Boat Deck, thus creating a virtually unobstructed view for almost 350 feet. The Smoking Room had walls of delicately matched, cross-veneered walnut panels, each framed with elaborate inlaid sycamore borders and impressive carvings. All along the tops of the walls was a richly carved bas-relief frieze depicting stylized dolphins. This room was divided by two well-hidden ventilator uptakes, creating a larger room aft, with three sitting recesses beneath large arched windows on each side and alcoves at the ends. The smaller, forward section of the room was dominated by a finely carved fireplace mantle, the sides of which were lined with slabs of green marble, a faithful reproduction of an original by the Florentine sculptor, Della Robbia. Even the basket grates and irons were facsimilies of those found at the Palazzo Varesi. The perimeter of each of these main rooms contained an elaborate plaster frieze, which supported a massive, vaulted glass-panelled ceiling. At either end of these rooms two semi-circular paintings depicted 'Old Liverpool' and 'Old New York'.

Directly forward the Lounge, again through bevelled glass doors, was the First-Class Grand Entrance, also modelled in the late Italian Renaissance style. The room was notable for the recessed, elaborately carved, walnut seat and the ornate lift cages crowned by a 14 ft 6 in circular glass domed skylight. These cages, also adopted from a 16th Century design, were made entirely of aluminium, the first instance of this metal being used in such a large quantity on board a ship. The use of this new, light metal around the staircase and on each of the five landings, saved an estimated twenty tons in weight.

Further forward, through glass-panelled doors, was the elegant Louis XVI style First-Class Library and Writing-Room. Its walls were of perfectly matched, silver-grey stained sycamore panelling, decorated with carved rondels and gilt mouldings. A 15 by 19 ft 6 in oval glass-domed skylight was positioned between a white marble fireplace, surmounted by an arched mirror and a gilded grille bookcase across from it. Large semi-circular bays supported by tall carved Corinthian columns at either end contained comfortable writing tables.

On 17 September 1907, without any public announcement, the *Mauretania* left her berth on the Tyne to begin somewhat secretive preliminary trials in the North Sea. These lasted until 21 September and according to an article in *Sea Breezes* (January 1971) the builders in Wallsend were kept informed of the daily results by carrier pigeon. The objective of these pre-trials was to detect any major problems that might disrupt the ship's first scheduled sailing date a month later. The problem that was discovered had been the builder's greatest fear — vibration. Apparently it was quite severe, and when the ship returned, adjustments were made in the weight distribution in the hull and the construction of the stern was reinforced. These modifications helped, but the problem ultimately was with the design of the propellers, which were not changed until May 1908, when a broken propeller blade forced Cunard to take action.

On 22 October 1907, surrounded by tens of thousands of cheering spectators, the *Mauretania* prepared to leave Wallsend for her trip around northern Scotland to Liverpool. She carried a distinguished complement of company officials and men responsible for her building. As a fitting tribute to the turbine's development in only ten years, the *Turbinia* was brought alongside the *Mauretania* so that she could accompany the *Mauretania* down the Tyne. Ironically, this proved to be the *Turbinia's* last trip under her own power. At the very last minute, the *Turbinia's* temperamental air pump failed, and the *Mauretania* had to leave unescorted.

Once the *Mauretania* reached Tynemouth, Mary, Lady Inverclyde officially signalled the start of the voyage with a command from the bridge, and the pleasant trip lasted two days. Upon arriving, the *Mauretania* was dry-docked in the new Canada Graving Dock from 25-30 October, at which time her hull was cleaned before she left for her official trials on 3 November 1907.

The *Mauretania's* official trials are already adequately described on pages xiii and xiv of this volume. Suffice it to say that the *Mauretania* exceeded the Admiralty's requirements by steaming 1,216 miles in two days at an average speed of 26.04 knots (29.97 mph), developing a maximum shaft horsepower of 78,273 at 189.7 rpm. On 6 November she ran the 'measured mile' at Skelmorlie, averaging 26.75 knots (30.79 mph), leaving Cunard and the shipbuilders triumphant.

Despite dismal weather, 16 November 1907 was a day filled with excitement and anticipation in Liverpool as the *Mauretania* prepared to leave on her maiden voyage. An atmosphere of pride and confidence prevailed as Englishmen anxiously anticipated a better performance from the English-built *Mauretania* than that of her Scottish-built sister, the *Lusitania*. For many years a rivalry existed between the shipbuilding centres of the Clyde and the Tyne, and now the *Mauretania* would at last have her chance only seventy days after the departure of the *Lusitania* on her now legendary maiden voyage.

To add to this excitement, the departure was delayed for

* The persistent problem of dodging centrally located dead spaces of funnel casings and ventilators was not solved until 1913, when the *Vaterland* introduced divided boiler uptakes, which allowed for the first time an unobstructed central axis view.

fifty minutes by the late arrival of a special boat train which carried to the *Mauretania* some £2,750,000 in gold bullion* intended to ease the money crisis in America. Insurance cover, taken out on the ship just before departure, amounted to nearly $5,000,000.

To see her off approximately 50,000 spectators were on hand at the newly renovated Prince's Landing Stage. The port authority had only recently dredged 20 square miles of the river bed, removing over 200,000 tons of mud, rock and sand to accommodate the new twin express steamers. *The New York Times* (17 November 1907) gives this account of the events that evening: 'Several hours prior to the vessel's departure, the landing stage on the river front was thronged with thousands of sightseers, who, with umbrellas upraised, bravely held their ground under the most cheerless conditions. The blaze of the illumination from stem to stern as the "Mauretania" was berthed at the landing stage presented a magnificent spectacle. The signal for departure was given shortly before 8 o'clock, and the vessel glided down the river to the accompaniment of intermittent bursts of cheering and the din of hooting sirens'.†

As the lights of Liverpool disappeared over the horizon, the dinner bugle summoned the passengers to their first meal and the voyage began. Across the Irish Sea the passage was extremely smooth, and at 9 o'clock the next morning, Sunday, the *Mauretania* reached Queenstown, to embark passengers and mail. The ship departed two hours later, and by noon Monday had covered an easy 571 miles, with each day promising more as the engines assumed their routine. However, this voyage was anything but routine, as she began to encounter, head-on, a not-unusual November gale. Winds of 50 mph and mountainous waves lifted her bow 60 ft, only to drop it again, breaking the spare anchor loose on the foredeck. For two hours the *Mauretania* made only three knots, with her back to the wind and only enough power to steer, conditions which nevertheless enabled her crew to secure the dangerously sliding anchor. Several promenade deck windows were smashed, railings above the bridge were twisted, and carpets were stained with seawater, all testifying to the peril of a winter crossing. Although the possibility of a record crossing time faded, the ship managed a very respectable 464 miles that day. The next day, even though still feeling the effects of the storm, she covered 563 miles and, by noon Thursday, had spanned 624 miles in only 25 hours. This was six more than the *Lusitania's* best day's run, and represented a new record for distance covered in one day. Toasts to the captain were made by elated passengers in the First-Class Dining Saloon, and one grateful American on board, Mr W. J. White, presented the stokers with $1,000 for their fine work.

The renewed hopes of achieving a record passage with the next day's run were dashed when the *Mauretania* encountered heavy fog near Sandy Hook and was forced to anchor at 11:13 am. This was one adversity the captain wanted her to wait out, and she was able to dock at 6:15 that evening. Her passage from Daunt's Rock (Queenstown) to Sandy Hook took five days, five hours, ten minutes, averaging 21.22 knots which, considering the circumstances, was very good.

On Saturday 30 November, one day out on the return leg of the maiden voyage, fog again slowed the ship for thirty hours, off the Banks of Newfoundland. Once it cleared up, on Tuesday, the *Mauretania* logged 556 miles, two more than the *Lusitania's* best. The next day the *Mauretania* passed the *Baltic* which had left New York two days before her. By the time the *Mauretania* passed Daunt's Rock a new eastward record had been set at four days, 22 hours, 29 minutes, at an average speed of 23.69 knots — 21 minutes better than the *Lusitania's* fastest eastward passage. And so the Blue Riband was hers.

The *Mauretania's* coal consumption was far less than expected. On this first voyage, instead of using an estimated 1,000 tons a day, she consumed only 856.5 per day westward, and 917.13 tons per day for the return trip. Although consumptions of 1,000 tons per day were reached occasionally on subsequent voyages, this was rare.

Certainly the *Mauretania* had demonstrated that she was not only a fine, seaworthy ship, but also a fast one. Throughout her long and brilliant life she continued to impress people, not only with her great speed, but also with the amazingly consistent punctuality of her performance.

In May 1908 one of the propellers lost a blade, so for that voyage** and the next seven, she ran on three screws, still producing decent times. On 27 May the *Mauretania* left Liverpool and managed to turn around in New York, loading 6,000 tons of coal in twenty hours, and return to Liverpool in only thirteen days, twelve hours.

* *The New York Times* reported this figure to be £2,800,000 in bullion. Nevertheless, at that time it was the largest amount of gold ever transported on a ship.

† Copyright © 1907 by The New York Times Company. Reprinted by permission.

** The term 'voyage' usually refers to a round trip crossing, unless otherwise specified.

In October she was taken out of service to be fitted with new eighteen ton, four-bladed one-piece cast propellers which raised her speed a full knot after she returned to service on 24 January 1909. The design of these propellers was so effective that every one of the thirty crossings that year was completed in less than five days, as her fifteen westward voyages averaged 25.39 knots, and her fifteen eastward voyages averaged 25.47 knots. Of the 88 crossings made from January 1909 to the end of November 1911, seventy averaged over 25 knots, and of those 32 averaged 25½ knots, while two averaged over 26 knots.

As the *Mauretania* continued to better her times the two fastest crossings prior to World War I are still quoted frequently. On her 26th voyage, departing from Liverpool on 25 September 1909, she crossed in four days, ten hours, 51 minutes, averaging 26.06 knots. A year later, on 10 September 1910, again departing from Liverpool, the crossing was made in four days, ten hours, 41 minutes, also averaging 26.06 knots.

The two fastest eastward crossings prior to the First World War were on 16 June 1909, when she raced to Liverpool in four days, seventeen hours, 21 minutes, at an average of 25.88 knots, and again on 4 August 1909, when she shaved a minute off that time, averaging 25.89 knots.

With her new propellers, and faster coaling in New York, the *Mauretania* continued to shorten her 'turn around' so that on one occasion, in December 1910, for the first time a complete round trip from Liverpool took just a few hours over twelve days.

In May 1911 the *Mauretania* averaged 27.04 knots (31.12 mph), for a whole day's run and although in June she was surpassed in size by the *Olympic*, the *Mauretania* continued to be the fastest ship for another eighteen years.

With the same confidence they showed in the punctuality of express trains, passengers depended on the *Mauretania*. Not only was her speed uniform, but out of 88 crossings of over 3,000 miles, not one voyage varied in length by more than five miles. Most of the voyages had a deviation of only one or two miles, and out of fourteen made in 1911 the mileage was exactly the same for ten.

By the end of 1913, having completed 86 voyages, the *Mauretania* had sailed on every advertised day except one. Her first six years were glorious, yet she still had so much more to offer. A new phase in her life was about to emerge, beginning with an eight-week overhaul that kept her out of service until the beginning of March 1914.*

With the *Mauretania's* reappearance in March, Queenstown had been replaced by Fishguard, allowing special trains to speed up by many hours the delivery of mail and passengers to London. The old *Campania*, which had served with the *Lusitania* and the *Mauretania* on the New York run, was replaced at the end of May with the new *Aquitania*, a slightly slower but substantially larger ship than her consorts. She was 111 ft 6 in longer, and some 13,709 tons greater than the *Mauretania*, and the cost of her construction, unlike that of her 'sisters', was assumed by Cunard.

After seven years the Cunard Line had finally realized its original dream of a formidable trio servicing the North Atlantic. This was, however, to be short-lived, as Europe was bracing itself for the First World War, which would leave the Cunard fleet shattered.

The day Germany declared war on Russia on 2 August 1914 the *Kaiser Wilhelm der Grosse* was requisitioned by the Germany Navy as an auxiliary cruiser. The following day, while the *Deutschland* was also being converted, Germany declared war on France after having sent the Belgians the infamous ultimatum demanding that German troops have unimpeded passage through their country. The *Kronprinz Wilhelm* left New York quickly that day with orders to meet the cruiser *Karlsruhe* in the West Indies, which would supply the *Kronprinz Wilhelm* with two 81mm guns and ammunition, and over the next 250 days the *Kronprinz Wilhelm* steamed 20,000 miles, sinking 26 Allied ships totalling 58,201 tons.

When German troops entered Belgium on 4 August Britain declared war on Germany. The *Mauretania* was *en route* to New York, so she diverted to Halifax, making that port her destination for the next three voyages.

After a one-hour battle with HMS *Highflyer* on 26 August, the reconditioned, now auxiliary crusier, *Kaiser Wilhelm der Grosse* was scuttled by her crew. On 14 September SMS *Cap Trafalgar* was sunk after a fierce ninety-minute duel with the *Carmania*. After these events, it was apparent to the

* The *Mauretania* was scheduled to return to service on 14 February 1914, but an accident occurred involving a gas cylinder explosion which killed four men and damaged the starboard high-pressure turbine.

† Under the terms of the 1903 agreement, using the ship's speed as a basis, the Government would pay Cunard the top rate of 25 shillings per month for each registered gross ton. This amounted to approximately £40,000 per month, or £1,333 a day, and if the crew and officers were included Cunard would be paid £48,000 per month, or £1,600 per day, excluding conversion costs or any damages incurred.

Admiralty that the loss of the *Mauretania* in her original role as an auxiliary cruiser or, worse still, her capture, must be avoided at all costs. Although fast, she was a large target, and very expensive to operate.†

Following her last voyage from Halifax on 21 October, the *Mauretania* was requisitioned by the Admiralty, taken out of service, had her fittings dismantled, and was laid-up pending the Admiralty's decision as to her fate. The fiasco of the Dardanelles campaign in early 1915 precipitated the decision. She was converted into a troop transport and made three voyages to the Aegean island of Lemnos in May, July and August, carrying a total of 10,391 troops. It was while on one of these trooping voyages that she narrowly avoided a German torpedo, which missed her by an estimated five feet.

In September, she was re-fitted at great expense as a fully equipped Red Cross hospital ship, her hull painted white with a green stripe and red crosses, her buff funnels towering overall. She made three round trips to nearby Mudros, ironically transporting back to Southampton the same men she had brought over earlier that year, a total of 6,298 wounded, plus a medical staff of 2,307. After completing her third voyage to Mudros, the HMHS *Mauretania* was reconditioned once again as a troop transport. She made two voyages in October and November 1916 between Halifax and Liverpool, carrying a total of 6,214 Canadian soldiers to England.

The year 1917 saw the *Mauretania* dismantled and laid-up on the Clyde in Gareloch, Scotland. With the entry of the United States into the war that year, American troops needed to be transported and the *Mauretania* was called back into action. This time she operated as an armed transport and, beginning in early 1918, made seven voyages to New York, carrying 33,610 officers and men. It was also about this time, for camouflage purposes, that she was renamed HMS *Tuberose** by the Admiralty. After the war was over she again carried troops, this time returning 19,536 soldiers to America, until she was released from service on 27 May 1919. She had transported a total of 69,751 troops during the war, with an additional 8,605 wounded, plus medical staff.

The *Mauretania* was now ready to begin another phase in her career. She was cleaned, repainted and her original fittings reinstalled with new carpets. Everything but the engines received attention, and on 6 March 1920 she steamed to New York from Southampton, her new home port. Of the seven voyages made that year, and the four in 1921, her fastest average speed was only 21.97 knots, and her slowest 17.81 knots. This was largely due to mechanical fatigue, however, and the slowest speed was attributable to a malfunctioning propeller. Many thought her record-breaking days were over.

Ironically, good fortune came in the form of a six-hour fire on 25 July 1921 while she was berthed in Southampton. It had been sparked by a careless worker using flammable cleaning fluid, and it gutted every First-Class cabin on the Main Deck, buckling the Dining Saloon floor on the deck above. The decision was made not only to repair the damage, but also to take advantage of her being out of service by converting her boilers to oil-firing. This alone cost over £250,000. When she returned to service on 25 March 1922 her average speed began to show some improvement, as the engineers became familiar with the new system. The 4,400 tons of oil that was now consumed on a typical voyage produced more heat energy, and a greater steam pressure, which in turn increased horsepower. Other advantages of oil were the much shorter refuelling time in port, as well as the great savings in labour costs, as her boiler room crew was now drastically reduced from 390 to ninety.

In 1921 the US Government enacted the Quota Act, also known as the Three Percent Act, which restricted the number of immigrants entering America to three per cent of each nationality already living there, based on the 1903 census. Since the majority of passenger accommodation on the *Mauretania* was for Third-Class passengers, Cunard, along with other companies, faced a serious problem. The solution was the creation of a 'Tourist Third Class' which, less restrictive than the Third, upgraded cabin accommodation that would appeal especially to the new generation of American tourists and students.

While the details of these new arrangements were being considered in 1923, Cunard revived the old German custom of 'cruising', beginning with an extravagant, nine-week chartered luxurious Mediterranean cruise sponsored by the American Express Company. The passenger list on this 10,132-mile voyage included many millionaires, among them the Director of Steel Trust who paid $25,000 for his suite. The idea of cruising became very popular, especially in the Prohibition era, and over the next eleven years the *Mauretania* took 31,517 passengers on 54 cruises, travelling 252,040 miles. She also eventually cruised to Havana, Nassau, Halifax, the West Indies, Gibraltar, Bermuda,

* According to Sir Arthur H. Rostron, the Captain of the *Mauretania* at that time, the *Mauretania's* new name was spelt: 'HMS *Tuber Rose*'

Casablanca and Madeira.

In order to undertake these cruises, the *Mauretania's* turbines had to be overhauled and so, after her 151st transatlantic voyage ending on 4 November 1923, she was taken out of service. The turbines were dismantled, carefully inspected, and worn rotor blades replaced, but due to a strike the work had to be finished in Cherbourg. It was while being towed powerless, by six Dutch tugs across the English Channel, with her turbines dismantled, that the *Mauretania* was almost lost in a storm. The cost of the engine overhaul amounted to one-third of the entire cost of the original ship.

The *Mauretania* returned to service on 31 May 1924, sailing from Southampton to New York. However, when only one day out one of the outer propeller shafts snapped off, dropping the propeller, yet she still managed to average 22.67 knots on three. After this was repaired, her performances once again began to top 25 knots, with one crossing in August 1924 averaging 26.16 knots.

By this time, many new liners, including White Star Line's *Majestic* (ex-*Bismarck*) and *Homeric*, United States Line's *Leviathan* (ex-*Vaterland*), and the French Line's *Paris* and *De Grasse* had been skimming their share of business from Cunard, with the threat of more ships such as the *Ile de France* and the new *Lafayette* forthcoming.

Cunard's response to the recently launched, very stylish *Ile de France* was a six-week renovation and redecoration of the *Mauretania* at the end of 1926. When she resumed service on 9 February 1927 new carpeting and large palms had been added to the Lounge, new smaller tables, linoleum flooring and palms to the Dining Saloons, and the old Verandah Café was replaced by a new indoor greenhouse. Two new propellers were fitted and Cunard advertised that one hundred staterooms had been refurbished, many with private baths, an important addition as it was the lack of private bathrooms that, in the end, contributed heavily to her decline in popularity. The greatest threat looming, however, again came from Norddeutscher Lloyd, who were now planning two super express liners, the *Bremen* and the *Europa*, which were designed to take back the Blue Riband lost in 1907.

Cunard was aware of the Germans' intentions to set a new speed record so, in November 1928, the *Mauretania* was taken out of service for seven weeks in order that secret adjustments could be made to her turbines, and new pumps and condensers installed, which would raise her shp to 90,000. On her first voyage after the engine alterations were completed on 2 January 1929, the *Mauretania* again encountered a severe winter storm which smashed wheelhouse windows, flooded the chartroom and ripped off four feet of teak deck railing.

On 22 June she passed the *Bremen* which was returning from her trials. The *Bremen* was indeed a powerful ship, since her twelve turbines were designed for a normal output of 110,000 shp with a maximum of 130,000 shp. This meant she was at least 69 per cent more powerful than the *Mauretania* and, as the first ship with a bulbous bow, she slipped through the water even faster. In addition, the *Bremen* at 932 ft 8 in overall, was 142 ft 8 in longer, 13 ft 11 in wider and 19,718 tons larger than the *Mauretania*.

So it was no surprise that the *Bremen* took back the Blue Riband on her maiden voyage crossing, 16 July 1929, when she averaged 27.83 knots. What was surprising, however, was the *Mauretania's* response to that voyage, her 227th, commencing on 3 August 1929, during which she beat her own westward record by 3 hours, 50 minutes, crossing in four days, 21 hours, 44 minutes, averaging 26.9 knots. With the help of her secret engine modifications made the year before, and not used until now, her propellers revolved at 210 rpm, thirty more than they were designed for. This enabled her on 5 August to cover 680 miles, averaging 27.2 knots, and the following day 687 miles, averaging 27.48 knots.

As impressive as this new record was for the *Mauretania*, her return voyage was even faster, as she averaged 27.22 knots (31.33 mph), crossing in only four days, seventeen hours and 50 minutes. To top this exceptional transatlantic performance, the *Mauretania* finished the voyage with the run from Eddystone to Cherbourg, a distance of 106 miles, at an average speed of 29.7 knots (34.184 mph), which is incredible, considering she was almost 22 years old, and designed for 25 knots! Although the *Bremen* retained her record as the fastest ship, the *Mauretania* had once again demonstrated that every metre of the Blue Riband she held for almost 22 years had been earned through much hard work, giving consistently better performances.

During the years 1930-1932 cruising became more prevalent in the *Mauretania's* itinerary, as 'booze cruises' gained in popularity. Fast four-day runs to Nassau between turn arounds in New York complicated the crew's lives, as their free time vanished. Longer, twelve to thirteen day cruises to the West Indies followed, as the *Mauretania* began to desert her transatlantic sailings. It was for these longer cruises that her hull was painted white, but the lack of air-conditioning, private bathrooms and swimming pools made passengers uncomfortable. The end was near.

Although old now, the *Mauretania*, working harder than ever, maintained a strong will to survive. On one cruise, she steamed from New York to Havana in 47 hours, 50 minutes, beating the previous record set by the *President Roosevelt* by thirteen hours, 28 minutes. Again, on 19 July 1933, she left Havana and averaged 27.78 knots on the first day, with one 112 mile segment averaging 32 knots, or 36.83 land miles per hour!

As a result of the North Atlantic Shipping Act of 1934, the Cunard and White Star Lines merged on 28 March 1934 as Cunard White Star Ltd. This merger was a prerequisite for a government loan to finish the construction of the *Queen Mary*. The *Mauretania* had become a liability in those hard times, and Cunard could not afford to keep her.

On 26 September 1934, the day the *Queen Mary* was launched, the *Mauretania* left New York on her last transatlantic voyage, number 318. After a 24.42 knot crossing which lasted five days and twenty hours, she berthed at Southampton, one month short of 27 years of service.

Rust-stained and dirty, on 2 April 1935 she was sold for scrap to Metal Industries Ltd, of Rosyth, Scotland. Her beautiful fittings were sold at public auction on 14-17 and 20-23 May 1935, with many entire rooms going to corporations, hotels and pubs. One man even bought, for $20 per letter, a set of the *Mauretania's* large brass bow letters that spelt her name.

On 1 July 1935, with her masts cut down to stumps so that she could clear the Forth Bridge, the *Mauretania* left Southampton for the last time. She made the 488-mile run to Rosyth at an average speed of only 12.51 knots. It was the end of the physical ship, but only the beginning of her legend.

MARK D. WARREN
NEW YORK, APRIL 1987

In the course of my research, the following document from The Cropley Collection at the Smithsonian Institution in Washington, DC was introduced to me by Jim Knowles, now retired. I include it in the story of the *Mauretania* as one instance of the kind of admiration and affection that she inspired. At the request of his cousin, Ralph Cropley*, President Franklin D. Roosevelt dictated this essay† to his secretary, Marguerite (Missy) Le Hand, at Hyde Park, New York, in August 1936. FDR wanted it installed along with the rest of his collection in the Smithsonian,** and insisted that it not be made public until 1950. Ralph Cropley fulfilled FDR's wishes by having it published (although somewhat edited) in *Sea Breezes*†† in June 1950. FDR entitled this work, 'The Queen With A Fighting Heart', and in part, it reads:

'For twenty-eight years the "MAURETANIA" played a poignant part, not only in the maritime history of the world, but in its business life as well as being of unreckoningable service to the United States in time of war. When she was born in 1907, the MAURETANIA was the largest thing ever put together by man. For twenty-two years she remained the fastest liner he had ever produced. When she had long ceased to be the largest ship — when after a gallant struggle in her old age, she no longer was the fastest Atlantic liner, still during another five years of hard work, she remained the world's most famous steamship.

Neither size nor speed alone could have given the MAURETANIA her fame. That rested on something more secure and intangible — on her PERSONALITY. For the MAURETANIA was a ship with a fighting heart. First and foremost, she was not just a great & successful liner. She was THE MAURETANIA.'

'Almost shaping history, the MAURETANIA made history as a carrier of human freight, bringing men and women, as well as American and Canadian soldiers, to and fro across the Atlantic. And through the difficult years of history she lived in, the MAURETANIA never fell short of success. For she was a marked individuality which moved successfully across twenty-eight years, a period during which success was not readily found.'

FDR continues, stating: 'Personally, I had always disliked to travel on the MAURETANIA and her near-sister, the ill-fated LUSITANIA. WHY? Heaven knows! Yet, not for one minute did I ever fail to realize that if there ever was a ship which possesed the thing called "soul", the MAURETANIA did.'

'Every ship had a soul. But the MAURETANIA had one you could talk to. At times she could be wayward and contrary as a thoroughbred.'

'Dislike to travel on her or not, the MAURETANIA always fascinated me with her graceful yacht like lines — her four enormous black topped red funnels — her appearance of power and good breeding. And especially was this so in the latter years of her life when she was painted white for cruising and became known as the "WHITE QUEEN", or as some of her crew have said, "looked like a bloomin' wedding cake".'

'As Capt Rostron once said to me, she had the manners and deportment of a great lady and behaved herself as such.'

'I'm sure that thousands of others besides myself and Ralph Cropley, found it hard on July 2, 1935 when we read that the MAURETANIA was on her last voyage to the shipbreakers to be turned into shot and shell for the next war. It seemed almost blasphemous that a Royal Queen should have for her Valhalla, only a newspaper paragraph.

Granted the MAURETANIA had outlived her usefulness. Granted she had become economically unprofitable, killed by the public craze for needless swimming pools and private baths passengers rarely used the whole trip (other than the toilet) after they'd paid heavily for the "foolish" honor. But why couldn't the British have remembered the MAURETANIA's faithfulness — taken her out to sea and sunk her WHOLE — given her a Viking's funeral, this ship with a fighting heart?

It would have been easier on the living — a Viking funeral. For the living in their hearts will never forget the MAURETANIA. It would have been more inspiring to those who come here after, to know that a ship which was a ship and not a damned freighthouse or one of the present day unholy super de luxe firetraps like the "Normandie" — things nothing more than floating Atlantic Cities — had received decent treatment at her death.'

'But the tragic part of it all to me, is that with this 1936 War Scare in Europe, the steel of her is being recast into shells, guns and other machines of destruction to human life. Yet — well, even in death, her SPIRIT fights on. She never will be forgotten. For the glory that was hers and the traditions she left behind, will live on in the memories of man long after those of us who knew her or served on her, are gone.

'For the MAURETANIA did great things. And in doing them, she lived from one age of human history into another. Yet her greatest achievement alone, her speed, her reliability, her tremendous capacity for hard work, do not explain her enduring popularity nor her peculiar place in the history of ships.'

'Her epitaph might well be — "SHE HAD A FIGHTING HEART." And if I am dead in 1950, from the grave or wherever else Ralph Cropley and I may be in spirit — that is what both of us are going to think of her. May be in the spirit world we will be traveling on her.'

(Signed)
FRANKLIN D. ROOSEVELT

* Ralph Cropley was a banker turned merchant marine purser, who travelled on every ship he could. When FDR was stricken with polio in 1921, it was Ralph Cropley's daily letters about his various sea experiences that gave FDR a renewed interest in life. FDR, along with his wife Eleanor, would eventually collect memorabilia on ships, especially the *Mauretania*. Ralph Cropley went on to become FDR's personal naval spy in World War II, with the highest security clearance, as a result of his extensive knowledge of international shipping.

† The excerpts quoted here are written exactly as presented in the original typed manuscript. It may be noted here that many passages contained in FDR's essay are strikingly similiar to some found in Humfrey Jordan's book, *Mauretania*, published in 1936.

** On 2 July 1935 FDR donated his personal nautical collection to the Smithsonian Institution. Among the items were approximately one hundred photographs of the *Mauretania* (eleven of which are included in this publication), and an 18 ft white-hulled shipbuilder's model of the *Mauretania*, given to the President by Bob Blake, American Head of Cunard. It is currently on loan, and is displayed inside the *Queen Mary* at Long Beach, California. In the model's glass case, FDR had placed a brass oil lantern which hung in the *Mauretania's* 'Main Lobby' for 27 years.

†† Some of the passages quoted in this publication were not published in *Sea Breezes*.

ACKNOWLEDGEMENTS

I would like to acknowledge the assistance of those people who helped me in compiling the photographs in the new section, as well as in the production of the book. They include: in Salem, Massachusetts, Ms Kathy Flynn at the Peabody Museum; in Halifax, Massachusetts, Mr Ted Hindmarsh; in New York, Ms Joyce M. Nappi and Mr Kay Strater; in Washington, DC, Capt Jack Kalina USN (Ret'd) at the Smithsonian Institution; in Boynton Beach, Florida, Mr Everett Viez; in London, England, Ms Jill Rose and Ms Tina Surridge at The Science Museum, South Kensington; in Newcastle-upon-Tyne, Messrs R. French and A. G. Osler at The Museum of Science and Engineering; in Wallsend,

Mr Ian Rae at Swan Hunter and in Liverpool, Dr Alan J. Scarth of the Merseyside Maritime Museum.

Special thanks for most generous assistance go to: Laura F. Brown of The Steamship Historical Society of America Inc at the University of Baltimore Library, in Baltimore, Maryland; Mr Guy Plamondon of Ottawa, Ontario, Canada; Mrs Alma Topen at The Archives, University of Glasgow, Glasgow, Scotland, Messrs Martin Taylor and Terry Charman of the Imperial War Museum, in London; Messrs Bower & Brown of New Brunswick, New Jersey; Mr Stephan Gmelin of Cranford, New Jersey; Mr Allan Lang of International Book Marketing Ltd, New York; Messrs

Frank R. Gerety, PE and Thomas W. Coffey, also of New York; Mrs Catherine Stecchini of Princeton, New Jersey; Mr Jim Knowles (Ret'd) of the Smithsonian Institution in Washington, DC, who so kindly brought the FDR Collection to my attention; Swan Hunter, for the use of their photographic archives and original *Engineering* book used in the publication of this reprint, along with Mr Bryan Rayner, Public Relations Manager; and Mr Darryl Reach, Editorial Director of Patrick Stephens Ltd of Wellingborough.

PHOTOGRAPHIC SOURCES

Page vi: The Library of Congress, Washington, DC; Page vii: Trustees of the Science Museum, London; Page viii: Smithsonian Institution, Washington, DC; Page xvi: Swan Hunter, Wallsend, Tyne and Wear; Blueprint plan following Plate XXXII: Swan Hunter; Plate XXXIX: Swan Hunter (both); Plate XXX: Peabody Museum, Salem, Massachusetts (both); Plate XXXXI: Swan Hunter (both); Plate XXXXII: Cunard booklet, 'Lusitania — Mauretania' ca 1908 (both); Plate XXXXIII: Smithsonian Institution;

Plate XXXXIV: Swan Hunter; Plate XXXXV: Smithsonian Institution; Plate XXXXVI: Swan Hunter (top), Smithsonian Institution (bottom); Plate XXXXVII: Cunard Booklet, 'Lusitania — Mauretania' (left), Swan Hunter (right); Plate XXXXVIII: Swan Hunter (top), Smithsonian Institution (bottom); Plate XXXXIX: Swan Hunter (both); Plate L: Swan Hunter (both); Plate LI: Smithsonian Institution (both); Plate LII: Smithsonian Institution (both); Plate LIII: Swan Hunter; Plate LIV: Swan Hunter (both); Plate LV: Smithsonian

Institution (both); Plate LVI: Swan Hunter (both); Plate LVII: Swan Hunter (both); Plate LVIII: Swan Hunter (both); Pages 142/3: Original Advertisement from Cunard Line, Supplement to Daily Bulletin, 1908 (both); Plate LIX: Swan Hunter. Front cover: Trustees of the Science Museum, London; Back cover: 'Lounge, *Mauretania*' (from Cunard Line, Supplement to Daily Bulletin, 1910).

BIBLIOGRAPHY

Scientific American, Vol XCV — No 18, New York, 3 November 1906. *The New York Times*, New York, 10, 17 & 22 November 1907. *Shipping Illustrated*, Shipping Illustrated Co, New York, 23 November 1907. *Presbrey's Information Guide for Transatlantic Travellers* Ninth Edition: Frank Presbrey Co, New York, 1914. Rostron, Sir Arthur Henry, *Home From The Sea*: The Macmillan Co, New York, 1931. Aylmer, Gerald, *RMS Mauretania — The Ship And Her Record*: Percival Marshall & Co Ltd, London, 1934. Jordan, Humfrey, *Mauretania*: Hodder & Stoughton, London, 1936. Roosevelt, Franklin, D., 'The Queen With A

Fighting Heart': Hyde Park, New York, August 1936. *Sea Breezes* — The Ship Lover's Digest: Liverpool, Vol IX — No 54, June 1950; Vol X — No 56, August 1950; Vol 45 — No 301, January 1971. *The Cunard Express Liners Lusitania and Mauretania*: Reprinted by Patrick Stephens Ltd, London, 1970. Rowland, K. T., *Steam at Sea — A History of Steam Navigation*: Praeger Publishers, New York, 1970. Hughes, Tom, *The Blue Riband of the Atlantic*: Patrick Stephens Ltd, Cambridge, 1975. Kludas, Arnold, *Great Passenger Ships of the World — Vol 1: 1858-1912*: Patrick Stephens Ltd, Cambridge, 1975. Wall, Robert, *Ocean Liners*: E. P. Dutton,

New York, 1977. van Riemsdijk, J. T., and Brown, Kenneth, *The Pictorial History of Steam Power*: Octopus Books, London, 1980. Shaum, John H. Jr, and Flayhart, William H. III, *Majesty at Sea*: Patrick Stephens Ltd, Cambridge, 1981. Maxtone-Graham, John, *The Only Way To Cross*: Patrick Stephens Ltd, Cambridge, 1983. *Turbinia*: Tyne and Wear County Council Museums, Newcastle-upon-Tyne. *Turbinia — The World's First Turbine Driven Ship*: Parsons Marine Turbine Co, Wallsend, Northumberland.

RMS "MAURETANIA" PASSING THE STATUE OF LIBERTY – CIRCA 1909.

A TRIBUTE TO THE 'TURBINIA'

"TURBINA" UNDER FULL STEAM.

THE single greatest innovation in marine propulsion since the invention of the reciprocating steam engine was the turbine engine, developed in 1894-1897 by the Hon Charles A. Parsons. After ten years of research and development of steam turbines for generating electricity in ships and land-based power stations, Parsons realized the potential of turbines for propelling ships. This new power source was lighter and could produce more power with less vibration than the standard reciprocating engines then in use.

In early 1894 Parsons established the Parsons Marine Steam Turbine Company for the purpose of demonstrating the practical application of his turbine propulsion theories. The results of his research were demonstrated in the *Turbinia*, the first turbine-powered vessel in the world, built later that year.

The *Turbinia* was a sleek 44-ton vessel, one hundred ft long, nine ft wide, with a draught of only three ft.* The original design of 1894 had her powered by a single radial-flow steam turbine driving one propeller shaft. After 31 separate speed tests, using seven different designs and arrangements of the propellers, the results were disappointing. With three propellers on one shaft, the highest speeds attained were only 19¾ knots. The problem was discovered to be cavitation, or the vaporization of water created by the high speed of the propellers, which greatly reduced their effectiveness. By the end of 1895, further study of cavitation using stroboscopic photography resulted in the creation of a new propeller design and arrangement.

By February 1896, the *Turbinia* had been newly fitted with

* The *Turbinia* was designated in 1981 as an 'International Historical Mechanical Engineering Landmark' by the American Society of Mechanical Engineers. The vessel has since been fully restored and is scheduled to be moved in late 1987 to the Museum of Science and Engineering in Newcastle-upon-Tyne, where it will be permanently displayed.

three turbines driving three shafts, each with three 18 in propellers. This arrangement produced regular speeds of 32 knots, with a maximum of over 34 knots, and by April 1897 final tests proved the *Turbinia* to be the fastest and most powerful vessel of her size in the world.

Parsons took the opportunity to demonstrate publicly the wonders of his vessel by making a surprise appearance on 27 June 1897 at the International Naval Review, held at Spithead in honour of Queen Victoria's Diamond Jubilee. The *Turbinia* streaked past rows of warships at unprecedented speeds of up to 34 knots (39.134 mph) leaving representatives from almost every navy astonished. Even Queen Victoria was amazed as she observed the event through a telescope in the Osborne House.

Parsons had very effectively made his point: turbines were to be the future of marine propulsion.

TURBINE-DRIVEN QUADRUPLE-SCREW CUNARD LINER "MAURETANIA."

First-Class Smoking-Room Forward Section

GENERAL INDEX.

LIST OF ILLUSTRATIONS.

LIST OF ADDITIONAL ILLUSTRATIONS

THE TRIALS OF THE "MAURETANIA."

By way of preface to the complete description of the Mauretania, we may give details of the official trials, run preparatory to the departure of the ship on her first trans-Atlantic voyage, on the 16th November. The official trials extended over four days, terminating on the 7th November, and for forty-eight hours the vessel steamed at an average speed of 26.04 knots, and, later, made a series of progressive speed runs on the measured mile at Skelmorlie, on the Clyde, up to 26.035 knots, followed by two long-distance runs at a mean speed of 26.17 knots.

The Mauretania ran her 48-hours' trial on a course of 304 nautical miles—between Corswall Point Light, on the Wigtownshire coast, in Scotland, and the Longship Lighthouse, in Cornwall, England. She began with a mean draught of 32 ft. 6 in., which corresponds to a displacement of 36,630 tons —the condition the ship will be in at the beginning of her second day out from Queenstown. The draught conditions therefore assimilated to those in mid-Atlantic. We have thus here a measure of the possibilities of the ship under the most favourable conditions and with a well-organised and adequate staff of trained officers and men. The results on the runs may be first tabulated.

Run.	Distance.	Time.		Speed.	
	Miles	h.	m.	knots	knots
First (southwards) ...	304	11	34	26.28	25.77
Second (northwards)	304	12	2	25.26	
Third (southwards) ...	304	11	6½	27.36	26.31
Fourth (northwards)	304	12	2	25.26	
Totals and mean speed	1216	46	44½	26.04	

The course was selected because its length could be traversed in about twelve hours, so that tidal influences on the north and south runs would balance each other. As regards weather interference, the first run south was affected by adverse conditions. A moderate gale of force 7 was blowing; for the first two hours four points on the port bow, and for the remainder of the twelve hours right ahead. The night, too, was dark. On the run northwards on Monday there was a light breeze astern with a calm sea, but with adverse tidal currents for most of the time. On Monday night's run to the south there were light head winds, and the early part of the night was thick, with rain falling, but it cleared off in the morning hours. On the return run on Tuesday the weather was favourable, although a head wind sprang up late in the afternoon and tidal currents were more adverse.

These facts regarding tidal and weather conditions partly explain the improved speed on the second day—26.31 knots against 25.77 knots. It should also be remembered that with the consumption of coal the ship's draught and displacement became less. The chief consideration, however, was the greater power—193 revolutions against 188. From first to last the machinery worked splendidly. The coal was partly South Wales and partly Yorkshire. The stoking was well organised. In view of the large power developed it should be stated that at no time did the draught pressure in the ashpits exceed ¾ in. Allen's fans supplied 900,000 cubic feet of air per minute. The temperature of the feed-water entering the heaters was 85 deg. Fahr., and at the feed-pumps 200 deg. Fahr. The steam pressure was well maintained, the mean for the forty-eight hours' trial being 180 lb. It is, interesting to record the pressure at the various stages of expansion within the turbines when the engines were making 194 revolutions per minute. These intermediate pressures were read off the indicator, having the four-way cock and connections described in our article on the turbines. With 150 lb. at the high-pressure receiver, the pressure at the end of the first stage of expansion was 113 lb. ; at the end of the second, 87.5 lb. ; at the third, 63 lb. ; at the fourth, 43 lb. ; at the fifth, 31.5 lb. ; at the sixth, 21.5 lb. ; at the seventh, 13 lb. ; and at the low-pressure receiver, 5 lb. At the end of the first stage of expansion of the low-pressure turbine the pressure was that of the atmosphere ; at the end of the second stage there was a vacuum of 4 in. ; at the third, 9¾ in. ; at the fourth, 16.5 in. ; at the fifth, 21.5 in. ; at the sixth, 24 in. ; at the seventh, 26 in. ; and in the condenser, 28 in. The barometric reading was then 30.1 in.

The turbines worked with remarkable steadiness. On the 48-hours' trial they started at about 186 revolutions, but steadily increased, and for hours ran at 192 to 193 revolutions, with very slight variation. The maximum reached was 198 revolutions. The significance of this result will be better appreciated when it is here recalled that the weight of the revolving mass in the low-pressure, turbine casing, for instance, is 126 tons, that the peripheral speed was over 9400 ft. per minute, and that the clearance was only $\frac{8}{100}$ in. In the case of the high-pressure turbines it was less. These facts carry their own encomium as to workmanship and design. There was no untoward feature about the 48 hours' work ; the bearings were always cool. The oil pressure at the bearings was only from 3 lb. to 5 lb., and less at the thrust-bearings.

The mean results on the 48 hours' trial should be tabulated, as they are unexcelled :—

Steam pressure at boilers...	180 lb. per sq. in.
Steam pressure—high-pressure receiver	145 ,, ,,
Steam pressure—low-pressure receiver	4 ,, ,,
Vacuum	28 in.
Barometric reading...	30 ,,
Revolutions of turbines	190 per minute
Speed of ship	26.04 knots

This long-distance trial terminated on Tuesday evening about eight o'clock, and the vessel anchored until the morning near to the Skelmorlie measured mile, to await daybreak for the carrying out of a series of progressive speed trials.

Runs were made at progressive speeds from 18 knots to full speed, and it was specially remarkable that the last, as shown in the table, were confirmative of the 48 hours' trial, revolutions averaging about the same, and speed was 26.03 knots. It was next decided to make runs between Holy Isle Light and Ailsa Craig Light further down the Firth of Clyde, where there was more sea-room. The mean of two runs there made was 26.17 knots. The results on the measured mile and between the lights are tabulated.

Direction.	Time.	Speed.
Northwards	3 min. 13 sec.	18.65 knots
Southwards	3 ,, 20 ,,	18 ,,
Mean speed, 18.32 knots ; mean revolutions, 123 per minute.		
Northwards	2 min. 50 sec.	21.17 knots
Southwards	2 ,, 54 ,,	20.69 ,,
Mean speed, 20.93 knots ; mean revolutions, 139 per minute.		
Northwards	2 min. 35½ sec.	23.17 knots
Southwards	2 ,, 40 ,,	22.5 ,,
Mean speed, 22.83 knots ; mean revolutions, 156 per minute.		

Direction.	Time.	Speed.
Northwards	2 min. 21⅖ sec.	25.46 knots
Southwards	2 ,, 19⅖ ,,	25.82 ,,
Mean speed, 25.64 knots ; mean revolutions, 180 per minute.		
Northwards	2 min. 21 sec.	25.53 knots
Southwards	2 ,, 15½ ,,	26.54 ,,
Mean speed, 26.03 knots ; mean revolutions, 190 per minute.		
Ailsa to Holy Isle ..	37 min. 35 sec.	25.6 knots
Holy Isle to Ailsa ..	35 ,, 54 ,,	26.75 ,,
Mean speed, 26.17 knots ; mean revolutions, 192 per minute.		

This completed the interesting day's work, in the course of which opportunity was afforded of testing the governor gear. This gear is normally set to come into action in the unlikely event of any of the turbines exceeding 230 revolutions per minute. It was, however, brought into use at a speed of 190 revolutions per minute, and under these circumstances the gear, which is described in this volume, in connection with the steam-distribution system, instantly closed the main stop valves, and the ship was brought to a state of rest in a few lengths. The steering mechanism also proved most satisfactory, and with the rudder hard over, and all propellers running ahead, the diameter of the turning circle was but 3¾ lengths—a very good result.

Excepting for the swell from the Atlantic which was experienced when the vessel was running between the Tuskar and the Longship Lighthouse on her four long-distance runs, there was no opportunity of testing her behaviour in a seaway. The periods of the roll and of the pitch were, however, found to be so long that even the maximum amplitude possible need not be disturbing to passengers. The period of the single swing varied from 10 to 12 seconds, according to the weights on board and their distribution, and that of the single pitch was about 4 seconds.

A more important question, from the point of view of the comfort of the passenger, has reference to vibration, and as so much has been said on this subject, especially by the uninformed, it may be well to consider the problem from the general standpoint before recording the results of careful observations on the Mauretania's trials. It is not many years since attention was prominently directed to the problem, and here, as in many other instances, the special conditions of warship service offered the required stimulation to investigation. In torpedo craft vibration became so serious as to make the vessel inefficient. Dr. Otto Schlick, Mr. Yarrow, Mr. Thornycroft, and other workers established the fact that much of the vibration which had been popularly attributed to propeller action was due to faulty design—to unbalanced moving weights setting up mechanical couples which tended to produce longitudinal movements in the structure. Dr. Schlick, in collaboration with Mr. Yarrow and Mr. John Tweedy, produced as near an approximation as was possible to a balanced engine by the proper adjustment of cranks and the relative positions and motions of the parts of the machinery. And now we have the turbine, which of itself is a perfectly balanced engine. In the earlier turbine-driven vessels, with machinery running at a high rate of revolution, vibration practically disappeared, and it became a popular belief that the use of turbines was a perfect cure for the troubles formerly experienced.

This view left out of account the influence of the propeller on the structural vibration. Even with the screw perfectly balanced, as is now the aim, it has to revolve in water set in motion by the advance of the ship, and in the "frictional wake" the forward motions of the particles of water disturbed by the passage of the vessel vary according to their distance from the hull. Consequently there are variations in the effective thrust on each unit of blade area as the rotation is performed ; and as a consequence a succession of impulses is produced, reacting on the structure of the ship. The "frequency" of these impulses is dependent upon the number of revolutions, the number of blades, and the number of screws. Reciprocating engines revolving three-bladed twin screws 85 times per minute may create about 510 impulses per minute. Four three-bladed screws making, as in the new Cunard liners, 190 revolutions may cause over 2250 impulses per minute. The impulses due to one screw may so synchronise with those produced by other screws that the cumulative effect will be great, and vibratory motion may result, as shown in the part of the records taken on the trials of the Mauretania by the Schlick pallograph, reproduced on the next page. From the foregoing remarks it will be seen that with the most perfectly balanced engines and propellers the tendency to vibration is unavoidable, owing to the variation in the frequency of impulses due to variations in thrust on individual units of blade area as they revolve. This explanation must not be taken as apology for the two Cunard liners; there is no need for any. The extent of the vibratory movement in the ships, considered as elastic structures, is exceptionally small when compared with the corresponding movements in ships fitted with well-balanced reciprocating engines. The high frequency of the impulses, however, tend to produce certain local movements in the lighter parts of the superstructure; but these movements have been overcome by local supports or stiffening, involving small additions to steamers and the natural period of vibration of the ship's structure, or with the period of vibration of individual items of fittings or equipment, it is possible, of course, that a maximum accumulation of motion may occur. In such case change in the rate of revolution of the engines or in the number of blades, or other means of destroying such synchronism, will greatly reduce, if not prevent, serious accumulation of motion. Twinscrews of different pitches, and, therefore, of different rates of revolution, have given good results. In one case a three-bladed and a four-aft, in the centre of the athwartship line between the two wing propellers, when they were making from 192 to 194 revolutions per minute. The wavy irregularities of the vibration lines are due to the ship rolling; the vertical and horizontal vibrations are of very small amplitude.

This diagram, with the records of speed and power, give the fullest promise of splendid performances on the Atlantic. They confirm in every respect the anticipations of experiment and calculation. A comparison, too, of the results on the measured mile, when the hull was clean, against

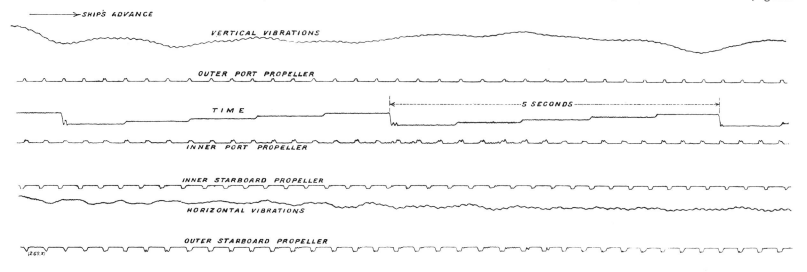

weight. Again, in certain of the fittings—notably, electric-light pendants, shutters, windows, &c.—care is being taken to obviate that chatter and noise which suggest to the uninitiated abnormal vibration, when they are really due only to high frequency rather than to amplitude of motion.

The entire elimination of variation of impulse, which would produce an absolute absence of vibration, is an ideal condition, which is wrongly considered to be attainable by the adoption of the completely balanced turbine. When synchronism of the period occurs between these comparatively small impulses in turbine-driven bladed propeller have been fitted to a twin-screw steamer. But our analysis of the situation must not, as we have already said, be taken as apologetic, or even specially applicable to the Lusitania and Mauretania. Both ships are remarkable for the comparative absence of any structural vibration set up by the propellers, and in many parts of the ship it was difficult to realise that she was steaming at 26 knots, and that the engines were developing about double the power hitherto exerted in the propulsion of any ship. The pallogram given above is proof: it was taken on the promenade deck the performance with a year's marine growth coating the skin of the ship, further justifies the deduction made from model results, as at full speed the resistance due to dirty hull involved 15 per cent. more power than when clean, and at lower speeds about 20 per cent. The final result is, undoubtedly, a great triumph for British shipbuilding, and in departing from the subject now we offer congratulations to the Cunard Company, to its chairman—Mr. William Watson—and to the builders and engineers; and specially to Mr. G. B. Hunter, D.Sc., Sir William White, K.C.B., and Mr. Andrew Laing.

Photo. by Elliott and Fry.

William Watson

QUADRUPLE-SCREW TURBINE-DRIVEN CUNARD LINER "MAURETANIA."

Seat in First-Class Grand Entrance, Boat Deck.

THE CUNARD TURBINE-DRIVEN QUADRUPLE-SCREW ATLANTIC LINER "MAURETANIA."

THE Mauretania and Lusitania are sister-ships. They are, however, the production of different firms, both experienced in merchant shipping work, and distinguished for originality, so that the vessels differ in a hundred and one details. No apology is therefore needed for entering upon a description of the Mauretania so soon after our comprehensive review of the design, construction, and performance of the Lusitania, especially as we propose to devote particular attention to these variations, and to some details which have important influences in the development of maritime practice. The Lusitania has given full promise in her Atlantic performance of achieving the highest expectations of all concerned, and of realising in service the splendid results got on the trial. In looking forward to the fulfilment of these aims the scientist is more patient than the "man in the street," because better informed, and more conscious of the difficulties of securing at once the precision in organisation essential in all ships, but more especially in vessels like the new Cunarders, with such extensive machinery, made up of immense units, and necessarily distributed over such a large area as 600 ft. by 88 ft.

The Mauretania, in her preliminary trials, has given promise of equally good results, and next year we shall probably have a very interesting friendly competition between the two ships. Such data as may become available must influence future progress, because of the differences in the form of stern in the two vessels and in the proportions of the propellers, which have had very careful consideration on the part of both firms. Those interested in marine propulsion do not require to be reminded that results vary also with differences in the longitudinal position of the propellers, their distance from the hull, the size of boss, the ratio of blade to disc area, and of pitch to diameter. The comparative propulsive efficiency realised in these two vessels may therefore be analysed with considerable gain.

We do not propose again to review the development which the Mauretania, like the Lusitania, signalises in Atlantic shipping. That has been done time and again, and quite lately in connection with the latter vessel (see ENGINEERING, August 2, 1907), but it is important, in view of much that has been written during the past few weeks about the enormous coal consumption of modern liners, to make some analysis of the progress in thermodynamics from this particular standpoint. It is easy to offer comparisons between the coal consumption of an immense Mauretania and the relatively small and slow steamer of twenty or thirty years ago. The important consideration is the expenditure for work done, and this is a point too often lost sight of. When effort is made, even with a moderate approximation to accuracy, to reduce Atlantic economy to a common standard of comparison, it is found that the efficiency of the new ships reflects the highest credit on engineering. What one has to consider is the coal burned per unit of work done, or per ton-mile, as the railway statistician has it. If higher speed is demanded, increased size is essential, since even with the best result every 100 horse-power added involves an addition to machinery weight of approximately 14 tons, and to the area occupied of about 40 square feet. To accommodate this the ship must necessarily be larger. This in turn involves a further addition to power to maintain the same speed, and thus the one reacts upon the other. The displacement is also influenced by the passenger accommodation. It is not enough to know that in about thirty years the number of cabin passengers carried has increased from 210 to 1027 ; what is more important is that the average cabin accommodation per passenger has increased by over 250 cubic feet, and that the public, with the growth of wealth, seek for greater luxuries, and are willing to pay for them. The average fare for first-class passengers in our latest ships is as high as 40l. The value per square foot of deck area is, therefore, as great as formerly, and it is possible also that the earning power per ton of displacement is as great, since the progress in engineering, and in propulsive efficiency or economy, has advanced almost at the same rate as the size of the ship. Certainly, with human nature as it is, the fastest ships can always command a good revenue, and thus the Cunard Company are sure to earn that high financial reward which their enterprise merits —at all events until the new ships are excelled.

Confining ourselves now to the question of propulsive efficiency, we give in Table I. a suggestive record of progress of Atlantic steaming at the end of each decade since the advent of the Cunard Company in 1840. The reader, in noticing the coal burned, should reflect carefully on the great cost in power of large additions to speed.

TABLE I.—*Progress of Atlantic Steaming.*

1.	2. Time on Outward Voyage.			3. Average Speed.	4. Displacement.	5. Indicated Horse-Power.	6. Indicated Horse-Power per Ton Displacement.	7. Coal Burned per 100 Tons Displacement per Nautical Mile Propelled.
—	days	hr.	min.	knots	tons			lb.
1840	14	8	0	8½	2,050	710	0.346	22
1850	11	3	0	12	3,620	2,000	0.552	21
1860	9	6	0	12½	7,130	3,600	0.505	18
1870	8	4	0	14½	6,900	3,000	0.434	12
1880	7	10	47	15¼	9,900	6,300	0.626	10
1890	5	19	18	20	13,000	18,500	1.42	12
1900	4	23	0	23½	23,620	40,000	1.69	12
1907	4	12	0	25	38,000	68,000	1.79	11

We have given the results at the end of each decade rather than with reference to each ship, as this more unusual division affords a clearer indication as to the rate of progress in speed and efficiency. In the second column there are given the times taken on the outward voyage, and in the third column the average speeds. It will be noted that the progress, while steady, has been at a diminishing rate in recent years, but it must be remembered that the power necessary to add to 22 and 23-knot speeds is enormously greater than to the 20 knots of seventeen years ago. This is made clearly evident by the fourth and fifth columns, which give respectively the displacement tonnage and the indicated horse-power of the propelling machinery. The proportion of power to displacement is stated in column 6, and here we have at once a measure of increase in power required for higher speed. It will be noted that in forty-seven years the speed has doubled, but the power per unit of displacement has multiplied more than three times. This is a very satisfactory result, and still more so is a comparison with the ships of seventeen years ago. Two factors account for this higher propulsive efficiency : one, the increase in the length of the ship ; and the other, the better results attained with present-day propellers, not only because of their more satisfactory proportions, but because of their deeper immersion. Very little advance had been made between 1840 and 1880 upon the length of ships, 450 ft. to 500 ft. being about the limit, while the draught was seldom over 23 ft. In the period from 1880 to 1883—when there was a great step in advance owing to the construction of Cunard, Guion, and White Star liners—this restriction, prescribed by the dimensions of the docks, severely handicapped the designers. Even the Umbria and Etruria were only 500 ft. in length, with a draught of 23 ft. Since then, however, progress has been marked. The Campania was made 600 ft. long ; the Germans added 100 ft. more in their series of very fine ships, and arranged for a draught of 29 ft. Once again the Cunard Company have forced the pace by making their new vessels 790 ft. long over all, with a draught of 33 ft. 6 in. The harbour authorities are awaking to the fact that this increase in length and of draught is an improvement from the propulsive point of view, and consequently are arranging for suitable docks and deeper river and harbour approaches.

The most interesting figures in the table, however, are in the last column, giving the coal burned per 100 tons of displacement per nautical mile. This, the nearest approximation possible to the consumption of fuel per unit of work done, is instructive, as it brings within compass not only the gain from the less resistance consequent on greater length and finer lines, and from deeper immersion of propellers, but the advantages of higher steam pressures, heated air for draught, feed-heating, fuller utilisation of steam expansion, and other contributing influences towards economy in marine machinery. It is truly a striking fact that in the 67 years speed has been multiplied threefold, while the coal used per 100 tons of displacement per mile has been reduced by 50 per cent. This fact alone is important, in view of what has been written regarding the heavy coal bill of modern ships.

The influences at work have been many. In the early Atlantic liners the steam pressure in the old side-lever paddle-wheel engines was 12 lb., and although this increased to 25 lb. in the 'sixties, the same type of machinery was adopted, cylinders having increased from 72½ in. to 100 in. in diameter, and the piston stroke from 82 in. to 144 in. Then came the era of the screw propeller : first, with horizontal trunk engines, driving direct, as in the Inman liners ; with oscillating geared engines in the early Cunard liners ; and finally, with the inverted or hammer type, as we know it to-day. The cylindrical boiler meanwhile took the place of the box tubular type. The compound engine was not early adopted on the Atlantic. In 1880, when the first "greyhounds" were built, they had three inverted cylinders and three cranks, working compound, with a pressure of 100 lb. They were the first of the vessels with only nominal cargo capacity. The triple-expansion engine was adopted on the Atlantic in 1887; quadruple expansion engines were fitted in the Ivernia in 1899. By 1890 pressures had increased to 180 lb., and although they attained a maximum of 225 lb. in the Kaiser Wilhelm II., there has been a decrease for the turbine machinery of the later ships.

The Mauretania, like her consort, represents undoubtedly a high effort at steam economy, and this probably accounts for the remarkable result suggested in the last column, in view particularly of the high speed attained. It is realised that in turbine efficiency higher vacua and, consequently, fuller expansion are more important than very high steam pressures, since every inch of vacuum above 26 in. is equal to a reduction of about 6 per cent. in the steam consumption per brake horse-power, whereas experience showed that in reciprocating practice high vacua may occasion an actual net increase in steam consumption. Again, in the new Cunarders, the exhaust steam from the many auxiliaries is utilised for heating the feed-water in the surface feed-heaters. The exhaust from the turbo-generators is utilised in the contact feed-heater, as is also the vapour from the feed make-up evaporators. The use of the heaters results in the temperature of the feed-water being raised to over 200 deg. Fahr. Another element in the economy is the heating of the furnace gases on the Howden system. The stokeholds are arranged with fore-and-aft baffle-plates, so that the air from the cowls passes down the outer compartments to near the level of the stokehold floors, and returns in the centre along the boiler uptakes to the fan-inlets; so that, before even it enters the nest of tubes in the uptakes, to be heated by the escaping hot gases from the furnace—an important part of the Howden system—it attains a fairly high temperature. Thus the temperature of the draught at the furnace door is about 250 deg. Fahr.

By the introduction of a supplementary dry-air pump in addition to the ordinary Weir pump, a high vacuum is attained. Experience on the Cunarders shows that with this system a vacuum of over 28 in., with a barometric reading of $29\frac{3}{4}$ in., is easily realised. There are many other instances of modern developments to ensure high efficiency, but enough has been said to show the general trend, and explain in some measure the high economy attained in present-day Atlantic liners, as indicated by the last column in Table I.

HIGH SPEED IN MERCHANT AND NAVAL SHIPS.

British engineers must be awarded the credit for this economy, and it is satisfactory to reflect that, alike in size and speed, we now hold the premier position. We have all along contended that only the opportunity was required to enable the British marine constructor to attain first place, because an analysis of the fastest ships in the merchant service, as well as in the various naval fleets, shows that Britain still holds the field. From Lloyd's list we have prepared Table II., which shows that while Britain owns forty-eight steamers which exceed 20 knots in speed, foreign countries possess only thirty vessels, and ten or eleven of these were constructed in this country. It is true that in ocean liners our position is

TABLE II.—*List of Steamers Exceeding 20 Knots' Speed in the British and Foreign Merchant Fleets.*

—	United Kingdom.	Belgium.	France.	Germany.	Holland.	Russia.	United States.
Over 10,000 tons	6	—	3	5	—	—	4
Between 5000 and 10,000 tons ..	1	—	—	—	—	1	—
Between 1000 and 4999 tons ..	30	7	3	1	3	—	1
Under 1000 tons	11	—	2	—	—	—	—
	48	7	8	6	3	1	5

not so favourable, as Germany possesses five vessels of between 22 and $23\frac{1}{2}$ knots, against our six, and, excepting the Mauretania and Lusitania, the fastest of our ships is of 22 knots speed. In Channel steamers, however, we have long held the premier position, and the problems which have been solved in the design of the thirty vessels between 1000 and 5000 tons gross register, some of them steaming from $23\frac{1}{2}$ to 24 knots, have eminently fitted British builders for undertaking the work of constructing a Lusitania or a Mauretania, so that it is fair to reckon these smaller vessels in making a comparison of fast merchant craft.

British supremacy is further indicated by a corresponding consideration of the number of warships of over 20 knots' speed owned by the various Powers. We have 82 vessels exceeding 20 knots in speed, whereas the other Powers combined have but 211. Practically all of these ships are over 1000 tons. Thus there are 293 naval ships of over 20 knots' speed, as compared with 78 merchant vessels of this speed. This comparison once again demonstrates the stimulating influence on naval architecture and marine engineering arising from the demands of naval defence, and this influence reflects also upon the merchant marine. One-fourth of the high-speed ships owned by foreign navies have been constructed in British yards, so that of the 293 vessels nearly one-half are the product of British marine works. This is gratifying, as is also the fact that of vessels exceeding 25 knots' speed, we have, in addition to the Mauretania and Lusitania, eleven cruisers, while foreign Powers possess only three, and these are small craft; between 24 and 25 knots we have three, and foreign Powers five; and between 23 and 24 knots we have eighteen, of which seventeen are armoured, a condition which severely handicaps the marine constructor in the development of speed. Foreign Powers have six armoured ships of this speed, and twenty-seven ordinary cruisers, and of these we have constructed about half.

TABLE III.—*British and Foreign Warships (excluding Torpedo Craft) with a Speed of over 20 Knots.*

—	20 to 21 Knots.		21 to 22 Knots.		22 to 23 Knots.		23 to 24 Knots.		24 to 25 Knots.		Over 25 Knots.	
	Armoured Ships.	Cruisers.	Armoured Ships.	Cruisers.	Armoured Ships.	Cruisers.	Armoured Ships.	Cruisers.	Armoured Ships.	Cruisers.	Armoured Ships.	Cruisers.
Britain	1	26	4	5	9	5	17	1	3	—	—	11
Argentina	2	2	—	—	—	2	—	1	—	—	—	—
Austria - Hungary	2	4	—	3	1	—	—	1	—	—	—	1
Brazil	—	1	—	—	—	3	—	1	—	—	—	—
Chili	—	1	1	2	1	1	—	—	—	—	—	—
France	1	13	10	3	3	3	5	3	—	1	—	—
Germany	3	3	2	7	2	3	—	11	—	—	—	—
Italy	5	5	—	4	6	1	—	—	—	—	1	—
Japan	4	6	1	3	3	3	1	2	—	—	—	—
Portugal	—	1	—	—	—	1	—	—	—	—	—	1
Russia	2	3	4	1	—	2	—	7	—	1	—	—
Spain	3	4	—	—	—	1	—	—	—	—	—	—
Sweden	—	3	1	—	—	—	—	—	—	—	—	—
Turkey	—	1	—	—	—	3	—	—	—	—	—	—
United States of America	—	3	1	1	14	1	—	1	—	3	—	—
	22	50	20	24	30	24	6	27	—	5	1	2

Thus, as regards the number of fast war and merchant ships, Britain occupies a favourable position; and with the advent of the Mauretania and Lusitania we have recovered the first place on the Atlantic, which has been held by Germany for ten years. Not for over fifty years had the winning flag been separated from the Union Jack, and even then it was only for a very short time. Germany undoubtedly deserves its place because of its commercial enterprise, and we welcome German competition in the belief that it will continue to stimulate British ship-owners.

THE "MAURETANIA" AND HER COMPETITORS.

In giving the dimensions of the Mauretania, in Table V., we place side by side corresponding figures, not only for the sister-ship Lusitania, but for the fastest ships of other nations. The data given are suggestive of the great advance which we have made since the Campania and Lucania were built by the Fairfield Company fourteen years ago, and particularly of the advance made on the German results.

Table V., on the opposite page, is suggestive from many points of view. The new Cunard liners have a length of 8.65 times the beam, whereas the high-speed German ships have a length of 9.23 times the beam, and the American ship of 8.50 times the beam. Too much importance, however, should not be attached to this proportion of length to beam. Dock accommodation has had a restricting influence of varied degree. German ships, owing to the limited draught in the North German ports, are placed at a disadvantage, and therefore the tendency has evidently been to accommodate the need for great displacement in length rather than in depth. There are those who doubt whether the German lines will attempt to excel the Mauretania and Lusitania with a correspondingly large ship; the impression prevails, rightly or wrongly, that if they essay the task they will attempt to do so with a moderate-sized vessel on the lines of the Kaiser Wilhelm II., reducing the size by eliminating all but first-class passengers. The difficulty, however, is one of accommodating machinery, and we should welcome such an enterprising move by our German friends, as it would throw considerable light, not only upon the possibilities of practical success, but also upon the financial balance.

Another point which will interest the reader is the relation between power and displacement, but as we have entered upon this question already, we may pass on to the ratio of grate surface to heating surface, and of heating surface to power developed. In the case of high-speed German ships it will be seen that the ratio of grate surface to heating surface is 1 to 34, whereas in the Mauretania it is 1 to 38.8. The boilers in the Kaiser Wilhelm II. are, however, worked on the open stokehold system, whereas the Cunard liners are worked on the Howden system. In the case of the Deutschland, which is on the Howden system, the ratio of grate surface to heating surface is 1 to 38. The French builders, who also adopt the Howden system, have a grate area of 1 to 37 of heating surface. As to the proportion of heating surface to power, it will be noted that in the Mauretania there is for each unit of power 2.33 square feet of heating surface, as compared with 2.68 square feet in the open stokehold boiler system of the Kaiser Wilhelm II., 2.35 in the Howden boiler arrangement in the Deutschland, and 2.25 in the Howden system in the United States fastest steamers.

More interesting, however, is the performance of the ships on the Atlantic, and even at the risk of repeating ourselves, we think it well to give here a short statement of the recent record performances, including the best so far made by the Lusitania. This last ship, however, along with the Mauretania, will, we are convinced, still further reduce the time, and will maintain on the ocean an average speed of 25 knots under normal conditions.

TABLE IV.—*Some Recent Atlantic Record Performances.*

Record-Breaking Steamers.		Time.			Speed	Best Day's Run.
		days	hrs.	min.	knots	
In 1840, Britannia' strip—Liverpool to Boston		14	0	0	$8\frac{1}{2}$	—
In 1862, Scotia's trip—Liverpool to New York		8	22	0	13	—
Servia, 1884 ..	Outwards	7	10	47	—	—
	Homewards	6	23	57	—	—
Oregon, 1884	Outwards	6	10	9	—	—
	Homewards	6	16	59	—	—
America, 1884. Homewards ..		6	14	18	—	—
Umbria, or Etruria ..	Outwards	6	1	44	19.3	501
	Homewards	6	3	12	19.1	—
Paris, or New York ..	Outwards	5	14	24	20.7	530
	Homewards	5	19	57	20.1	—
Campania, or Lucania, 1904	Outwards	5	7	23	21.82	562
	Homewards	5	8	38	22.01	533
Kaiser Wilhelm der Grosse, 1902	Cherbourg-Sandy Hook	5	15	20	22.81	580
Kaiser Wilhelm der Grosse, 1901	Sandy Hook-Plymouth	5	10	0	23	553
Deutschland, 1903 ..	Cherbourg-New York	5	11	54	23.15	—
" 1900	New York-Plymouth	5	7	38	23.51	—
Kronprinz Wilhelm, 1902	Cherbourg-Sandy Hook	5	11	57	23.09	581
Kronprinz Wilhelm, 1901	Sandy Hook-Plymouth	5	8	18	23.47	561
Kaiser Wilhelm II., 1904	Cherbourg-Sandy Hook	5	12	44	23.12	583
Kaiser Wilhelm II., 1906	Sandy Hook-Plymouth	5	8	16	23.58	564
Lusitania	Outwards	4	18	40	24.25	618
	Homewards	4	22	53	23.61	—

The Deutschland's westward mean speed of 23.51 knots, made over a long course, and not, therefore, a record in point of time, is equivalent to steaming from Queenstown to Sandy Hook in about 4 days 23 hours; and the Kaiser Wilhelm II.'s homeward mean speed of 23.58 knots would bring her to Queenstown in a few minutes' less time.

THE CONCEPTION OF THE "MAURETANIA": THE CONTRACT.

The Lusitania's achievement is the first fruit of several years of careful consideration, not only of the economical, but of the practical, possibilities of such a high speed. As we have pointed out on previous occasions, the British nation, in view of its long record of successes in merchant shipping and ship-owning, looked with something of disappointment at the success in speed of the German ships, and consequently they welcomed the completion of an agreement between the Government and the Cunard Company for the construction of two ships which should be capable of maintaining British commercial prestige. As these vessels will perform useful service in the event of war, and will carry the mails, the financial arrangement between the British Government and the Cunard Company is based on sound commercial principles, and cannot be regarded in any sense as a shipping subsidy. The payments made are for work done; nor are they excessive for the duty to be discharged. Apart altogether from the advantage of high-speed for the carrying of mails on such a service is very exten-

industry, which dates back about fifty years, the work carried on, with some exceptions, was the construction of cargo steamers; but in recent years there has been a distinct advance, and we find in the list of ships turned out each year a greater variety, and a larger number of the higher class. It is true that one or two firms have, by making warship work a speciality, achieved great success; but here we are concerned with merchant-ship work.

The Cunard Company, as has always been the case, were guided by experience, and it should be remembered that the contract for the Mauretania was largely a consequence of the proved success of previous Cunard liners built and engined by the Tyne firms named, and by intimate acquaintance with the producing facilities of the establishments

North-East Coast was supplied from the Wallsend Slipway and Engineering Company; and it is a further significant fact that the manager of the establishment, who is responsible for the design of the machinery—Mr. Andrew Laing—was associated not only with those six ships, but with many of the Cunard liners built at Fairfield on the Clyde. The confidence, therefore, which the Cunard Company had in ordering the machinery from his firm was the result of intimate acquaintance with his work. Great developments have been made in the equipment of the establishment. The chairman of the company, Mr. Thomas Bell, whose portrait we give on page 6, has by his great commercial experience contributed much to this improved status of the company, and, along with his co-directors, has encouraged the policy of

TABLE V.—SHOWING DIMENSIONS OF THE " MAURETANIA " AND HER COMPETITORS.

Name of Ship ..	" Mauretania."	" Lusitania."	" Kronprincessin Cecilie."	" Kaiser Wilhelm II."	" Deutschland."	"Campania" and " Lucania."	" St. Paul " and " St. Louis."	" La Provence."
Name of builders ..	Swan, Hunter, and Co., Wallsend-on-Tyne	John Brown and Co., Clydebank	Vulcan Company, of Stettin	Vulcan Company, of Stettin	Vulcan Company, of Stettin	Fairfield Company, Glasgow	Cramp, of Philadelphia	S. des Chantiers et Ateliers de St. Nazaire
Name of owning company ..	Cunard	Cunard	North German Lloyd	North German Lloyd	Hamburg - American	Cunard	American	French
Year when built ..	1907	1907	1907	1903	1900	1893	1895	1906
Length over all ..	790 ft.	785 ft.	706 ft. 4 in.	706 ft. 6 in.	684 ft.	622 ft.	554.2 ft.	597 ft. 1½ in.
Length between perpendiculars ..	760 ,,	760 ,,	682 ft. 9 in.	683 ft.	662 ft. 9 in.	600 ,,	535.8 ,,	
Breadth.. ..	88 ,,	88 ,,	72 ft.	72 ,,	67 ft.	65 ft. 3 in.	63 ft.	64 ft. 7½ in.
Depth, moulded ..	60 ft. 6 in.	60 ft. 4½ in.	44 ft. 2 in.	52 ft. 6 in.	44 ft.	41 ft. 6 in.	42 ft.	41 ft. 8 in.
Gross tonnage.. ..	32,000	31,000 tons	19,400	20,000 tons	16,502 tons	12,500 tons	11,629 tons	13,750 tons
Draught	33 ft. 6 in.	33 ft. 6 in.	30 ft.	29 ft.	29 ft.	25 ft.	26 ft.	26 ft. 9 in.
Displacement	38,000 tons	38,000 tons	27,000 tons	26,000 tons	23,620 tons	18,000 tons	16,000 tons	19,160 tons
Number of passengers (first) ..	563	552	729	775	693	600	320	442
,, ,, (second) ..	464	460	343	343	302	400	200	132
,, ,, (third) ..	1138	1186	740	770	288	700	800	808
Machinery makers ..	Wallsend Slipway and Engineering Company	John Brown and Co., Clydebank	Vulcan Company, of Stettin	Vulcan Company, of Stettin	Vulcan Company, of Stettin	Fairfield Company, Glasgow	Cramp, of Philadelphia	St. Nazaire Company
Type of engine ..	Parsons turbine	Parsons turbine	4 sets, four-cylinder quadruple-expansion	4 sets, 4 - cylinder quadruple - expansion	6-cylinder, quadruple-expansion	5-cylinder triple-expansion	6-cylinder quadruple-expansion	
Number of cranks ..	..	..	6	6	4	3	4	4
Diameter of cylinders ..	..	..	Four of 37.40 in. ; four of 49.21 in.; four of 74.80 in.; four of 112.20 in.	Four of 37.4 in.; four of 49.2 in.; four of 74.8 in.; four of 112.2 in.	Two 36.61 in.; one 73.6 in.; two 106.3 in.	Two of 37 in.; one of 79 in. ; and two of 98 in.	Two of 28 in. ; one of 55 in. ; one of 77 in. ; and two of 77 in.	Two of 47.2 in. ; two of 76.2 in. ; and four of 88.18 in.
Stroke of piston ..	..	..	70.87 in.	70.86 in.	72.8 in.	69 in.	60 in.	66.9 in.
Number and type of boilers ..	Cylindrical : 23 double-ended ; 2 single-ended	25 cylindrical; 23 double-ended; 2 single-ended	12 double-ended ; 7 single-ended	12 double-ended ; 7 single-ended	12 double-ended ; 4 single-ended	12 double - ended ; 1 single-ended	6 double-ended ; 4 single-ended	21 single-ended
Number of furnaces ..	192	192	124	124	112	102	64	84
Steam pressure ..	195 lb. per sq. in.	195 lb. per sq. in.	220.5 per sq. in.	225 lb. per sq. in.	220 lb. per sq. in.	165 lb. per sq. in.	200 lb. per sq. in.	206 per sq. in.
Total heating surface ..	159,000 sq. ft.	158,350 sq. ft.	101,900 sq. ft.	107,643 sq. ft.	84,468 sq. ft.	82,000 sq. ft.	40,320 sq. ft.	58,342 sq. in.
,, grate area ..	4,060 ,,	4,048 ,,	2,970 ,,	3,121	2,188 ,,	2,630 ,,	1,144 ,,	1,571 ,,
Draught	Howden's	Howden's	Open stokehold	Open stokehold	Howden's	Open stokehold	Howden's	Howden's
Total indicated horse-power ..	68,000	68,000	45,000	38,000 and 40,000	36,000	30,000	18,000	30,000
Highest mean speed on Atlantic passage	25 knots*	25 knots*	23.5 knots *	23 to 23.5 knots (estimated)	23.25 to 23.51 knots	22.01 knots	21.08 knots	22 knots*
Revolutions per minute ..	180	180	82	80	76	..	..	80

* Designed.

sive, the new ships are important acquisitions from the naval point of view.

The ships have been designed and built under the direction of the Admiralty to meet naval conditions, and the work from beginning to end has been supervised by Mr. C. G. Hall, a member of Sir Philip Watts' staff. The machinery is entirely under the water line, the steering-gear and the rudder are similarly protected, while the coal - bunkers are arranged to still further reduce the possibility of damage from artillery. The ships, moreover, are each to carry twelve 6-in. quick-firing guns (see Fig. 53 on the two-page Plate XXXIV. They have thus an armament equal to some of the modern first-class cruisers costing a million sterling. The Mauretania and her consort may not be able to carry on a long fight, but with their immense speed, and with a radius of action at full speed equal to that of some modern cruisers at less than half the speed, these vessels will be able to do great service as scouts. Moreover, 25 knots is the rate at which they can steam for about six days, whereas no cruiser will be able to maintain over 23 knots for more than 40 hours.

When the agreement had come to between the Government and the Cunard Line negotiations were entered into for the construction of the two ships. At this time of day it is not necessary to repeat the story of these negotiations, however interesting. It is enough to say that throughout all vicissitudes there seemed continuity in the probability that one of the vessels would be built by Messrs. Swan, Hunter, and Wigham Richardson, Limited, and be engined by the Wallsend Slipway and Engineering Company, Limited. This fact and the success of the Mauretania, so far, carrying distinct promise of complete realisation of the requirements of the service, demonstrates more than any other circumstances the great advance in the shipbuilding industry on Tyneside. There is no gainsaying the fact that in the early years of the

and the experience of the staffs. The Mauretania is the seventh Cunard liner built in recent years on the North-East Coast, as shown in Table VI. It will be noted that the builders of the Mauretania were also responsible for the Ultonia, Ivernia, and the Carpathia, the two latter vessels of the intermediate class, which have proved most desirable

TABLE VI.—Tyne-Built Cunard Liners.

Year	Vessel	Shipbuilder	Engine-Builder	Displacement in Tons	I.H.P.	Speed in Knots
1898	Ultonia	Swan & Hunter, Limited	Furness, Westgarth, & Co., Ltd.	17,700	4,000	11½
1899	Veria	Armstrong, Whitworth, & Co.	Wallsend Slipway & Engineering Co.,Ltd.	7,330	2,500	11½
1900	Ivernia	Swan & Hunter, Limited	,,	24,400	11,000	16
1903	Brescia	J. L. Thompson & Sons	,,	7,400	2,500	11½
1903	Carpathia	Swan & Hunter, Limited	,,	22,760	8,500	15
1903	Slavonia	Sir J. Laing	,,	17,900	6,000	13¾
1907	Mauretania	Swan, Hunter, and Wigham Richardson, Limited	,,	38,000	68,000	25

ships from the point of view of economy. Indeed, these two steamers, which have quadruple-expansion engines, are regarded as exceptional in this latter respect. It was therefore not surprising to those conversant with the progress of Messrs. Swan, Hunter, and Wigham Richardson, under the direction and chairmanship of Mr. G. B. Hunter, D.Sc., to learn that his firm had been entrusted with the building of the Mauretania.

As regards the machinery builders, there was even less room for surprise. The machinery for six of the seven Cunard liners which originated on the

progress. In ten years since Mr. Laing's appointment the covered area of the works has been doubled and the production increased three-fold, while the class of work done is much higher.

The large measure of prestige which the Tyne, as a shipbuilding district, gains by the success of the Mauretania is, therefore, due to the association of Mr. G. B. Hunter and Mr. Andrew Laing in this, as in other important, work.

THE DESIGN OF THE SHIP.

The preliminary designs put forward by both contracting firms were naturally the subject of much consideration, and it was arranged by the Cunard Company that both ships should be, as far as possible, similar in design. There have thus been frequent conferences, and it is gratifying to say that the one aim of all the firms concerned was to achieve the best result without reference to individual or company credit.

The first design prepared by Messrs. Swan, Hunter, and Wigham Richardson, the builders of the ship, was got out in the latter part of 1901. The first proposal was for a vessel 700 ft. long to steam 24 knots on a draught of 30 ft. 6 in. In the next year the length and width were proportionately increased, the one to 750 ft. and the other to 75 ft., and at the same time, with a slightly reduced draught, the firm were prepared to guarantee 25 knots. Following upon this were a succession of models, most of them 750 ft. long, but varying in beam from 76 ft. up to 82 ft. In November of 1902 the Cunard Company invited proposals for a vessel 750 ft. long, 76 ft. in beam, and 52 ft. deep. From this point the advance to greater beam, proportionate to length, was a noticeable feature, and at the same time there was a steady development in the over-all length. So far, however, the idea was for reciprocating engines, driving three screws, and in July, 1903, when the second outline specification was issued by the Cunard Company, it was for two triple-screw steamers 750 ft. long by 75 ft. beam, to steam continuously at 24¾ knots. The present dimensions were arrived at early in 1904, and at that time a series of models were tested at the tank at Haslar, when the Swan and Hunter scheme for a vessel 760 ft. long by 80 ft. beam, and 60 ft. 3 in. moulded depth, proved most satisfactory. Ultimately, as the result of further experiments, the leading dimensions of the ship were fixed as follow :—

Length between perpendiculars... ... 760 ft.
Length over all ... ... 790 ,,
Breadth, extreme ... ... 88 ,,
Depth to shelter-deck ... ... 60 ft. 6 in.

The type of machinery was also the subject of very careful research, and the Cunard Company appointed a commission to inquire into the whole circumstances, and to offer suggestions on the question. Here also the story of the procedure is a familiar one, and has been reviewed in ENGINEERING. It is only right, however, that in such a complete review of the ship we should again name the members of the Commission. Mr. James Bain, the marine superintendent of the Cunard

To the experimental work in connection with turbines reference will be made in describing the machinery. But here mention ought to be made of the great service the Hon. Charles Parsons, C.B., has rendered in the invention of his turbine as adopted on these new Cunarders. To his genius, indeed, the success of the vessels is largely due, and the engineering world, no less than the firms concerned, render him full credit for this great advance in marine engineering.

EXPERIMENTS ON FORM OF SHIP AND PROPELLERS.

The long and valuable series of experiments carried out by Dr. R. E. Froude at the Government tank at Haslar, under the direction of Sir Philip Watts, K.C.B., Director of Naval Construction, yielded valuable results regarding the problems of ship resistance and propeller efficiency. The speed performances of the two ships have proved the accuracy of these experimental data. But Messrs. Swan, Hunter, and Wigham Richardson, and the Wallsend Slipway and Engineering Company, very properly decided, early in their

the forward part of the launch. As shown in Figs. 1 and 2, there were four shafts in the model, each driven by its separate motor, and with regulators for speeds varying from 150 to 950 revolutions. The coupling served as a self-recording torque dynamometer designed on a well-known principle (Fig. 5). The illustration shows three bevel-wheels, two of which are keyed to the motor-shaft and propeller-shaft respectively, while the centre wheel revolves on a swinging axis supported by a spring S, the extension of which is recorded by a pencil P on the drum D, which is made to revolve slowly during each trial. A representative diagram is shown in Fig. 4, representing the torque recorded during fourteen runs on the measured distance, as indicated by numbers, while a, b, c, d are tests with the launch moored in order to ascertain the zero line from which to measure the heights of the diagram, and thus to eliminate any errors due to friction, &c., in calculating the torque and shaft horse-power. The constant of the instrument was ascertained by frequent tests with a Prony brake on the pulley provided for this purpose (see Fig. 5). No appreciable differences in the scale of the records were found in these tests—a proof of the suitability

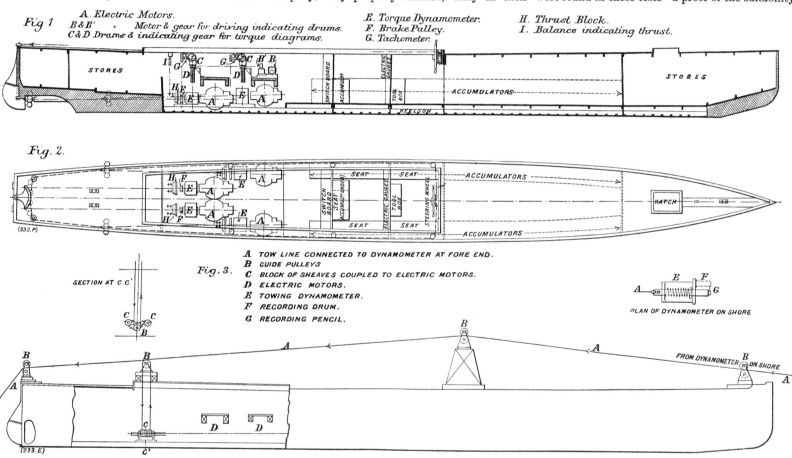

Fig 1
A. Electric Motors.
B & B'. Motor & gear for driving indicating drums.
C & D Drums & indicating gear for torque diagrams.
E. Torque Dynamometer.
F. Brake Pulley.
G. Tachometer.
H. Thrust Block.
I. Balance indicating thrust.

Fig. 2.

Fig. 3.
A TOW LINE CONNECTED TO DYNAMOMETER AT FORE END.
B GUIDE PULLEYS
C BLOCK OF SHEAVES COUPLED TO ELECTRIC MOTORS.
D ELECTRIC MOTORS.
E TOWING DYNAMOMETER.
F RECORDING DRUM.
G RECORDING PENCIL.

SECTION AT C.C'

PLAN OF DYNAMOMETER ON SHORE

FIGS. 1 TO 3. EXPERIMENTAL ELECTRIC LAUNCH.

Company, was the chairman—an appointment not alone due to his official position, but because of his intimate knowledge of the conditions of Atlantic steaming. Engineer-Rear-Admiral H. J. Oram, C.B., Engineer-in-Chief of the Navy, was able, by consent of the Admiralty, to act as a member, and his close contact with all scientific and practical questions in marine propulsion, as well as his initiative, enabled him to render very useful help. Other members were Mr. J. T. Milton, Chief Engineer-Surveyor at Lloyd's ; the late Mr. Harry J. Brock, of the firm of Messrs. Denny and Co., of Dumbarton; Mr. Thomas Bell, of Messrs. John Brown and Co., Limited ; Sir William H. White, K.C.B., of Messrs. Swan, Hunter, and Wigham Richardson, and Mr. Andrew Laing, of the Wallsend Engineering Company. It is not necessary again to review the work done by this Commission. Their recommendation was in favour of the adoption of the Parsons turbine, and this recommendation was accepted by the Cunard Company, and by the contracting firms, with commendable courage. The results have justified this step, but it would be idle to ignore the fact that the step taken involved grave responsibility, and necessitated a large amount of experimental work and care in meeting all the problems in the construction of units of such magnitude.

negotiations with the Cunard Company for the construction of the ship—now about four years ago—to carry out themselves experiments, which proved highly suggestive. With a 47½-ft. launch, an exact model of the proposed Mauretania, they were able to carry out tests impossible in the Government tank, as the model more closely approximated to the conditions and method of propulsion in the ship than do the experimental tank models. The launch was made to a scale of one-sixteenth of the size of the large ship, as compared with a forty-eighth in the case of the tank models, and the trials were carried out in the Northumberland dock on the Tyne. The depth of water in the dock is over 24 ft., so that with a draught of 2 ft. 0¾ in. the speed could not be appreciably affected by insufficient depth of water. Currents were naturally absent, which simplified the observations and was conducive to accuracy. The distance available for the speed trials was about a quarter of a mile, after allowing ample space at each end for regaining speed after turning. The drawings reproduced above show the general arrangement of the machinery. The boat was built of wood, and changes were thus easily made either in the entry or in the form of stern. The motive power consisted of electric motors, supplied with current from the storage batteries placed in

of this instrument for accurate measurement of turning moments. Fig. 5 also shows the arrangement for measuring the thrust on the propeller-shafts, the ball-thrust bearing being so supported that the thrust is indicated directly by a spring-balance. The number of revolutions of the shafts were ascertained in the trials by electrical counters and by tachometers (see Figs. 1 and 2). The speed was measured in the usual way, by running over a measured distance, and taking the time by a stop-watch. The velocity of the wind was measured during each run by an anemometer, while the mean direction of the wind was noted.

These wind measurements were found to be absolutely necessary to ensure accuracy of the results of speed and power, as it became evident after a number of tests that enormous errors can be made by taking simply the mean of two runs in opposite directions—i.e., with and against the wind. This is clearly illustrated in Fig. 7, which shows curves of revolutions for various speeds in a comparatively strong wind, in comparison to the results obtained during the next day, when the weather was practically calm. For 6¼ knots speed, the mean power with and against the wind, is in this case about 20 per cent. higher than in calm weather. These investigations were utilised for drawing conclusions with regard to the full-size ship, and a series of experiments were made with deck erections on board the launch equivalent in proportion to those of the ship. The results obtained were utilised for calculating, by means of the law of comparison, the effect of winds of various directions and velocities upon the progress of the ship at sea. To give some idea of the wind forces in question, it may be mentioned that the Mauretania, when travelling at 25 knots speed, will require about 12 per cent. more power against a 25-knot wind than is required in calm weather.

At the beginning of the electric-launch experiments considerable difficulties were experienced through the foulness of the launch's bottom, which increased irregularly after some time of exposure ; cleaning with a brush proved useless in dealing with this difficulty, as it was impossible to ascertain how far the cleaning extended, so that the amount of extra resistance due to fouling became

manœuvring qualities, &c., when taking the results comparatively would scarcely be diminished.

In addition to the resistance experiments, an elaborate series of trials were made with the launch when fitted with electrically-driven propellers. These, as well as the other experiments, were entrusted to Mr. M. Wurl, a member of the builders' professional staff, under the consultative guidance of Sir W. H. White, K.C.B., a director of Messrs. Swan, Hunter, and Wigham Richardson and Co., Limited. These latter tests were directed to ascertain the efficiency of propellers with different sizes of bosses, diameters, pitches, and blade areas, the influence of various athwartship and longitudinal positions for the propellers, the comparative advantages of ordinary twin, triple, and quadruple-screw arrangements, and other problems.

Tests were also made in regard to the effect of trim. The wave profile was measured at the various

Plate II. It will be noted that the blades are perhaps, narrower, especially at the root, than is the practice with turbine propellers. Importance was also attached to the proportion of the boss. Trials were also made with cones of various angles, and consequently of varying length, abaft of the propeller boss. It was ascertained, further, that the thickness of the blades of the propellers had influence on the efficiency. It is of considerable importance to note that the propellers proposed as most suitable by various authorities varied in efficiency as much as 12 per cent., which means that 8000 indicated horse-power might have been spent in excess of what is necessary to drive the ship at 25 knots at sea. The final achievement of these numerous propeller experiments was an increase of the number of revolutions per minute of the full-size propellers, from 145 to 175, without an appreciable reduction in propeller efficiency.

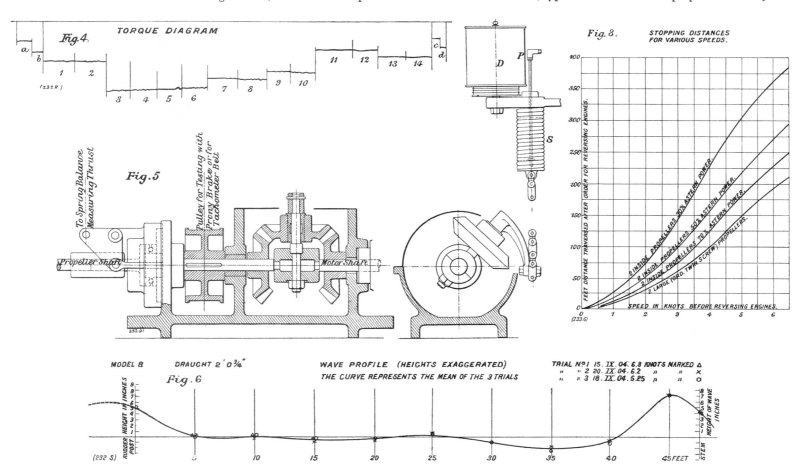

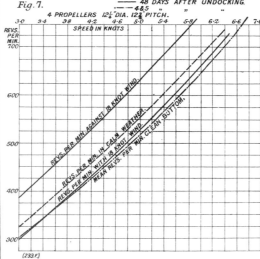

thereby less traceable. Several weeks of experimenting, however, furnished sufficient information with regard to the amount and the quickness of fouling that a way was found to overcome these difficulties. By avoiding foulness as far as possible, and by applying comparative tests for its measurement, the effect of fouling was practically eliminated from all the results. A reference to Fig. 7 will show the difference in the number of revolutions for a given speed, due to fouling after a period of about seven weeks, and it may be mentioned that the difference in power at full speed amounted to fully 25 per cent., and differences quite as large were obtained in about two weeks when the fouling was not interrupted by speed trials.

Although the indicated horse-power for the ship had been ascertained by tank experiments, as mentioned above, a verification was attempted with the launch. To apply the law of comparison, with correction for skin friction, the resistance of the launch had to be ascertained by towing. The method adopted for this purpose is illustrated in Fig. 3, showing the gear by which the launch was hauled along a rope (fixed on one end) whose horizontal pull, representing the ship resistance, was recorded by the dynamometer connected to the rope and fixed on shore. In applying the results to the full-size ship a satisfactory agreement with the previous tank experiments was exhibited. But even if this had not been the case, the value of the electric-launch experiments with regard to details in the design, by studying their effect upon speed, horse-power,

FIGS. 4 TO 8. EXPERIMENTAL APPARATUS AND RESULTS.

trials by means of floating weights along each side of the ship recording graphs, and one of these is produced in Fig. 6.

Tests were made with propellers of various sizes and proportions. These experiments confirmed the design of the propellers which have been fitted. These are well shown in the engraving on

Another interesting series of experiments had reference to the question of whether the propellers should turn inwards or outwards. The inner propellers were from first to last arranged to turn outwards, and it was found that there was no material difference with the outer propellers turning inwards or outwards. Inturning screws were adopted.

A problem associated with propeller efficiency had reference to the rate of flow of stream-lines from the propeller. The wake was measured by current-meters at various positions relative longitudinally and horizontally to the centre of the propeller. The experiments threw considerable light on the effect of the overlapping of propellers. It was found that the water disturbed by the forward propeller was spread over a large area before it reached the aft propeller. In the Mauretania the forward propellers are 78 ft. 11 in. in advance of the aft propellers. This distance was decided upon as the experiments showed that in such case the forward propellers would not appreciably interfere with the efficiency of the aft propellers.

With regard to the distance between the forward propellers and the side of the ship, various experiments were made, and on these the arrangement adopted in the Mauretania was based. The question of the relation of the propeller to the manœuvring of the ship was also carefully considered, and a series of trials were made to measure the diameter of the circles with various rudders, and also with and without the deadwood cut away forward of the rudder. The diameter of the circles, by altering the aft body and the size of the rudder, was reduced to 75 per cent. of that of the circle made with the first launch model. Tests were also made of the turning circle of twin and quadruple screws using the rudder, and the quadruple screws were found to give better results.

The various questions and problems experimented on may thus be briefly summarised :—

1. Effect of aperture in deadwood between inside propellers.

2. Effect of cutting away the deadwood as adopted for both the full-size ships.

3. Effect of position of outside propellers longitudinally and of their distance from the hull.

4. Comparative efficiency of proposed four-screw arrangement, and of ordinary twin-screw arrangement with large propellers, as used with reciprocating engines. The experiments showed that the efficiencies of both systems are about equal in this case.

gain general information regarding the intricate problems of ship resistance and propulsion.

It may be added that since all questions connected with the design of the Mauretania were investigated, Messrs. Swan, Hunter, and Wigham Richardson, and the Wallsend Slipway and Engineering Company, are, with characteristic enterprise, continuing the experiments on the same lines in connection with propeller problems.

THE SUPERVISION OF THE WORK FOR THE CUNARD COMPANY.

Valuable suggestion has from first to last been made by practically every official of the Cunard Company, so that the ship embraces not only the experience of the firms responsible for her construction, but is the embodiment of many years of close study of the requirements of the Atlantic passenger service.

respected for his wide knowledge and eminently practical judgment. Cautious, yet progressive, his policy has ensured that great measure of reliability which has ever characterised the Cunard steamships, and has enabled them to attain such a high position of public confidence. Mr. L. Peskett, the naval architect for the Cunard Company, has naturally been intimately associated with the design, and particularly with the arrangement of the deck cabins ; while in the arrangement of the navigating appliances he has had the advantage of Captain Dodd's wide acquaintance with these matters. Mr. George Thompson, the superintending engineer of the company, will be responsible for the upkeep and maintenance of the machinery, and in a large measure also for its success on the Atlantic. He has had a splendid training for this work, having for a long time being associated with Messrs. Harland and Wolff's ships. The builders and engineers of the Maure-

5. Best direction of turning (inside or outside) for shafts with regard to propulsive efficiency.

6. Effect of dragging screws when part of the machinery be disabled.

7. Comparative distances and times for stopping ordinary twin-screw steamer and turbine vessel with proposed arrangement, and with the available astern power. The results are given in Fig. 8, page 5.

8. Astern speeds obtainable with proposed arrangement.

9. Steering and turning by rudder, and by screws.

10. Most suitable propellers, with regard to high number of revolutions and high efficiency. Twelve sets of propellers of different proportions were tried for this purpose.

11. Form of wave profile. The illustration, Fig. 6, shows the comparatively small height of bow and stern wave.

12. Various other measurements were made, as, for instance, measurements of the relative velocity of the water at different distances from the hull, including the speed of the wake at various positions longitudinally, also trials to ascertain the amount of skin friction on surfaces similar to those of the electric launch, and other experiments to

Mr. William Watson, the chairman of the Cunard Company, has from the beginning taken a close personal interest in the supervision of the work, being in the earlier stages associated with the late Lord Inverclyde, alike in the inception and carrying into effect of the ambition of the British nation to be supreme on the Atlantic. Altogether Mr. Watson's very long acquaintance with Atlantic transport has been particularly useful in connection with the work. He has had as close ally the vice-chairman of the company, Sir W. B. Forward, while Mr. M. H. Maxwell and Mr. J. H. Beazly, as members of the Shipbuilding Committee, have rendered useful services. The same remark applies to Mr. A. D. Mearns, the general manager of the company, and Mr. Dranfield, the secretary.

On the technical officers of the company there has fallen considerable responsibility in connection with the settlement of the details of construction, and their great experience and their enthusiasm for the Cunard Company have at all times enabled them to give most material help. Mr. James Bain is one of the *doyens* of the Atlantic service, and we are specially pleased to be able to give his portrait in this issue, as he is so well known and so deservedly

tania will feel ample reliance in confiding their work to the experienced staff of the Cunard Company.

The Mauretania in service will be commanded by Captain John Pritchard, a native of Carnarvon, who has been in the Cunard service for over twenty years. His appointment to the Mauretania makes it almost unnecessary to say that he has been in command of the principal ships of the fleet, and has thus gained a large experience in his work. He has been captain of the Carmania, Caronia, Campania, Lucania, Etruria, Saxonia, and Ivernia, so that he has already won the confidence of the travelling public. It is, perhaps, an interesting coincidence that Captain Pritchard, thirty years ago, took delivery (as captain) of the smallest ship ever built by Messrs. Swan and Hunter, and has now similarly taken away the largest vessel constructed by the company.

The chief engineer of the ship is Mr. John Currie, a native of Ayr, who has also been in the Cunard service for many years, and was employed in superintending the machinery for the Caronia and Carmania, of which he was formerly chief engineer. He has thus an intimate knowledge of the turbine system ; and it is also important to note that he was the head of the machinery department of the Lucania when she made her record voyages. He it was who developed such a high economy in the Ivernia, built and engined by the same firms as have built and engined the Mauretania. We append here a list of the crew of the Mauretania. It is significant that there are only 69 in the navigation department, while there are 393 on the engineering staff.

LIST OF THE CREW, DIVIDED INTO THE DEPARTMENTS OF NAVIGATION, ENGINEERING, AND PERSONAL.

TABLE VII.—*List of the Crew.*

Navigation :

Captain and officers	9
Quartermasters	8
Boatswains	3
Carpenters and joiners	3
Lamp-trimmer and yeoman	2
Masters-at-arms	2
Marconi telegraphists	2
Seamen	40
	—— 69

Engineering :

Engineer officers	33

TABLE VII.—*(continued).*

Refrigerating engineers	3
Firemen	204
Trimmers	120
Greasers	33
	—— 393

Personal :

Doctor	1
Purser	1
Assistant pursers	2
Chief steward	1
Chief steward's assistants	2
Chef	1

TABLE VII.—*(continued).*

Barbers	2
Cooks and bakers	28
Matrons	2
Stewardesses	10
Mail-sorters	7
Typists	2
Leading stewards, bar-keepers, &c.	50
Stewards...	367
	—— 476
Grand total	938

THE CONSTRUCTION OF THE SHIP.

THE BUILDERS OF THE SHIP.

The Wallsend Shipyard, where the Mauretania has been built, dates from 1872. Of this concern the late Mr. C. S. Swan was the principal partner, but soon after his death, in 1878, Mr. G. B. Hunter became the head of the firm. From the first, progress has been continuous, alike in the size and character of the vessels built. As a shipbuilder Mr. Hunter has the advantages of hereditary inclination and sound practical training. His forebears were connected either with the sea or the building of ships. This applies to his father, his grandfather on both the paternal and maternal sides, and to his other relatives. Indeed, he was born in a shipbuilding atmosphere, and served his apprenticeship as a shipbuilder with the Piles of Sunderland, a family which greatly contributed to the early prosperity of the industry on the North-East Coast, having been identified with the formation of Sir William Gray and Co.'s yard, and of Messrs. Furness, Withy, and Co.'s establishment. Mr. Hunter, when he completed his apprenticeship, although barely twenty years of age, was given charge of the drawing-office and of the work at Messrs. Piles' yard. But he wisely decided to widen his experience, and spent two years with Messrs. Robert Napier and Sons when Mr. (afterwards Sir) William Pearce was head of the constructive department. For a year or two after his return to the North-East Coast he was a partner in the shipbuilding works at Sunderland of Messrs. Austin and Hunter, and in 1879, as we have said, became a partner in the Wallsend Shipyard.

In 1895 the firm became a limited liability company, with Mr. Hunter as chairman, and with a strong board of directors. Since then developments have taken place, the works of Messrs. Schlesinger, Davis, and Co. being added to the Wallsend yard, while in 1903 the firm amalgamated with Messrs. Wigham Richardson and Co., of Neptune Works, Walker-on-Tyne, a firm which since 1860 had won a high repute, not only for the building of ships, but also of machinery. The repair work of the Pontoon and Dry Dock Company, founded in 1882, was also purchased, and the combined concerns now known as Messrs. Swan, Hunter, and Wigham Richardson, Limited, have a river frontage of some 4000 ft. and an area of 78 acres. They are located about three miles to the east of Newcastle, on the north bank of the river, at a point where there is a bend, so that little difficulty is involved in launching such large vessels as the Mauretania.

As to the recent progress of the company, the

table below of the output of the two establishments is interesting testimony. Prior to 1897, the output had only twice exceeded 40,000 tons—in 1889 and in 1893; whereas since 1897 the production has never been as low as this figure, and has often been twice as large, while in 1906 it was three times this total.

The Mauretania is herself the best testimony to the capabilities of the establishment, and when we come to describe the building of the hull we shall have occasion to refer to some of the outstanding features. There are four built-up berths in addition to the twelve open berths, making sixteen in all. The plater's shed is arranged close to these building berths. The new furnaces which have been built for dealing with angle-bars, &c., are heated by producer-gas, which gives uniformity of heat. Powerful hydraulic and electrically-driven tools are fitted in the sheds.

For installing the boilers on board ship the company have adopted a floating-crane with a lifting capacity of 150 tons. The pontoon on which this crane is mounted has its own propelling machinery,

and 68 ft. beam, was fitted with twelve Temperley transporters, and arrangements were made so that two warships could be dealt with at each side, and could be loaded with coal with great rapidity; indeed, the whole of the coal is mechanically manipulated.

The establishment, it may be added, includes the Wallsend and Neptune Shipbuilding Yards, which are contiguous (Fig. 13, Plate XXXIII.).

The marine engineering works at Neptune includes a dry dock 550 ft. long and 76 ft. beam, with a depth on the entrance sill of 26½ ft.; in addition there are two floating docks, to take

vessels up to 350 ft. long. The capacity of the works, which has now its 804th vessel on the stocks, is, however, more fully exemplified by a description of the building of the Mauretania than by any elaborate narration of the machine-tools fitted, and with this brief historical note, we shall return to our description of the work on the hull of the Mauretania. Here, however, we may interject the remark that in carrying out this work Mr. G. B. Hunter has more than proved the efficiency of the staff. It was peculiarly appropriate that the director most intimately associated with him in the actual work of construction

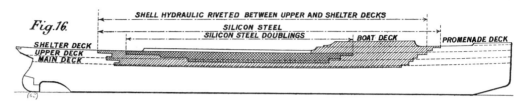

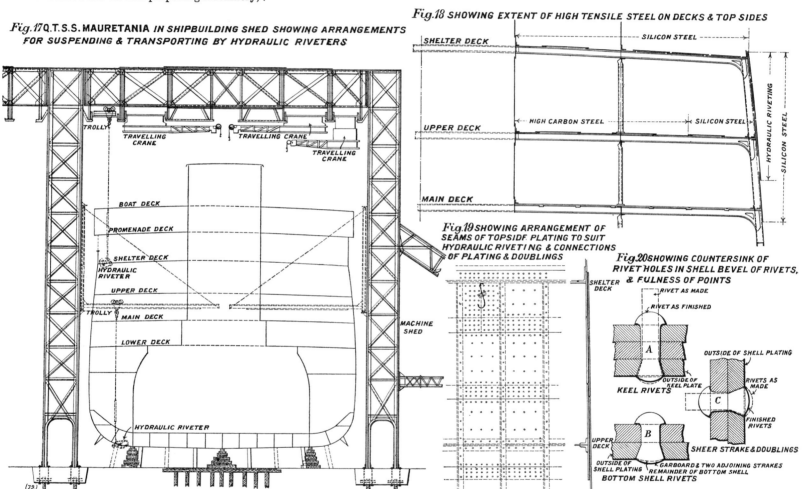

FIGS. 16 TO 20. CONSTRUCTIONAL DETAILS OF THE HULL.

so that it can be readily sent to any part of the river.

In Table VIII., annexed, a reference is made to outstanding work done during the past ten years. The firm have built many high-speed passenger ships in addition to those for the Cunard Company, to which reference has already been made. One of the notable ships is the Princess Victoria, constructed for the Canadian Pacific Railway Company, and capable of steaming at 22 knots. Note may also be made of the Osmanieh, for the Khedivial Mail Steamship Company, and of the turbine-steamer Immingham, for the Great Central Railway Company's North Sea traffic. Many floating docks have been constructed at the Wallsend yard, among the number being one of 16,500 tons capacity, for the British Admiralty, safely towed to Bermuda; another, of 12,000 tons capacity, was built for the Spanish Government, and sent to Havana. A third, of 11,000 tons capacity, was constructed for the Stettin Maschinenbau Actien-Gesellschaft Vulcan. Many others have been built for foreign and home clients, the dimensions ranging, as in the case of the Bermuda dock, to 545 ft. by 126 ft. in clear width. Mention should also be made of a floating coal dépôt, built for the British Admiralty, to take 12,000 tons of coal. This craft, 424 ft. long

TABLE VIII.—*Productions of Messrs. Swan, Hunter, and Wigham Richardson and Co., Limited, 1897-1907.*

Year.	Swan and Hunter, Limited.	Wigham Richardson & Co., Limited.	Swan, Hunter, and Wigham Richardson, Limited.	Prominent Ships, &c.
			total	
1897	48,570	18,217	66,787	Havana Pontoon Dock, s.s. Monarch, s.s. Idaho.
1898	68,696	27,320	96,016	T.S.-S. America Maru, t.-s.s. Ultonia, Stettin Pontoon Dock.
1899	42,522	28,751	71,273	T.-S.S. Ivernia.
1900	42,880	34,894	77,774	
1901	49,087	37,355	86,442	S.S. Lake Manitoba, s.s. Patrician, s.s. Lake Michigan, two pontoon docks.
1902	64,220	41,340	105,560	Four pontoon docks, s.s. Carpathia.
1903	—	—	66,452	Floating workshop for Natal, Durban floating dock.
1904	—	—	73,592	Coal dépôt for British Government, floating dock for Suez Canal.
1905	—	—	82,447	Nigerian floating dock, t.-s.s. Madonna.
1906	—	—	126,921	T.-S.S. Immingham, t.-s.s. Osmanieh, t.-s.s. Empress, q.-t.-s.s. Mauretania.

should be Mr. C. S. Swan, the son of the originator of the firm. Mr. Swan has brought to bear upon his work great skill and experience, together with tact in dealing with delicate questions, and has in a large measure contributed to the rapid and successful termination of this great undertaking. The yard manager, Mr. Christopher Stephenson, has tackled all the constructional problems with care and courage; and as regards the plans and the speed and strength calculations, Mr. E. W. de Rusett and Mr. J. Meuwissen deserve high commendation.

THE CONSTRUCTION OF THE HULL.

In the construction of the hull three outstanding features call for special description: the berth structure and the handling of materials, the use of silicon steel in preference to carbon steel for those parts of the ship subject to the most severe strains from hogging and sagging, and the hydraulic riveting of the principal parts of the structure. We propose to direct attention to these points.

To facilitate the construction of the ship Messrs. Swan, Hunter, and Wigham Richardson, Limited, themselves constructed a double berth, which is well shown in Figs. 14 and 15 on the two-page

Plate XXXIII., and on Fig. 17 on the previous page. The dimensions of the berths illustrated are as follow :—

	Ft.
Length of shed over all of columns ...	682
Length of roof, including overhang at each end	728
Width clear of west shed, under which Mauretania was built	95
Width clear of east sheds	100
Height of columns above ground to under-side of principals or girders, south end...	133
Height of columns above sloping ground to underside of principals or girders, south end	105

In the width there are three lattice posts at 56-ft. centres longitudinally. That in the centre is 10 ft. by 12 ft., and those at the sides 10 ft. by 11 ft., secured with 1⅜-in. bolts on concrete foundations, 18 ft. by 16 ft., with a depth of 5 ft., resting on eight piles driven 30 ft. to 35 ft. into the subsoil. There are cross-girders carrying the roof and sup-

for closing rivets in the double bottom, &c. This and the illustrations of constructional details, Figs. 16 to 20, are taken, along with much of the data given, from the papers read at the Institution of Civil Engineers and the Institution of Naval Architects by Mr. E. W. de Rusett, who, as naval architect of the builders, has been intimately associated with the design and construction of the Mauretania.

Below we reproduce comparative cross-sections of the Mauretania and the Great Eastern, from Mr. Foster King's paper, read at the spring meeting this year of the Institution of Naval Architects. The comparison is instructive ; it shows the greater beam of the new ship—87 ft. 6 in. against 83 ft.—and the flatter floor and bilge-keels, which make the modern ship steadier. It should be remembered that the Mauretania has two decks above the shelter-deck, so that in every way she is larger. The cellular structure of the Great Eastern reflects the genius of Brunel, and the variation in scantlings indicates the progress since made in metallurgy.

seams of the bottom shell-plating of the vessel, where hydraulic riveting was resorted to, are arranged clincker fashion, so that the machines could close the work strake by strake. The frame bottoms are joggled. The bottom shell-butts are double strapped, the inner strap having three rows of rivets, two of which are close pitched, the outer row being wider spaced. The outer strap is double-riveted, with edges bevelled, to reduce resistance.

There is very little rise in the bottom. The bilge-keel, to minimise rolling and to add strength at this part, is 240 ft. long and 3 ft. deep. For the three-fifths of the length of the ship, from near the stern forward, the frames to the shelter-deck are spaced 32 in. apart, while forward they are at 26-in. intervals, and aft 25-in. The side framing consists of 10-in. channel-frames extending from the tank margin-plate to the shelter-deck with closely-spaced web-frames. The beams on all the decks are also of channel section, and have turned knees to secure lightness.

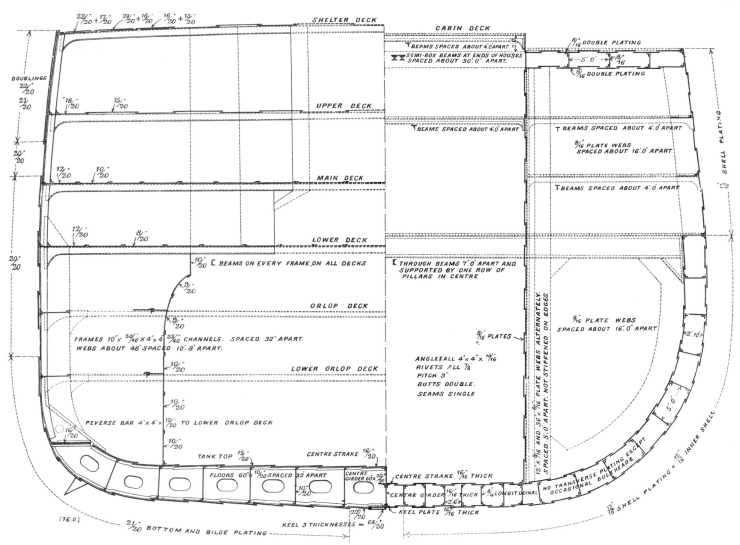

FIG. 21. COMPARATIVE SECTIONS OF THE "MAURETANIA" AND THE "GREAT EASTERN."

porting electric traversing-cranes. The berth is roofed over with glazing, and is well lighted by arc-lamps, so that work can proceed independently of weather or of natural light. A feature which distinguishes from others this berth, and the other constructed by the firm at an earlier date, is the arrangement of the cranes. The rails on which these run are on the bottom booms of longitudinal girders suspended from the transverse members supporting the roof principals. There are several tracks, and on these there are four 5-ton and four 3-ton electric travelling-cranes. These cranes are shown in Fig. 17. In each case the jib is suspended from the carriages and works horizontally ; the jibs of the 3-ton cranes are at a lower level, so that they may easily pass under the carriages of the adjoining 5-ton cranes. Several could be concentrated on a heavy load, and as much as 40 tons might thus be dealt with. In the earlier stages of construction jibs were fitted on the vertical members of the building berth, as shown in Fig. 17, for carrying the heavy gap-riveters utilised

The depth of the double bottom of the Mauretania is 5 ft. in the boiler-rooms and holds, and 6 ft. in the engine-rooms, extending well up to the bilge. There is a flat keel-plate 50 in. wide, made up of three thicknesses of metal, a total of 3¼ in. The middle plate is $\frac{1}{20}$ in. thicker than the garboards, to allow of their being placed in position after the keel-plates and longitudinal keelson bars were riveted. The butts of the keel-plate are not strapped, as it was found there would be sufficient margin of strength without doing this. By the omission of these straps about ¾ in. of draught was saved. This was of great importance considering the small margin of dead-weight that it is possible to allow in a vessel of this character on the given maximum draught of water. The centre strake is 1 in. thick, having on each side seven longitudinal girders $\frac{10}{20}$ in. thick, with intercostals $\frac{12}{20}$ in. thick, all secured together and to the shell and floor-plating by 4½-in. by 4-in. by 1$\frac{2}{20}$-in. to 1$\frac{0}{20}$-in. angles. The bottom shell-plating is $\frac{20}{20}$ in. thick ; the inner floor-plating $\frac{15}{20}$ in. The

The skin-plating is, on the side of the ship from $\frac{22}{20}$ in. to $\frac{21}{20}$ in. At the shear-strakes, as shown in Figs. 18 and 21, it is, for 105 ft. aft of amidships, and 120 ft. forward of amidships, 2$\frac{1}{20}$ in., and is for even a greater length doubled, of silicon steel, and hydraulically riveted. This precaution has been taken, as will presently be explained, because of the sagging and hogging stresses due to the vessel being supported alternatively on waves at bow and stern without complete support in the centre, and riding over a wave without sufficient support at the ends. These, with such a long structure, involved heavy bending moments, the maximum being slightly over a million foot-tons. The plating of the topside, where the doublings occur, had to be so arranged that the inner edge of the landing was kept as at the top, so that each plate could be riveted up in due order. This will be observed by reference to Fig. 19. The deck-stringers, &c., are correspondingly heavy. The heavier plates at the turn of the bilge and the sheer-strake are 40 ft. long, and weigh from 4 to 5 tons ; the ordinary

C

shell-plates are 34 ft. long, and weigh 2½ to 3 tons. A feature of the hull is, as we have said, the use of silicon steel : the extent to which it was adopted is shown by the hatching on Fig. 16, page 8, the double-hatching showing where the sheer-strakes are of double thickness. High-tensile carbon steel was also used for bulk-heads, &c., but chief interest centres in the silicon steel adopted where stresses were greatest. A saving in weight was also aimed at, but, determined to concede nothing in weight, it was laid down in the specification that such steel must have the following qualifications under normal conditions : — 1. An ultimate tensile strength of 34 to 38 tons per square inch. 2. An elongation of not less than 20 per cent. in 8 in. In addition, it should satisfactorily stand the following tests :—Temper tests ; cold-bending, normal, annealed and tempered ; fatigue tests ; and mechanical tests. This silicon steel was subject to special tests for ultimate tensile strength, elastic limit, and elongation, by Messrs. David Kirkaldy and Son, London, on strips 11 ft. long by 2 in. wide, having a length for extension of 100 in. The results proved to be quite satisfactory, the test-pieces being 0.77 in. and 1.49 in. thick respectively. The average of Lloyd's tests of high-tensile carbon and silicon steels made by Messrs. J. Spencer and Sons, Newburn, for ship purposes were as follow : —

TABLE IX.—*Results of Steel Tests.*

Normal Conditions.	High-Tensile Carbon Steel.	High-Tensile Silicon Steel.
Number of samples	60	5	86
Thickness of plates varied from	$\frac{6}{20}$ to $\frac{13}{20}$ in.	$\frac{10}{20}$ to $\frac{13}{20}$ in.	$\frac{13}{20}$ to $\frac{23}{20}$ in.
Average ultimate stress tons per sq. in.	36.4	37.3	36.35
Elongation n 8 in. per cent.	22.5	22	22.7
Elastic limit tons per sq. in.	22.2	20.8	21.6

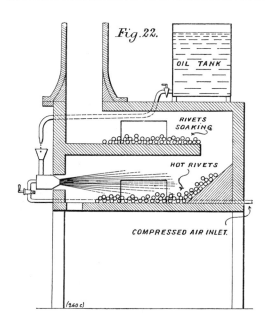

FIG. 22. SECTION OF RIVET-HEATER.

In view of the results attained, a further reduction of 10 per cent. in the scantlings where high-tensile steel is employed (making 20 per cent. in all) might have been reasonably made, as a fair margin of strength would still have been secured above the mild-steel basis, especially as the midship scantlings, and the tapering of the same towards the ends, were based on the static stresses the vessel would be subject to when mounting and leaving a wave of the abnormal length of 760 ft. by 38 ft. high from hollow to crest. In determining the extent of taper, due consideration was, of course, given to the fact that the moment of inertia of the end sections is necessarily less than that of the midship section, owing to the form of the vessel.

In carrying out the tests of the material, it was observed that to punch a hole ⅛ in. small and rimer out to full size reduced the strength of the sample less than if the hole had been drilled the full size, and because of this it was decided to punch the high-tensile steel plates up to ½ in. in thickness with holes ⅛ in. less in diameter, and then rimer them out to the full diameter required by the rivet. By punching the holes small and rimering them, as described, the saving in labour

was about 10s. per plate, or about 30 per cent. less than electric drilling. All the holes in high-tensile steel above ½ in. in thickness were drilled, and the rag of the hole was removed by a special tool, which at the same time removed the sharp edge of the hole and produced the requisite taper for the neck of the rivet.

High-carbon steel was adopted in all the main transverse and longitudinal bulkheads extending to the upper deck. The lower portions of these are $\frac{10}{20}$ in. thick, thence $\frac{9}{20}$ in. to the lower deck, $\frac{7}{20}$ in. to the main deck, and above this they are $\frac{6}{20}$ in. The stiffening bars are of ordinary mild steel, of channel or angle sections. Silicon steel was used for the top sides, and doublings where shown in Fig. 18, page 8 ; also for the stringers, decks, and doublings on the shelter deck for the full width between the ship's side and casings, and stringer and adjoining trake on upper deck for a width of

8 ft. 6 in., and for a length of about 500 ft. amidships on the shelter-deck, and about 480 ft. on the upper deck, tapering off at the ends. The remainder of the plating to the sides of the casings on the upper deck is of high-tensile carbon steel, extending for 400 ft. in length. By the employment of high-tensile steel a reduction of 10 per cent. on the basis of scantlings of mild steel was allowed, and a corresponding reduction in the thickness of the bulkheads where made of this material. The result has been a saving in weight of about 200 tons, with an appreciable increase of strength in the top structure. The silicon and high-carbon steel were not annealed. The edges of seams and butts were planed. Experience showed that high-tensile and mild steel would work well together.

The authorities at Lloyd's Registry, from their experience up to date, strongly recommended that the rivets used for the whole structure, including the silicon and high-carbon steel, should be made of mild ingot steel ; consequently this material was adopted, although it has since been urged by many that silicon steel might also have been used with better results, as in naval practice. The rods had an ultimate stress of 26 to 30 tons per square inch,

elongation not less than 20 per cent., and an elastic limit of 13 to 15 tons per square inch. The rivets are 1⅛ in. in diameter, and are spaced in accordance with Lloyd's rules for mild steel of equivalent strength. Considering that the rivets were softer than the high-tensile plates they connected, special provision was made to minimise the shearing effect on them by rounding the edges of the drilled holes by the special tool to which reference has already been made. A pressure of 50 tons was put upon the rivet when closing.

Hydraulic riveting was adopted in the following parts of the structure—viz., the keel-plates, centre keelson, garboard strake, and shell-plates within the range of the double bottom ; also the connection of shell to stem and stern castings, floors, frame bottoms and top bars, tank girders, web frames, reverse-bars to frames and tank side knees, and also the girders forming the engine-seating.

FIG. 23. STERN FRAMING IN THE WORKS OF THE DARLINGTON FORGE CO., LTD., DARLINGTON.

The topside plating and doublings were also hydraulically riveted for a length of 520 ft. amidships, and the shelter-deck stringer and doublings for a length of about 440 ft.

The eight hydraulic riveting-machines employed were of three sizes, having gaps 5 ft., 5 ft. 6 in., and 6 ft. respectively. The 5-ft. 6-in. gap machines were found to be the most serviceable for general purposes. They were each fitted with an adjustable arrangement by which the pressure could be brought to bear directly through the axis of the rivet at whatever angle the plating lay, the result being that very little trouble was experienced in pressing the rivets fairly into the countersink. The machines were supported by trolleys running in the roof of the shed under which the vessel was built, also from derricks which were guyed from the standards of the shed, as shown in Fig. 17, page 8, the trolleys and derricks being so arranged that they could be readily moved to any required position within their range of action.

The shell-rivets called for very careful consideration, both as regards the convexity of the head and taper of the neck, and their length in proportion to the thickness of the plates they connected.

THE BULKHEAD ARRANGEMENT OF THE SHIP.

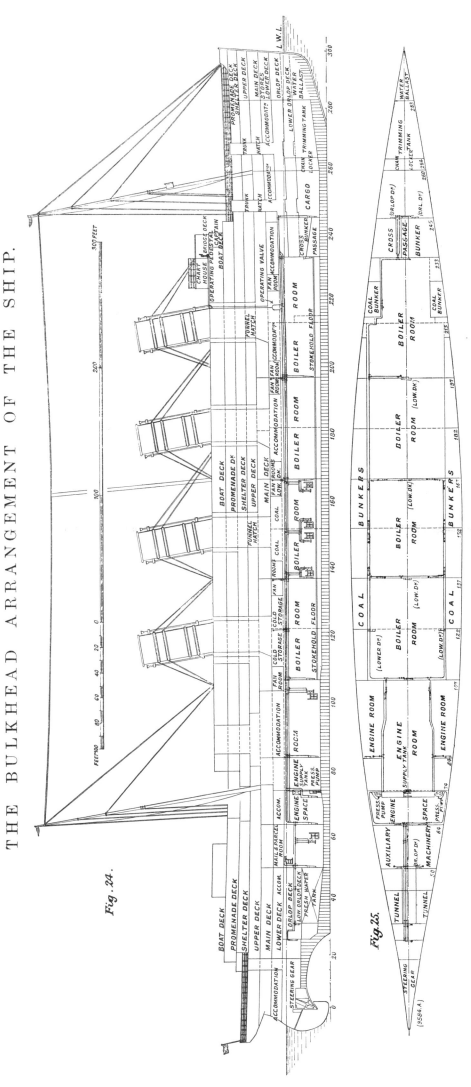

Fig. 24.

Fig. 25.

(9584-A.)

The proper relation of the bevel of the counter-sink to that of the neck of the rivet was a matter of much importance, otherwise a sound watertight job could not be readily obtained. And, further to ensure good work, any burr left on the edge of the countersunk rivet-head during manufacture was ground off. Fig. 20, page 8, shows the bevel of the countersink in the shell for neck and point of rivet, also the bevel of the neck and the rivet before being closed up. It is worthy of remark that it was found by experience that the bevel of the rivet-neck had to be less than that in the plate to ensure good closing, otherwise the material did not solidly fill the hole from the neck of the countersink in the shell for neck and root. The angles of these bevels are, for the neck of the rivet $18\frac{1}{2}$ deg., and for the plate 20 deg., each measured from the axis of the rivet. The proper length of the shell-rivets was a matter of experiment, as the rule for hand-laid rivets did not apply, on account of the great pressure employed in closing them, which amounted to about 50 tons. By reference to Fig. 20, it will be observed that the heads of the rivets in the keel were made fuller than those in the garboards and three adjoining strakes, while further up the bilge the heads were finished with only the usual amount of fulness, to afford as little resistance to the water as possible. The countersunk rivets in the bottom, shown at A

and B, were put in from the underside and clenched on the inside, and those on the topsides C were also clenched on the inside, the heads being rounded, as shown in the diagram. The deck-rivets were countersunk and flush on the top, on account of the deck-sheathing, and clenched on the under-side.

Upwards of 4,000,000 rivets were used, weighing fully 700 tons, a considerable proportion of which were hydraulically riveted. They were heated in oil furnaces, specially designed at the Wallsend Yard. Each furnace has a daily heating capacity of at least 3000 rivets, $\frac{7}{8}$ in. by 3 in. About 11 gallons of crude oil were consumed in each furnace per day. The oil is disintegrated by air drawn from the mains supplying the pneumatic tools. These furnaces may be readily regulated to work absolutely without smell or smoke, and they heat the rivets in a clear white flame. Of this furnace a section—not to scale—is reproduced in Fig. 22 on the opposite page. The rivets are first put into the upper part of the furnace to soak in the spent flame. From thence they are pushed down to the lower level, where they come into contact with the full blast. They are fed into and withdrawn from the furnace by sliding doors. The crude oil is kept in a tank placed on legs on top of the furnaces from whence it flows into a coned cup with wire-

gauze on top. The oil is then conducted into an ejector of ordinary design, where it is disintegrated and blown into the furnace by air, which is heated by pipes led along the inside of the furnace.

Before departing from this part of our subject, reference should be made to the steel stern-frame and bracket-castings, which constituted a most important part of the work. These, with the stern, weighed 161 tons. The stern-frame and bracket for the two inner propellers, as illustrated by Fig. 23, weighed 104 tons; the frames for the outer propellers, together 48 tons; and the rudder, with an area of 420 square feet, $63\frac{1}{2}$ tons. The heavy members were made by the Darlington Forge Company, Limited, Darlington, who also made the stem-bar, which is an ingot-steel forging, weighing $8\frac{1}{2}$ tons. It is rabbeted and tapered to suit the lines of the ship. The stem foot-piece is of cast steel, weighing $1\frac{1}{2}$ tons, making 10 tons in all.

The framing aft forms the termination of a considerable rise of keel, as shown in the longitudinal section of the ship above. This rise improves the turning circle of the ship, and gives a freer flow of water to the inner propellers. Abaft the propeller there is a downward curve to the main support for the rudder. The hull frames for the inboard shafting are of spectacle form, as in nearly all twin-screw vessels now. The upper part of the

same frames had also to be curved outwards to accommodate the connecting-rods and crosshead from Brown's steering-gear. This crosshead is attached to the top of the rudder-head, which passes through the stern-framing. The bossing out for the rudder, as well as the propellers, is very clearly shown in the view of the stern of the ship ready for launching.

The rudder, including the rudder-head, weighs $63\frac{1}{2}$ tons, and is of the balanced type, made up of a series of castings, bolted together with heavy ribs. The rudder-head is of forged ingot steel, of $25\frac{1}{2}$ in. diameter. There is only one gudgeon on the stern-framing, and the pintle—a single pintle in double shear—had to be made of very large size, its weight being over $1\frac{1}{4}$ tons. The pintle, however, can be withdrawn, to enable the bushes to be replaced, without disconnecting any part of the steering-gear or rudder.

The rudder-head is connected by two long rods, which are carried forward, to a dummy crosshead in the steering-gear compartment, being worked by the tiller, which is of the Brown type, the engines being placed above the tiller casting. The arrangement is shown in the orlop-deck plan on the two-page Plate XXXIV. The steering-engine is a duplicate of that supplied to the Lusitania, which has already been described in ENGINEERING.

THE BULKHEAD ARRANGEMENTS OF THE SHIP.

In the design of the ship the sub-division of the hull was a matter which received the most careful consideration, and the very conservative regulations of the Board of Trade Committee, which investigated this question and prepared rules, have been more than met in order to ensure absolute safety. There are 12 main transverse bulkheads, as shown on the elevation and plan on the preceding page, and intermediate wing bulkheads are fitted in the side bunkers, dividing them into spaces about 40 ft. long. There are thus 175 water-tight compartments or flats.

At the forward end the main compartments are small, so as to minimise danger due to collision. The longest of the compartments is the forward boiler-room, which is over 90 ft.; but as the width of the ship is considerably reduced owing to the fining of the lines here, the area of the compartment is not so great as might be suggested by its length. Any two of the compartments may be flooded without materially affecting even the trim of the ship. It will be noted, further, that the coal-bunkers are arranged alongside the boiler compartment right fore and aft, and that the main machinery space is divided into three compartments by longitudinal bulkheads, so that for nearly 350 ft. the ship has an inner and an outer skin, not only on the bottom, but on the sides, and sufficiently far apart to prevent the effect of collision, or grounding, making a rupture in the inner plating. This inner plating, too, has been as carefully constructed as the outer shell of the ship.

The pillars are of Mannesmann tube in all the 'tween-decks. Here, too, it may be noted that in the boiler-rooms strongly-built pillars of channel section are fitted immediately below the continuous girder, which forms the fan-room and casing sides between the lower and main decks. The shelter-deck forms the top member of the equivalent girder, the deck above being of comparatively light scantling. The pillars in all the 'tween decks are of Mannesmann tubes.

It has been impossible to dispense with bulkhead doors, especially in the machinery compartment; but the next best alternative has been accepted in the fitting of a system for controlling by hydraulic gear the doors through the bulkheads. The system adopted, the Stone-Lloyd, is constructed by Messrs. J. Stone and Co., Limited, Deptford, London. Hydraulic power is generated by pumps in the main engine-room, which are always in operation, and which maintain at all times water pressure in the hydraulic supply system shown in the sectional plan on the preceding page. The pumps discharge into a system of piping carried throughout the ship. These pipes extend to the forward boiler-room bulkhead, and here there is fitted a screw-down valve, the operation of which admits pressure into a subsidiary pipe-line, simultaneously closing all doors. This valve is operated by steel wire and chains from a pedestal on the bridge. The captain, or other officer, liberates the valve-handle by moving aside a clutch-gear, which until then retains the handle in the "open" position, and in turning pressure into the closing pipe causes the ringing of large gongs at each bulkhead-door station, as a warning to all in the compartment of the impending closing of all means of communication. The controlling valve, which is of the ram-and-slide-valve type, is arranged so that when pressure from the subsidiary pipe enters the valve-casing the slide-valve is driven to the position for closing the door. The valve has three ports, the central one being the exhaust, while the second admits pressure for opening, and the third for closing, the door.

The valve has been arranged so that in the event of the doors being closed from the bridge, the pressure may be relieved in any one case, in order that a man imprisoned within a water-tight compartment may release himself. For this purpose there is a spindle through the centre of the ram of the valve for the whole of its length. This spindle is at one end in contact with a lever, which can be operated by a handle working through wire connection on each side of the bulkhead. The lever drives the spindle through the valve-ram, and opens a small spring-loaded valve on the end of the ram, allowing the pressure water above the ram to escape down through four grooves cut in the spindle. At the same time the lever drives back the valve-ram, actuating also a slide-valve, which liberates the pressure water from the cylinder holding the door closed, and admits the pressure to the other side of the cylinder to open the door. When the man within the compartment releases the handle of the lever, in order to escape from the compartment, the pressure in the main system again shuts the small spring-loaded valve on the top of the ram, and forces the spindle outwards, so that the door is re-closed by the pressure in the main system. It will thus be seen that while all the doors may be simultaneously closed, the men in the compartments have at their hand the power to re-open the doors for a sufficient time to enable them to escape; but it is necessary that they should hold the handle operating the lever continuously if they wish the door kept open continuously, otherwise the main-pressure system will keep the door closed. The door in all cases closes slowly, and has considerable power to break up any obstructions.

THE LAUNCHING OF THE SHIP.

The launching of the vessel called for as much forethought and care as the solution of the problems of design and construction, especially in view of the immense weight, which on this occasion was 16,800 tons, including the launching-ways, and in view also of the comparative narrowness of the

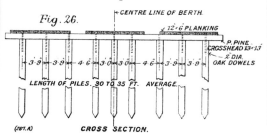

Fig. 26.

Fig. 27.

FIGS. 26 AND 27. DETAILS OF PILING OF SHIPBUILDING BERTH.

river into which the vessel had to be launched. In the first place, special provision had to be made to ensure a thoroughly sound foundation. The berth, therefore, was carefully piled, the number of piles driven being over 16,000. These were 13-in. by 13-in. timbers, and their length averaged from 30 ft. to 35 ft. They were driven at 4-ft. centres in the longitudinal line, and transversely, as shown in Fig. 26, above. Pitch-pine beams, also of 13-in. by 13-in. timbers, of a length of 36 ft., connected the piles, being secured by oak dowels, 3 ft. long and 2 in. in diameter. Over these horizontal timbers, again, there was, throughout the entire area of the berth, a floor of 12-in. by 6-in. timber. The gradient of this floor is shown in Fig. 27, above.

On this foundation were laid the keel-blocks, which were in groups of five, about 12 in. apart, with 3-ft. intervals between the groups. This arrangement facilitated communication from one side of the berth to the other. The cap-blocks were of oak, 12 in. by 8 in. As the floor of the ship was constructed, additional support was provided by four rows of shores under each alternate frame and on each side of the centre line. The bilge-blocks were at intervals of about 50 ft.

The keel was laid with a declivity of 0.494 in. per foot, and the standing ways forward of 0.545 in. per foot, and for the remainder of the length 0.564 in. per foot. The camber was 21 in. in the whole length of 794 ft. The standing ways extended from 64 ft. abaft of the fore perpendicular to 98 ft. abaft of the aft perpendicular. The sliding-ways had a bearing length from the fore end of the cradle to the heel aft of 635 ft., and as the width was 6 ft., the total area of bearing surface was 7620 square feet, which gave a pressure per square foot of 2.20 tons, when the total weight, including the cradle, was taken into consideration. There was, however,

at the moment the stern floated a pressure at the forward cradle of probably about 9 tons to the square foot; this pressure affected not only the fore cradle and the ways, but the floors and tank girder construction. Subsequent examination, however, showed that everything had been of sufficient strength to withstand the great thrust, which was calculated to be 3700 tons, decreasing to 1600 tons as the bow left the ways. The greatest statical lifting moment was when the forward perpendicular was about 209 ft. from the end of the ways. The greatest draught aft before lifting was about 33 ft., while the maximum moment against tipping was calculated at 420,000 foot-tons. These and other results and calculations are set out in the diagram, Fig. 43 on page 14.

The ways were placed at 25-ft. centres. They were constructed of pitch pine, excepting at the forward end; but because of the high pressure at the moment of lifting, the sliding-ways at the forward end, and the ground-ways at the after end, were of oak. Instead of using elm rubbers, spiked and bolted to the outer edge of the ways, as is more usual, the outer timber was 2 in. thicker than the others, and this formed a strong guide 2 in. deep, as will be seen by reference to the various sections of the ways reproduced opposite. The average length of the timbers forming the ways was about 35 ft., and the butts were connected by 3-in. iron straps, with two through-bolts at each side of the butt. For facility in moving the ways after the ship had floated, the sliding-ways were built up of three lengths on each side of the ship, the bolts being omitted at the junctions of these sections. The standing ways, it will be seen, were supported by side shores, as shown in Figs. 28 and 29, and by angle-stays and brackets between the ways to counteract any outward thrust. Another point in connection with the ways is their distance from the ground; and this is shown not only in the sections, but also in the following table :—

TABLE X.—*Distance Between Launching-Ways and Ground.*

	Way Ends.	Heel Casting.	Amidships.	Fore End Cradle.
	ft. in.	ft. in.	ft. in.	ft. in.
Standing ways above ground	1 5½	1 11	4 1	7 2½
" " below keel ..	5 8½	3 5	1 6	1 2
Keel above ground ..	7 2	5 4	5 7	8 4½

Standing-ways above ground at closest point 6 ft. aft A.P., 1 ft. 1½ in.
Sliding-ways below bottom plating at closest point, 3 in.

The construction of the forward and aft parts of the cradle are so well shown in the section that it is scarcely necessary to enter into any detailed description. It will be seen that a strong shelf plate of steel was attached to the skin-plating of the ship, and was supported by knee brackets in order to form a butting surface or a bearing for the vertical members of the poppets. The foremost timbers were slightly canted inwards. Four 2-in. tie-rods were fitted, as shown, to brace the port and starboard cradles together. The rods were connected under the keel by a pin through eye-bolts, which, when the vessel was afloat, could be withdrawn by levers, so that the port and starboard sides of the forward cradle could be separated from each other after the launch. It will also be noted that 3-in. round bar stays were put in from the keel to the upper part of the poppets, to prevent any canting outward at their heads in the event of the vessel being slewed by wind and tide prior to the fore part being water-borne. As a matter of fact, however, the wind at the time of launching was light, not exceeding five miles, and, moreover, was direct end on to the travel of the vessel. It will be noted from the cross-section also that five layers of soft wood, making a total thickness of 14 in., was laid over the sliding ways to facilitate the distribution of

— 13 —

DETAILS OF THE LAUNCHING-WAYS AND CRADLE.

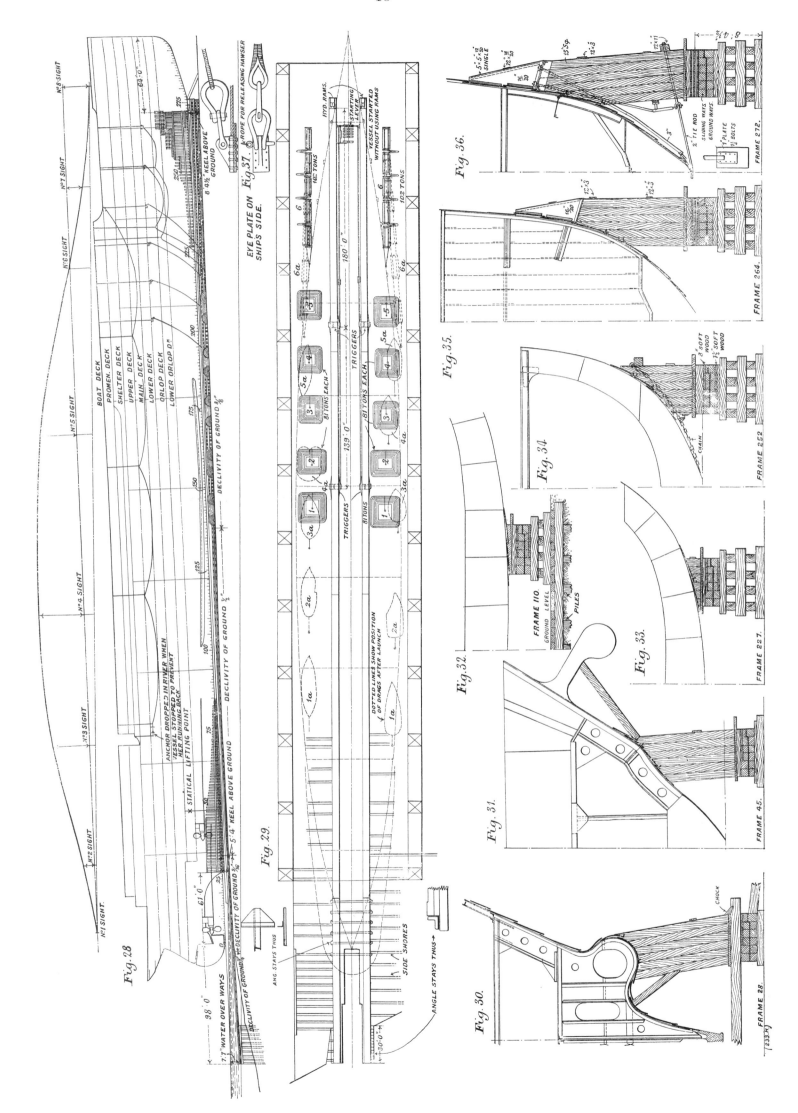

the thrust over the whole of the cradle. The vertical members of the cradle were connected by chain lashings, and by narrow plates and angle-bars, as shown in Figs. 34 and 35 overleaf.

The amidship part of the cradle is well shown. The driving wedges were of pitch-pine and about 7 ft. 6 in. long; here they were only single, but forward and aft they were double.

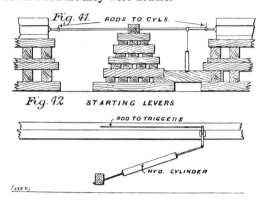

The aft cradle was constructed under the spectacle framing for the propeller shafting, and the vertical members were held in place by a large angle-bar riveted to the shell. The poppets here were also inclined inwards, and three large timbers were carried from side to side to prevent splaying.

On the standing-ways there was laid from 1 in. to $\frac{5}{8}$ in. of tallow, next $\frac{1}{4}$ in. of tallow and train oil mixed in the proportion of 2 to 1, then soft soap in blobs about 6 in. apart, with train-oil sprinkled on the top. On the sliding-ways there was laid, before they were turned in on the top of the permanent ways, $\frac{3}{8}$ in. of tallow and $\frac{1}{4}$ in. of tallow and train-oil, with soft-soap in blobs. The tallow was put on with brushes. The total quantity of tallow thus used was $14\frac{1}{2}$ tons, of soft-soap 1 ton 2 cwt., and of train-oil 113 gallons. This lubrication of the ways commenced about a month before the date of the launch; the weather was favourable.

The system of releasing the ship when all was ready for launching is illustrated by Figs. 38 to 40, annexed. There were eight triggers, placed four abreast, the forward set being 180 ft. aft of the foremost poppet, and the second set 139 ft. further aft. as shown on the plan, Fig. 29. As to the details of this arrangement, given on Figs. 38 to 40, it is sufficient to say that when the clip was pulled back by the rod, worked from the bow of the vessel, the casting shown in cross-section fell sideways, and the trigger dropped, leaving the vessel free. The rods from each pair of triggers were led to the bow and connected to a crank, which was turned by hydraulic power, so that all triggers were released simultaneously. There were hydraulic rams of 400 tons pressure abutting on the head of each of the sliding ways, to start the vessel if necessary, but they were not brought into use.

As shown on the diagram, Fig. 43, the time occupied in the first 6 ft. of travel was 7 seconds, while for the 794 ft.—the total length of the standing ways—the time was 55 seconds. The whole distance travelled by the ship was 951 ft., the total time taken being 70 seconds. The maximum speed was $23\frac{1}{2}$ ft. per second, equal to 14 knots, and the maximum acceleration was 0.87 ft. per second per second.

The bringing of the vessel to a state of rest was successfully accomplished. The principal method adopted is well shown on the elevation and plan, Figs. 28 and 29. There were six sets of drags on each side of the ship, consisting, in the case of five sets, of heaps of chains, weighing about 80 tons, and the remaining pair of armour-plates, weighing about 100 tons. The total weight of the drags was 1050 tons. Each heap was connected by an 8-in. steel-wire hawser to eye-plates fixed to the shell-plating, as shown on the elevation and Fig. 37. The chains were coiled, and the connecting strap was carried round the forward part of the heap, so that the heap had to be pulled over before being jerked along the ground. In this way the load was put on gradually. The first drag came into action when the vessel was about 30 ft. from the end of the ways, and the last when the ship had travelled 90 ft. from the ways. The vessel was stopped when the stem was 93 ft. from the end of the ways.

The draught forward was 11 ft. $7\frac{1}{2}$ in., and aft 21 ft. $4\frac{1}{2}$ in., with a mean of 16 ft. 6 in., the total weight being 16.250 tons, which excludes the 550 tons due to the launching-cradle.

In view of the width of the river relative to the length of the ship, it was important that the vessel should be as soon as possible swung into line with the channel, and to facilitate this a wire-rope was laid from the after end of the ship to an anchor near the up-stream bank of the river. The rope connecting the ship to this anchor was arranged to become taut soon after the vessel left the ways.

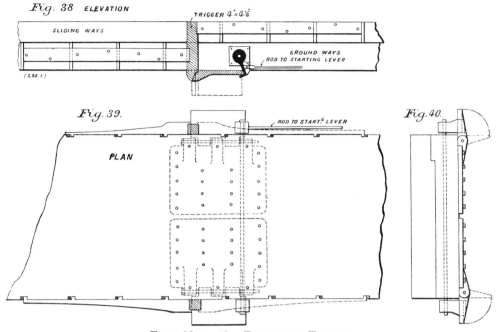

FIGS. 38 TO 40. DETAILS OF TRIGGER.

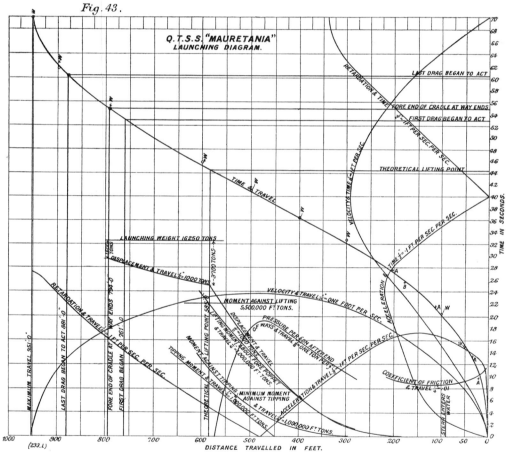

FIG. 43. DIAGRAM OF LAUNCHING.

The anchor was dragged 120 ft. without, however, having any appreciable effect upon the ship. The anchor was dropped from the bow of the ship to prevent the vessel returning too near the ways.

Six tugs took the vessel in charge, and brought her alongside the two large dolphins, which had been constructed in the river, as shown in the photograph reproduced on Plate III., to serve, in the absence of a wharf, as fenders for the ship during her fitting out. A special steel lattice-girder gangway had been constructed, and this was supported by shears built of steel work and used earlier in connection with the lifting into place of the stern-brackets, &c.

THE NAMING OF THE SHIP.

The honours of the launch were performed by the Dowager Duchess of Roxburgh, who named the vessel the Mauretania. This, it is interesting to recall, was in old times the name of the most north-western part of Africa looking right across to Gibraltar, the "Fretum Herculeum" of the Ancients. It corresponded to the present Morocco and the western portion of Algiers. Mauretania reached on the south to the Atlas Mountains, and was originally separated from Numidia on the east by the River Mulucha, now the Muluya, although at later date it extended as far east as the Ampsaga. In ancient times Mauretania produced large quantities of corn and valuable timber. The sister-ship Lusitania, it may be noted, takes her name from the old Roman province of the Spanish peninsula. Under the Emperor Augustus the peninsula was divided into three provinces. One of these was named Lusitania, and until quite recent times was regarded as practically identical with the present kingdom of

Portugal. As a matter of fact, however, the Roman province of Lusitania lay wholly on the south side of the River Tagus. It was famous for its wines, a fact which, it may be recalled, was recognised by Tennyson in "Will Waterproof's Lyrical Monologue." It will thus be seen that there is appropriateness in the selection of the names of two prosperous provinces, adjacent, yet belonging to two different continents, and their choice is consistent with the practice of the Cunard Company of taking the names of the ships from countries famous in ancient and classical history.

THE ARRANGEMENT OF THE DECKS.

There are nine decks in the Mauretania, seven of which are completely above the load water-line. The eighth, the orlop deck, is entirely given over to machinery, with the exception of the forward holds, where insulated space is provided in connection with the carriage of supplies for the cuisine department, and for perishable cargo (see Plate XXXIV.). The other decks, which are, as far as possible, given up to the accommodation of passengers, are designated by letters, from the boat-deck downwards. Corticine has been largely used for deck-covering in lieu of wood, to save weight. The boat-deck, which extends over the greater part of the centre of the ship, contains some of the finest *en suite* rooms, shown in Fig. 50, Plate XXXIV. At the forward end, well abaft these, are the first-class library, the grand entrance hall, the first-class lounge and music-room, and the first-class smoking-room. These are exceptionally fine apartments, the height of ceiling being 11 ft. 9 in., but in the centre in each case there is a large dome of great height, which gets rid of the cramped feeling experienced in even the public rooms on board ship.

The library extends across the deck-house, being 33 ft. long by 56 ft. The walls of the deck-house are bowed out to form bay windows, which is an improvement upon the ordinary flat walls characteristic of ships. The lounge is similarly treated, and this room is 80 ft. long over its greatest dimension, and 56 ft. wide. The smoking-room is all that such a room should be, as will presently be proved when we come to describe and illustrate it. It is 53 ft. long and 50 ft. wide. Abaft this is the veranda café, which, as in the Lusitania, is sure to prove a popular resort. There is formed in the roof a dome, which makes the veranda bright and attractive. The second-class lounge, it will be seen, is accommodated in the deck-house aft on this level, and forms also the entrance to the second-class quarters. There is splendid promenading space on this boat-deck, and the boats, if an obstruction from some points of view, afford protection from wind and sun for passengers on the deck chairs.

The promenade-deck, which is designated B, is without a single public-room, except at the stern, where the second-class drawing-room and smoking-room are located. In the first-class space there are arranged a large number of cabins. In this part of the ship there are, on port and starboard, the regal suites, while along each side of the main deck-house are *en suite* rooms. In all there are on this level six rooms with single berths, sixty-four with two berths, and thirty-two with three berths. An interesting feature here, as in the Lusitania, is the closed-in gangway at the forward end of the deck-house. The front of this is closed, so that passengers, even when they are not allowed on deck in stormy weather, may from this vantage point view the splendid effects of the ship driving through a head wind and storm at full speed. In front of this point of observation is the forecastle head, as shown in the plan, with all the anchor gear, &c., to be described later. To provide better deck space on the promenade and boat-decks, these decks have been extended 20 in. beyond the line of the shelter-deck—an arrangement which was adopted in the previous Cunard vessels, the Ivernia and Carpathia—built at Wallsend.

On the shelter-deck there is not a single cabin in the first-class quarters. Right at the forward end are the very powerful Napier engines for working the anchor gear; abaft that, on the starboard side, is the general room or lounge for the third-class passengers, and on the port side the smoking-room, with a companion-way leading to the third-class dining-saloon below, and to the third-class cabins on the main and lower decks. The third-class galleys are accommodated in the main deck-house, and close by is a set of the refrigerating machinery used in connection with the rooms for the storage of supplies for the kitchen department. Alongside also is the very extensive lavatory for the third-class passengers, and, still further, the grand stairway to the third-class rooms. The side of the ship for a considerable distance aft of this is plated up to the promenade-deck level, so that the third-class passengers have not only convenient rooms, but a protected promenade, and abaft that an open promenade. Indeed, the arrangements made for the third-class passengers are exceptionally fine, so far as public and private rooms are concerned. Coming now to the accommodation on the deck-house for the first-class passengers, it will be seen that on the grand stairway there is a children's dining-saloon and nursery, with adjacent compartments for the stewardesses and other servants attending upon the children.

With access from the grand entrance are the doctor's and purser's offices, and abaft is the upper floor of the first-class dining-saloon. This is one of the finest features of the ship. It has a sitting accommodation for 142 persons, and surrounds the well, which is surmounted by a dome. This, under some conditions, may be adapted as an *à la carte* restaurant. The Cunard Company have preferred to follow the usual course, with this important modification—that passengers may elect to dine at any hour, and may choose for themselves from an ample list a special menu without extra charge; this arrangement has proved very popular, and the company are to be commended for their enterprise in this direction.

It will be seen from the plan of this deck that the hospital accommodation is put abaft the fourth funnel and entirely separated from the other part of the ship. The engineers, it is interesting to note, are located around the engine hatches in very complete and roomy state-rooms, with a separate mess-room. They are thus near their work, a fact which is also noticeable in connection with the navigation officers of the ship. These are housed on the navigation bridge abaft of the chart-room, &c., with a separate mess-room, so that the officers, whether on or off duty, are easily within hail of the officer on the bridge. The captain's room is immediately below at the forward end of the boat-deck, with a good look-out ahead. Right aft, the shelter-deck is given up to the second-class passengers, and here, it will be noted, there are several very fine rooms.

On the upper deck there are dining-saloons for all three classes of passengers, that for the third-class being forward, for the first amidship, and for the second near the stern, while the remaining part of the deck amidships is occupied with first-class state-rooms. Around the engine-hatch are the quarters of the kitchen department, including the immense galley, and abaft the second-class dining-room there are more state-rooms for the passengers, the extreme stern being given up to the stewards and officers in the ship. The first-class dining-saloon on this deck has a length of 87 ft., and a width of 87 ft. 6 in., while the height is 11 ft. The principal saloon, it may be interpolated here, is 62 ft. 6 in. by 66 ft., with a height of 9 ft. 3 in. There is sitting accommodation in the lower saloon for 328 passengers, so that in all, excluding the accommodation in the children's room, there is space provided for 470 first-class passengers. In the second-class dining-saloon 251 passengers may dine at the same time.

The main deck is given up entirely to state-rooms, and as figures are given on the plan on Plate XXXIV., showing the accommodation in each department, it is scarcely necessary here to particularise. It will be noted that the firemen and other engine-room and stokehold workers are located above the machinery, with separate entrance and exit to and from their work. Promenade space is provided for them on the shelter-deck, fenced off from the third-class and second-class passengers. The whole of the lower deck forward is arranged for state-rooms for third-class passengers, while amidships is a coal-bunker, with one compartment under the engines for the storage of supplies. The coal-trimmers are accommodated alongside the engine-casing, and abaft are the mail-rooms, with accommodation for stewards, &c. The orlop-deck, as we have already said, is devoted entirely to machinery, with coal-bunkers on each side of the boilers, to provide against the effects of collision, or of penetration by an enemy's shot when the vessels are used for scouting or for Admiralty duty. This orlop-deck well shows the arrangement of the steering-gear, to which we shall refer later.

By way of summarising the accommodation we annex Table XI., showing the number of rooms, of the different sizes, on each deck. It will be noted that there are 253 rooms for the accommodation of the 563 first-class passengers, 133 rooms for the 464 second-class passengers, and for the 1138 third-class passengers 278 rooms.

TABLE XI.—*Passenger Accommodation on each Deck.*

—	One-Berth Rooms.	Two-Berth Rooms.	Three-Berth Rooms.	Number of Passengers.
First-class—				
Boat-deck state-rooms ..	3	26	..	55
,, en suite ,, ..	..	4	..	8
Promenade-deck state-rooms	6	64	16	182
Promenade-deck en suite rooms	..	..	16	48
Promenade-deck regal suites	8	..	..	8
Upper-deck state-rooms	10	13	39	153
Main-deck rooms ..	8	19	21	109
Shelter deck		(Children's room.)		
Total	35	126	92	563

Total of first-class rooms 253
Total of first-class passengers 563

—	Two-Berth Rooms.	Four-Berth Rooms.	Number of Passengers.
Second-class—			
Shelter-deck ..	—	24	96
Upper-deck ..	14	25	128
Main-deck ..	20	50	240
Total	34	99	464

Total number of second-class rooms.. 133
Total number of second-class passengers 464

—	Two-Berth Rooms.	Four-Berth Rooms.	Six-Berth Rooms.	Eight-Berth Rooms.	Number of Passengers.
Third-class—					
Main-deck permanent rooms ..	13	118	10	4	590
Lower-deck permanent rooms..	—	18	6	—	108
Lower deck portable rooms ..	18	79	6	6	436
Lower-deck open berths ..	—	—	—	—	4
Total	31	215	22	10	1138

Seating Accommodation of Dining-Rooms.

First-class upper	142	persons
First-class lower	328	,,
Second-class dining	251	,,
Third-class dining	520	,,

THE DECORATION OF THE SALOONS.

If it were possible to give a complete description of the first-class saloons on the Mauretania, the reading of such particulars would, perhaps, prove tedious to many; but it is nevertheless desirable to attempt a somewhat detailed account of the work for two reasons. In the first place, never has the interior of a ship had more careful thought bestowed upon it, nor has such an earnest desire after purity of style been manifested; and, second, much of the work having been carried out in the sixteenth-century style of François Premier, and the Italian Renaissance of that period, a few leading thoughts may— to those less initiated in the art of those times—prove helpful to a fuller appreciation of what the directors of the Cunard Company have sought, and succeeded in effecting.

The portion of the work of the ship to be first described is that carried out by the firm of Messrs. W. Turner Lord and Co., London. The original designs for all the first-class saloons were prepared by the well-known architect, Mr. H. A. Peto, the styles which he first suggested having been adhered to throughout, and he is to be congratulated upon the admirable results attained. Some idea of the extent and importance of the work with which Messrs. Lord have been entrusted may be obtained from the list following:—The dining-saloon; restaurant, or upper dining-saloon; smoking-room; the staircase entrances to the promenade, upper, shelter, and boat-decks; the cages of the Waygood electric lifts; and aluminium grille enclosing the well of staircase; the two suites of regal rooms; and fifty-four *en suite* rooms.

THE STAIRWAY AND ENTRANCE HALLS.

We give first a description of the staircase and grand entrances, since these portions of the ship are the first to be visited, as from them access is

TURBINE-DRIVEN QUADRUPLE-SCREW CUNARD LINER "MAURETANIA."

FIG. 58. THE GRAND ENTRANCE ON THE BOAT-DECK.

gained to all the principal rooms, as well as to the alleyways leading to the state-rooms. In visiting this colossal ship one has need to be prepared for surprises everywhere, and one of these surprises will be the grandeur of the stairways and approaches. Except in the Mauretania's sister-ship, never has there been in a vessel a stairway of such size, and resembling so nearly that of a private mansion; while the fact that, in the well of the staircase, there are two separate lifts will make clear to the reader the perfection of comfort that has been provided by the Cunard Company for travellers. A view of the entrance hall on the boat-deck is given in Fig. 58, and of a nook facing the lifts in Fig. 59, annexed.

The staircase and entrances are in the Italian style of the sixteenth century. The woodwork is French walnut, the panels being veneered with wood of exceptionally fine figure. Messrs. Lord inform us that they had the utmost difficulty in obtaining a sufficient quantity of veneers for so extensive a work, both England and France being searched for what was needed. The carving of the woodwork on the staircase and entrances is much less extensive than in the dining-saloons, but the panels that contain carving are very chaste in design and workmanship. The carved capitals of both pilasters and columns are also most interesting. There is quite a variety of designs in these, and as in the dining-saloons so on the staircase and entrances, Messrs. Lord deserve praise for giving so much varied detail. In the whole of the work of the staircase and entrances there is the charm of simplicity; no one piece, or panel, of carving or woodwork

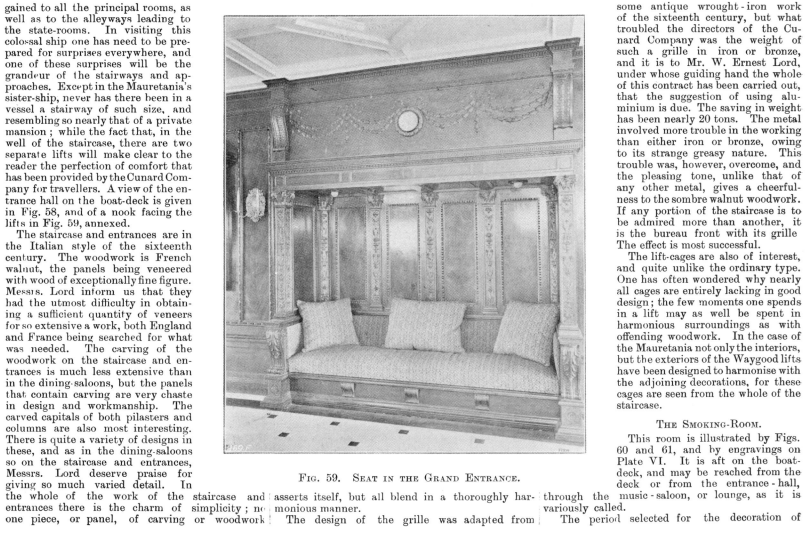

FIG. 59. SEAT IN THE GRAND ENTRANCE.

asserts itself, but all blend in a thoroughly harmonious manner.

The design of the grille was adapted from some antique wrought-iron work of the sixteenth century, but what troubled the directors of the Cunard Company was the weight of such a grille in iron or bronze, and it is to Mr. W. Ernest Lord, under whose guiding hand the whole of this contract has been carried out, that the suggestion of using aluminium is due. The saving in weight has been nearly 20 tons. The metal involved more trouble in the working than either iron or bronze, owing to its strange greasy nature. This trouble was, however, overcome, and the pleasing tone, unlike that of any other metal, gives a cheerfulness to the sombre walnut woodwork. If any portion of the staircase is to be admired more than another, it is the bureau front with its grille The effect is most successful.

The lift-cages are also of interest, and quite unlike the ordinary type. One has often wondered why nearly all cages are entirely lacking in good design; the few moments one spends in a lift may as well be spent in harmonious surroundings as with offending woodwork. In the case of the Mauretania not only the interiors, but the exteriors of the Waygood lifts have been designed to harmonise with the adjoining decorations, for these cages are seen from the whole of the staircase.

THE SMOKING-ROOM.

This room is illustrated by Figs. 60 and 61, and by engravings on Plate VI. It is aft on the boat-deck, and may be reached from the deck or from the entrance-hall, through the music-saloon, or lounge, as it is variously called.

The period selected for the decoration of

TURBINE-DRIVEN QUADRUPLE-SCREW CUNARD LINER "MAURETANIA."

FIG. 60. FIRST-CLASS SMOKING-ROOM, LOOKING AFT.

the smoking-room is the same as the staircase — viz. :—sixteenth century Italian; but it differs, inasmuch as it is far richer in the carvings, and, in addition, is relieved round all the panels with an inlaid border. An unusual feature in the main portion of the room is a jube extending along the length of the room, divided into recesses with divans and card-tables (Fig. 60), the two recesses at one end of the room being fitted up with writing-tables, giving the users perfect seclusion. The windows in these recesses are of unusual size for ship-work, and have been most successfully treated with semicircular arches, giving every appearance of the windows of a private house.

In the centre, at the forward end of the room, is perhaps the main feature of the scheme—namely, the chimney-piece, surmounted with a carved hood (see Fig. 62, Plate VI.). The frieze of this chimney-piece has been modelled and carved from a fine example of Della Robbia in the Museum at South Kensington, and the interior is lined at the sides with massive slabs of "verte antique" marble, the basket grate and handsome fire-dogs being reproduced from the originals at the Palazzo Varesi. Another feature not to be overlooked is the treatment of the doors, with their carved columns having clear glass between. The carved architraves and pediment overdoors are most successful, as will be seen from Fig. 60, annexed.

FIG. 61. FIRST-CLASS SMOKING-SALOON, STARBOARD SIDE.

What is most helpful in this room is its grand height, which is greatly enhanced by the wagon-headed roof. This roof is divided into three sections, with some most beautifully-modelled plaster-work, which also runs as a frieze round the lower part of the wagon immediately above the carved-wood cornice, and embraces at the extreme ends of the room two pictures, one representing "Old New York," and the other "Old Liverpool." This roof, with its plaster-work, has been all finished a vellum colour.

The strengthening girders between the shafts to the engine-room have afforded the artists a fine opportunity of producing a most pleasing effect, the sides being filled in with open-work jube, giving snug corners for small parties, and the space over the central opening is surmounted by a flat coffered ceiling, terminating with a cresting, the upper part being left clear, with fine columns on each flank. Fig. 61, annexed, will give an idea of these details.

THE DINING-SALOONS.

Perhaps the most important rooms decorated by Messrs. W. Turner Lord and Co. are the dining-saloon and upper dining-saloon, these two rooms, with the open-well between, being so designed as to carry out one complete scheme. These rooms are illustrated on Plates VII. and VIII. Dating back to the sixteenth century, the style chosen for these two saloons is that known as François Premier, the type most closely followed being between the years 1540 and 1550, selected

D

from the more crisp models which are so acceptable to true lovers of art.

To appreciate fully the work it will be well to carry our mind back to the period which gave birth to this style, and to try and realise what forces were at work to render the general form and feeling so much akin to the Italian work of the same period. As far as art in France was concerned, for many years prior to the dawn of the sixteenth century the Gothic style had reigned supreme. The workers had produced a variety of designs, which call forth from us of the present day the greatest admiration for their wonderful inventive skill and their pure conception of the highest art ; but, as in all things, "familiarity breeds contempt," so it was with the French artist and craftsman of about 1480. The Gothic style seemed to have reached its zenith, and was now on the decline, and the workers were ready and anxious to take advantage of any new suggestion coming in their way. At such a time, therefore, it was of the highest importance that the genius of the nation should be turned into a right channel, and fortunately for those who love the beautiful, we find that the French and Italian nations, both possessing such natural gifts in art, were thrown together, and an influence was brought to bear upon the minds of the French which quickly resolved itself into the style we have now under consideration. At first the two styles were not easily merged, and one may find existing examples of work when a series of panels are alternated—one pure Gothic and one Italian, each keeping its

taken in seconding the artist's wishes. An art critic in going through the rooms said that never before had he seen such delicious rendering of François Premier. Some of the most delightful and delicate work is that upon the stiffening bulkheads, which run at right angles to the outer sides of the ship. When one considers that all the carving has been worked out of the solid wood, we realise that, apart from the skill of the carver, the work must have been most laborious.

By the help of photographs we are enabled to give some illustrations of these two rooms (Plates VII. and VIII.), but at best the idea they convey must be imperfect. They will, however, help the readers to gain some insight into the scheme of decoration, and it may be seen how the designer's aim has been to keep the larger and lower room richer in carving, leading up to the simpler treatment of the upper dining-saloon, and finishing with the crowning feature of the groined dome. The interlacing of the groins has been most carefully planned, with small plaques at the cross-sections introducing signs of the Zodiac. The centre portion of the dome is raised upon a number of balustrades, terminating in a gilded convex disc which forms the flat, or ceiling. Against this the electric light is reflected, shedding a soft warm glow over the whole room. A word, too, may be said here about the sconces in the upper dining-saloon, which are well worthy of attention, being reproduced from a fine pair of antique silver ones. Even the design of the carpet Messrs. Lord reproduced

carved mouldings, is upheld by mahogany and gold columns, of exquisite workmanship, each with its cap and base of rich gold, encasing the stanchions, which are unavoidable in so large a space. On three sides of the room are panels of Aubusson tapestry, on which many weavers have been working during the past year. By their perfect colouring and exquisite design these tapestries, which are illustrated in Plate IX., give a final note of perfection to the whole. From the ceiling hang chandeliers of gilt bronze and crystal, so cleverly arranged that, although the crystals appear to hang loose, and have the light effect of such hanging, no motion of the ship disturbs them, and the lights themselves are completely hidden. The curtains, hanging with their soft folds against the dull gold of the carved curtain-boxes, are of a charming cream silk, and, with their flowered borders, give a tone both sumptuous and refined. The carpet is of a slender trellis design, with blush-pink roses trailing over a pearl-grey ground, and forms a perfect foil to the splendid furniture with which Messrs. Mellier have embellished the room. The chairs, of polished beech, with their costly coverings of eighteenth-century brocades, are the epitome of luxury and comfort, and they are fitly matched by the parquetry-panelled occasional tables placed at convenient intervals.

THE LIBRARY.

It is with reluctance that one leaves this room to go to the library, of which three views are given

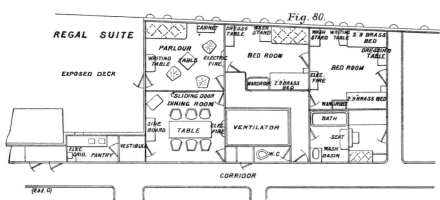

Fig. 80.

REGAL SUITE

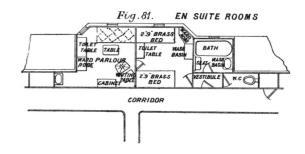

Fig. 81.　EN SUITE ROOMS

own character. This was, however, soon to be overcome, and within a short time we trace how well the French workers assimilated the Italian designs, imparting, however, their own natural rendering. One is tempted to mention examples to show how this influence of the Italian was working in the minds of the French craftsmen ; but to do so would be a digression, and the study must be left to those enough interested in art to seek it out for themselves.

To return now to the panelling of the dining-saloons. After the final acceptance of the scheme of decoration by the directors of the Cunard Company, the next decision was as to what wood should be used. One of the first objects to be attained was lightness ; and as white painted woodwork was to be avoided, sycamore was suggested. This, however, proved to be impossible, and the choice finally fell on oak, which was to be kept light in tone ; and Messrs. Lord are to be congratulated upon the pleasing colour which they have, after various experiments, been able to produce, it being entirely free from that disagreeable yellow tone which too frequently makes the oak-work of the present day so common and uninteresting. The next consideration was the preparation of a variety of designs and models, one of the greatest charms of the early French work being that no piece of carving is an exact reproduction of its neighbour. A casual glance proves how well the artist has realised these traditions of the style. Even now all was not accomplished. To produce designs is an all-important factor ; to find models is also an absolute necessity ; but the greatest difficulty was yet to present itself—namely, to find men artistic enough to be entrusted to give the true feeling to the work, for, while many men are available to carry out the later styles, few can be found to give the right expression to that of the sixteenth century. The work, however, had been confided to a firm with a high reputation for reproducing the feeling of the styles of days gone by, and the result proves how well the carvers must have entered into the spirit of their work, and what keen interest they must have

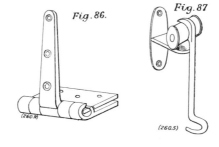

Fig. 86.　Fig. 87.

from a fine antique Italian velvet. The colour is a most pleasing tone of cerise, which again adds to the cheerful and comfortable appearance.

THE LOUNGE.

The lounge and the library have been decorated by Messrs. Ch. Mellier and Co., Albemarle-street, London, and upon entering them one is transported in a moment from the cold realities of a modern steamship to the exquisite taste of a French *salon* of the eighteenth century. Thick carpets, comfortable chairs, soft colourings, and bright, but carefully-shaded, electric lights, all combine to give an atmosphere of luxury and beauty hitherto considered impossible even in modern steamships. The style is influenced by the revived appreciation of the beauties of the Louis Seize period, but the colouring is original in its charming blending of harmonising tints.

Altogether, the lounge, which is illustrated on Plates IX. and X., gives a wonderful impression of quiet grandeur, with its panels of beautifully-grained mahogany, dully polished a rich brown, each lit by its surrounding moulding of gold, and relieved by slender pilasters of fleur de pecher marble of a lilac hue, with caps and plinths of sombre ormolu (Figs. 69 to 72). The mantelpiece (Fig. 72), of the same materials, is in itself a work of art, and accentuates the feeling that one is in some great palace of a past age. The white ceiling of simple design, with boldly-

on Plate XI. ; but here again a scheme of decoration no less effective greets the eye. The first impression is that of a shimmering marble ingrained with silver, but in reality the panels are of sycamore, stained in a delicate grey, and treated in a novel and beautiful manner, the whole impression being one of lightness and grace. The eye wanders with pleasure from the magnificent carvings to the handsome bookcase with its semi-circular doors and gilt trellis.

Carrying out the general scheme of softness of colour, the mantelpiece here (Fig. 73) is of pure white statuary marble, which, together with the grate of toned ormolu, conveys a feeling of great refinement. As in the lounge, the glass-panelled swing-doors, with their delicately chased and gilt-bronze mouldings, are worthy of observation. The ceiling is again white, and the effect of the elliptical dome, with its slender tracery of design, is exceptionally beautiful. The cool grey and gilt tones have a charming relief in the deep rose pink of the curtains and carpet, and in the exquisite designs and colourings of the chairs, the frames of which are of light mahogany. These are specially worthy of mention, as, without exception, they are authentic Louis Seize designs, and one at least is an exact copy of the beautiful original in the possession of the decorators. It is impossible to speak in terms of too great praise of the architect, Mr. H. A. Peto, under whom Messrs. Mellier have worked. His exquisite taste and ingenuity have overcome what seemed at first insurmountable difficulties. It is, indeed, hard to believe, when gazing upon the beauties of these rooms, that underneath the costly and magnificent woodwork is hidden the crude iron-work of a modern steamship.

THE REGAL SUITES.

Coming to the regal rooms, one is immediately impressed by an air of delicate refinement throughout the suite, which comprises drawing-room, dining-room, two bed-rooms, bath-room, and private corridor, all starting off from the main alleyway on the promenade-deck, arranged as shown on the plan on this page (Fig. 80). The period selected for decoration is a simple form of the Adams style, which is admirably suited to rooms of this scale, and has been as charmingly carried out by Messrs. Lord. Four illustrations of the regal suite are given on Plate XII. On the port side the drawing and dining-rooms, with their wide communicating sliding-doors, are both panelled in East India satin-wood, the veneers of panels being laid across the angles converging to centres with just sufficient carving to make the rooms interesting. In the drawing-room gilding has been added, and a silk tabouret, in a charming tone of green, has been used in the wall-panels, the carpets throughout the suite being also green. The rooms are supplied with statuary marble chimney-pieces and electric radiators.

The two bed-rooms are Georgian in character, with carved mouldings, the wall panels being covered in silk, corresponding to that used in the two reception-rooms. They are finished entirely in white, while the furniture is mahogany, the whole effect being so thoroughly homelike that it is difficult to imagine oneself on board ship. On the starboard side the suite is carried out in very similar style, with the exception that a delightful tone of rose is substituted for green, and in the case of the two reception-rooms, the wood chosen for the dining-room is fiddle-back sycamore, most charmingly treated and inlaid.

The drawing-room, also in fiddle-back sycamore, of a soft grey tone, is inlaid very delicately with holly wood ; this colour of wood, with the warm rose carpet and silk hangings, is very pleasing.

SPECIAL EN SUITE AND STATE ROOMS.

We next come to the special state and *en suite* rooms, some 54 in number, many of which have likewise been entrusted to the firm of Messrs. W. Turner Lord and Co. to decorate and finish. These rooms, with the regal suites, were, however undertaken by Messrs. Morison, their Edinburgh branch. A plan of an *en suite* room is given in Fig. 81. The style selected throughout these rooms is the same as in the case of the Royal rooms, but a most interesting variety has been obtained by a judicious choice of woods, silk hangings, and general colouring. Without going into minute details, one feels at a glance the daintiness prevailing, and it is indeed difficult to say which effect is the more pleasing. To our mind, one of the most charming is the pear-tree room, with its inlay of holly wood and its cream and green upholstered surroundings. Then, again, we have the fiddle-back sycamore, which delicate colouring is relieved with inlays of green wood in the pilasters and frieze panels, and with its refined moulded cornice and panelled ceilings, silk hangings, and carpets, carefully selected to be in harmony, this forms a very agreeable room. Another noticeable room is that in which the sycamore is of a soft grey colour ; in this case the relieving inlay is in holly and pear tree. Then, again, there are several varieties of white rooms, the mouldings being carved, and in some cases the furniture is in fine mahogany. Other rooms are panelled in satin-wood, which is always a satisfactory wood to use. This is inlaid with faded mahogany, which gives a good result.

No one can fail to realise the immense care which has been devoted to secure the comfort of the traveller in every way. Most of these rooms have recesses, curtained off from the room, fitted up most luxuriously with washstand in fine onyx marble. In many of the rooms the wall panels have been covered with cream silk, with, in some cases, a border of embroidery, taking up the colours of inlays on panelling and on the carpets ; in other cases the panels are framed with a fine lace laid on a contrasting colour, and embroidered at the sides.

THE NURSERY.

The nursery, which has been furnished and decorated by Messrs. J. Robson and Sons, of Newcastle-on-Tyne, has been most appropriately treated. It is in mahogany, enamelled white, and the panels have a series of quaint paintings of the well-known legend of " Four and twenty black-birds baked in a pie," by a happily-inspired artist. His work is sure to be a continuous source of delight to the little ones. Dining-tables and seats of suitable height for the little passengers are provided. As in the public rooms generally, the windows are square. A lavatory and pantry,

besides rooms for four stewardesses and two matrons, open off the children's room.

PUBLIC ROOMS FOR THE SECOND-CLASS PASSENGERS.

A well-known authority on steamship decoration who happened to enter the public rooms for the second-class passengers before reaching the saloons for the first-class passengers was, later, surprised when told that he had not been in the principal rooms of the ship, so satisfactory did he consider these second-class rooms. This may be appreciated by a glance at the engravings which we publish on Plate XIII., illustrating the smoking and drawing-rooms for the second-class passengers. A suggestion of the variety of treatment here, as well as in the first-class, is afforded by the fact that no fewer than thirty varieties of timber have been used, and that throughout there has been a determination to seek for effect from the natural grains of the various woods. Consequently very careful selection had to be made to ensure the desired results. Mahogany of African growth, and oak from Austria, have been extensively used. Of the latter, something like 50,000 square feet have been cut up for parquetry flooring, while sycamore, satin-wood, high-figured teak, birch, beech, ash, and pear-wood have been used in the ship with very satisfactory results. All the rooms for the second-class passengers, as well as several for the first-class, have been carried out by Messrs. Swan, Hunter, and Wigham Richardson, Limited. The smoking-room, illustrated by Fig. 82, opens aft from the grand entrance on the promenade-deck, and is decorated in accordance with the ideas of the late Georgian period. The work is carried out in mahogany, inlaid with English boxwood and burr mahogany. The upholstering of the chairs and sofa seats is in dark blue velvet-pile morquette. Over the inlaid linoleum on the floor are dark blue Brussels carpet runners. Overhead is a dome, which is well shown in our engraving.

The drawing-room for the second-class passengers, which is illustrated by Fig. 83, Plate XIII., is on the same level, opening from the grand entrance forward. Here a fine effect is produced by the adoption of maple with gold decorations. The general style is of the Louis Seize period. The dome, of obscured glass, with gilded metal framework, enhances the general appearance of the large square windows, and assists still further the illusion that the room is in a country house rather than on board ship. These windows are of special construction, patented by the shipbuilders, and are fitted with an obscured glass screen in front, which can be lifted or closed at will. The upholstery is in crimson frieze velvet, the Brussels carpet and curtains being in tints to harmonise.

The second-class dining-saloon on the upper deck opens direct from the grand entrance, and, as we have already said, has a length of 61 ft., is the full width of the ship, and has a height of 10 ft. Here also the Georgian period is simulated in furniture and decoration, the design being carried out in oak and parquetry flooring to suit. In the centre of the room, and rising to a height of 19 ft., is a dome, from the centre of which there is suspended an electrolier. A feature of the room is the massive carved oak sideboard.

On the boat-deck level there is a lounge, and from this level there is the grand staircase leading to the various decks below. The floors of the entrance halls are laid with rubber tiling in a simple design of black and white ; the staircase is in teak.

STATE-ROOMS.

We reproduce on Plate XIV. two representative state-rooms, one for the first-class and the other for the second-class passengers. A comparison of these two rooms is most striking, and demonstrates the great comfort ensured for the second-class passengers. Several of the first-class suite-rooms have been decorated by Messrs. J. Robson and Sons, of Newcastle-on-Tyne, while the others, including that illustrated, have been carried out by Messrs. Swan, Hunter, and Wigham Richardson. The first-class state-rooms, as a rule, are carried out entirely in one wood, either mahogany, oak, walnut, or satin. The lower beds are, in many cases, in brass, and the upper bed folds up. The first-class room, it will be noted, has the lavatory in a recess, curtained off from the room itself, an arrangement which will commend itself to all passengers. In other rooms, where a recess has not been possible, there has been fitted the usual folding-down basin,

with fold-down table over it. The chests of drawers in most cases have also a table that may be drawn out. In the berths under the shelter-deck advantage has been taken of the space between the frames to construct a cupboard which will always be useful. There are abundant conveniences for stowing away the articles required on the voyage in these cupboards, in the wardrobes, in the lavatory recesses, &c., as well as in the chests of drawers. There are many other small commendable features. For instance, the ordinary hook for securing the door slightly ajar rattles with every movement of the ship, and is disturbing both by day and night to nervous passengers. Messrs. Swan, Hunter, and Wigham Richardson have adopted the Phipps patent cabin-hook (Fig. 87). The feature of this, the invention of their former joiner, is the spring which holds the hook perfectly rigid in the eye-bolt, in which there is also a rubber lining. On the inside of the wardrobe-doors there is a tension-lever to prevent the door closing when it is left open at any position. The lever works in a slotted guide, which is arranged to offer sufficient frictional resistance to prevent the door itself moving. There is in each state-room a metal fitting to allow a small table to be secured for the use of passengers, either for dining, writing, or reading. But it is impossible within reasonable limits to indicate the originality of many of the forty-two articles of hardware in the ordinary first or second-class cabin. In Fig. 86 we illustrate a butt-hinge, which is employed in many instances. Notice, too, may be taken of the angle of the handles on the drawers, which conform to the natural angle of the hand when moving the drawers.

THE ROOMS FOR THE THIRD-CLASS PASSENGERS.

The public rooms for the third-class passengers are on the upper and shelter-decks forward, and the sleeping accommodation on the lower and main decks. Two main staircases extend from the main to the upper deck, one giving direct access to the dining-saloon on the upper deck. This dining-saloon is 84 ft. long and the full width of the ship. The height of the apartment—10 ft.—makes it both light and airy. Revolving-chairs are provided, and 330 persons can be accommodated at one sitting ; but the other rooms may also be used for diners. The dining-room proper is panelled in polished ash with teak mouldings, and the floor is covered with corticine. The sidelights are screened by sliding sashes fitted with coloured obscure glass.

On the shelter deck two other apartments—the smoking-room and the ladies' room—are provided for the use of third-class passengers. The smoking-room on the port side is 50 ft. long, 24 ft. wide, and over 9 ft. high. The ladies' room, on the starboard side, is 50 ft. long, 20 ft. wide, and over 9 ft. high. Both are panelled in polished ash, with teak mouldings, are provided with revolving chairs, and are generally similar to the dining-saloon.

THE KITCHENS.

The galleys, pantries, bakery, confectionery-room, and knife-cleaning room for the first-class accommodation extend for a distance of 130 ft. the full width of the ship, and the fittings are for the most part by Messrs. Henry Wilson and Co., Limited, Liverpool. Situated on the upper deck between the first and second-class dining-saloons, a handy service is ensured to both. Electricity plays a large part in the culinary operations on board the vessel. The main cooking range, heated by coal fire, is 24 ft. long by 8 ft. wide. In addition, there are four large steam boilers, twelve steam ovens, three large electric grills, and various roasters driven by electric motors. The pantries are fitted with carving-tables, bain maries, electric egg-boilers, electric hot-plates, electric grids, and electric plate-washers. In the baker's shop there are numerous ovens and an electrically-driven dough-mixer. The confectionery-room is fitted with a long marble-topped table, an ice-cream machine, &c. Four electrically-driven knife-cleaning machines are provided in the room specially set apart for this operation. Lifts are arranged from the galley to the engineers' and officers' mess-rooms on the deck above and to the store-rooms below. The third-class galley, on the shelter-deck, is 48 ft. long by 28 ft. wide, and is fitted with large cooking-range, vegetable-cookers, steam boilers, &c. The galley is connected by means of a lift and a staircase with the third-class pantry below. In connection with the commissariat department there are extensive cold-storage chambers, and two complete installations of refrigerating machinery have been supplied by the Liverpool Refrigeration Company, Limited. The installations are of the carbonic anhydride type, that for the storage of ships' provisions being in connection with chambers having a total area of 13,000 cubic feet; but as these installations correspond exactly with those on the Lusitania, it is unnecessary here to give a further description.

HEATING AND VENTILATION.

The whole of the ventilation and heating of the Mauretania, as of the Lusitania, was carried out by the Thermo-Tank Ventilating Company, Glasgow, and is probably the best thought-out scheme yet applied to any steam-ship. Air is supplied either in a heated or cooled state, according to the outside temperature, to every room and every alleyway, while the foul air is exhausted. The system has been described previously in ENGINEERING,* but the drawings which we reproduce on this and the opposite page are of exceptional interest, as they indicate the arrangement of a typical installation—that at the casing of the funnel second from the bow.

It will be noted from the section of the second funnel-casing (Figs. 88 and 89) that there are three thermo-tanks arranged on the port and starboard sides respectively. All of these three thermo-tanks are inter-connected by means of a trunk fitted with a valve, so that, if found necessary, one thermo-tank may be arranged to assist the other by the mere opening or closing of the valves. From each of these thermo-tanks a vertical trunk is led down in the light and air spaces, with branches along the beams, and with connections to forward and aft in the main trunk, boxed in out of sight behind the woodwork. An examination of the drawing will show the louvre where air is admitted or extracted, as the case may be. As a certain amount of loss of temperature takes place in the transmission of heated air through the trunking, it was necessary to arrange for other thermo-tanks situated on the lower decks for supplying air to the third-class accommodation. It will be noted on examination of the trunks, indicated with a dotted hatch-line, that the fresh air is drawn in at the top of the first-class and third-class promenade-decks, this being done to prevent the admission of smells or dust, which are often associated with the funnel and galley hatch-deck.

The air, in most cases, is admitted in the centre of the ceiling of the first-class state-rooms, the louvre being worked by means of a controlling handle arranged in a convenient position on the panels of the state-rooms. When the warmed or cooled air is being supplied to the cabins, the air is extracted by means of the light and air-casing communicating with the funnel-deck, and as the whole of the bath-rooms and w.c.'s are connected to powerful exhaust-fans, there is no possibility of vapour or smells permeating the living quarters. It will be noticed that the louvres are placed at the level of the decks in the public rooms, and, as a general rule, this method has been adopted throughout. In the state-rooms, however, the louvres are arranged in the ceilings, as it is found from experience that the positions indicated give the best results.

In arranging the trunking near the funnel-casings, great care has been taken to prevent any heat being carried through the trunks from the funnel-uptakes, as, of course, in hot weather, when the air has to be delivered cold to the rooms, it would be impossible to do so if the trunks were carried too near the funnel-casings.

The first-class accommodation is ventilated and heated by 29 thermo-tanks, placed, as we have said, on the top of the boat-deck, half the trunks for these being led into the public and state-rooms. The second-class accommodation is served with nine thermo-tanks on the boat and shelter-decks, while the third-class, including officers' and crew's quarters, are served by 15 thermo-tanks, making a total of 53 in all.

As stated above, the fresh-air supply to the various thermo-tanks is obtained from gratings opening out on the promenade and shelter-decks, in order that soot from the funnels, or smells from the galleys which exhaust above the boat-deck, may not find their way into the passengers' quarters through the

* See ENGINEERING, vol. lxxxiv., page 143.

thermo-tanks. On the other hand, when exhausting, the thermo-tanks discharge the vitiated air from the public rooms and cabins above the boat-deck. The electrically-operated fan at the top of the thermo-tank apparatus, when supplying air to the rooms between decks, draws it from the atmosphere, passing it through tubes in which, if the temperature is cold, steam is supplied so as to heat the air, the pressure of the steam being about 30 lb., with a relief-valve to blow off at 100 lb. There are valves for controlling the passage of air and for regulating the steam-pressure, and consequently the temperature. At the same time, the air is humified by means of a special valve admitting steam in a fine spray through the small needle-holes in the copper hoop surrounding the heater. The thermo-tanks are capable of changing air, either

from above, as owing to the situation of the thermo-tank no trouble is likely to arise from the presence of coal-dust or smells. It will be noticed that in this thermo-tank a water-proof cowl-head is fitted, so that in the case of wet or stormy weather no rain or spray is carried down to the rooms below. On the left-hand side of the nearest thermo-tank there will be noticed the steam and exhaust-valves, the exhaust-valves being fitted with a steam-trap designed so as to pass only water, and thus prevent any wastage of steam, should the steam or exhaust-valve be carelessly set. On the steam-valve there will be noticed the relief-valve, already described, and on the front the three air-regulating valves. By the movement of these valves the thermo-tank may be either set to exhaust or to supply air, or the temperature

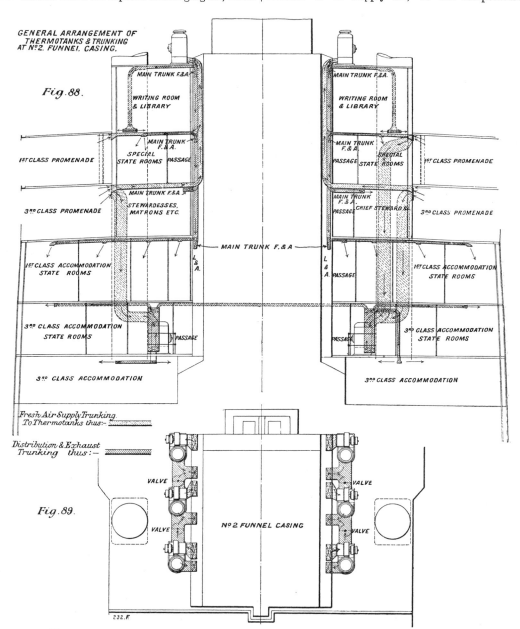

FIGS. 88 AND 89. GENERAL ARRANGEMENT OF THERMO-TANKS AND TRUNKING.

by exhaust or supply, in the various compartments to which they are connected from six to eight times per hour, and of maintaining a temperature of at least 65 deg. Fahr. with an exceptionally low temperature outside. The thermo-tanks are inter-connected, so that on the breakdown of any one the supply can always be obtained from another.

Fig. 90 illustrates one of the thermo-tanks situated in the third-class quarters. The electric motor for driving the fan will be seen on the left of the illustration, with the special controller for starting it and regulating its speed.

Fig. 91 illustrates the bottom-suction type thermo-tank placed on the top of the boat-deck house. In this particular thermo-tank the valves are set so that the air is exhausted from below, as will be noted from the mushroom over the heater being open.

Fig. 92 illustrates the top-suction deck type thermo-tank—that is to say, the air is being drawn

may be varied to suit the requirements of the rooms below.

THE ELECTRIC LIGHTING.

For supplying electricity for lighting the ship, and for running the large number of motors used for various purposes—for hoists, ventilating fans, and other appliances in the machinery-room, to be referred to later—there is an electric generating station abaft the main engine-room. There are four turbo-generators, each of 375 kilowatts capacity at 110 and 120 volts, fitted by Messrs. C. A. Parsons and Co., Limited, Heaton-on-Tyne. The turbines were designed to give full load when exhausting into a back pressure of 10 lb. They run the dynamos at 1200 revolutions, and are capable of an overload of 10 per cent. for two hours. These turbo-generators gave very satisfactory results on trial. At half-load the water consumption was 60.60 lb. per kilowatt hour, at three-quarters load 52 lb., at full load 46 lb., the back-pressure in each case being about 5 lb. The other most interesting feature of the electric installation is, perhaps, the switchboard.

starboard sides of the ship respectively, illustrated in Fig. 93, on the next page. These are separated by a bulkhead, so that any accident to the electric supply is isolated, though disconnecting switches allow them to be worked together

other generator panel. The diagram of connections given for the port board, Fig. 94, shows the arrangement and equipment adopted. The generators, which are all similar, 375 kilowatts, 115 volts, shunt-wound turbine-driven machines,

FIG. 90. THERMO-TANK IN THIRD-CLASS QUARTERS.

FIG. 91. BOTTOM-SUCTION TYPE THERMO-TANK.

FIG. 92. TOP-SUCTION DECK-TYPE THERMO-TANK.

supply the bus-bars through automatic overload and reverse-current time-limit circuit-breakers, one on each pole. The relays operating these breakers are of the Ferranti moving-coil type, and are set to bring out the machine after an overload of 85 kilowatts has lasted for 15 seconds, 145 kilowatts for 10 seconds, or 200 kilowatts for 5 seconds, a dead short-circuit being broken, of course, practically instantaneously. If, for any cause, the machine should be taking current instead of supplying it, it would be isolated by the action of the same relay after a number of seconds, varying inversely with the strength of the reverse current. As the full-load current of each of the machines is over 3250 amperes, it will be understood that such large circuit-breakers require a good deal of effort to close, and the handle is, therefore, placed in the best position in view of this, and connected to the circuit-breaker proper by means of link-gear at the back of the board. The design of the heavy type of circuit-breakers avoids practically all the faults usually found in this class of apparatus. In the first place the carbon blocks are a very long distance away from the main current-carrying contact; and, further, the construction is such as to reduce as much as possible the weight, which acts at a large radius. The subsidiary contacts are also so arranged as to form an ample protection to the main contacts of the circuit-breaker. All the current-carrying parts of the board are exceptionally massive. Each bus-bar, for example, is of 4 square inches section, and the cables and leads are correspondingly heavy. The feeders are designed to carry 600 amperes each, and are controlled through automatic switches with overload relays. The feeder circuit-breakers have double trip-coils, a shunt and a series. The object of this is as follows:—

The feeder circuits at other parts of the vessel are protected by means of fuses. The fuse, as is well known, has a certain time-lag. The circuit-breaker, therefore, on the switchboard ought also to have a time-lag. On the other hand, in the event of a bad short it is advisable that the circuit-breaker comes out as instantaneously as possible. The series trip-coil is therefore set high, so that it does not come into operation at all unless there is an overload of the nature of a short-circuit on the

The switch-gear for a vessel of the size of the Mauretania constitutes an equipment which would serve for many a power-station on land. The switchboard, which has been constructed by Messrs. Ferranti, Limited, of Hollinwood, Manchester, consists of two similar boards for the port and

under normal circumstances. Exclusive of the disconnecting panel, each board contains two generator panels and twelve feeder panels. The disconnecting panel on each board is naturally that nearest the bulkhead; next to it is a generator panel, then the twelve feeders, and, finally, the

SWITCHBOARD IN ELECTRIC GENERATING-STATION.

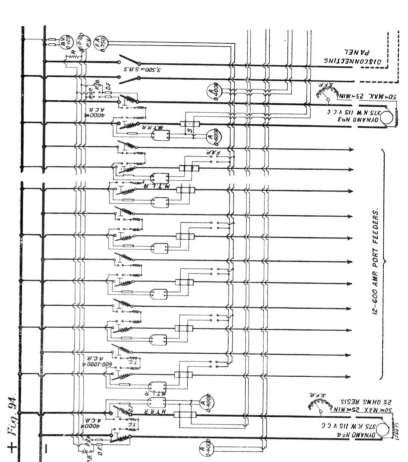

FIG. 93.

Fig. 94.

led to each hold, and a small fan draws air through these pipes every quarter of an hour. Should any fire occur, the smoke issues from the pipe, and a connection is fitted so that a steam-pipe can be coupled to any of the pipes and steam blown into any compartment where fire may occur. Pearson's automatic fire-alarms are fitted in the mail and baggage-rooms.

TELEPHONE SERVICE.

The Mauretania, like her sister ship, is equipped with an extensive telephone system, furnished by the National Telephone Company. It can be connected with the Liverpool or New York Exchanges when the vessel is in port, so that the passengers have, until departure or upon arrival, all the facilities of communication possessed by residents on shore. The express Cunarders are, we believe, the only ocean-going vessels on which an equipment of this nature has, as yet, been provided. On the Mauretania there are at present 89 stations and 10 exchange lines, connected to a switchboard having a capacity for 200 stations and 20 exchange lines. The instruments are fitted in the regal and first-class state-rooms, as shown in the illustrations on Plate XIV., the cabins of the ship's doctor, purser and chief steward, and in the bureau. The receivers are clipped in the switch-hooks, and the latter are pivoted horizontally, so that the motion of the ship does not cause the instrument to swing about, nor does it shorten the effective length of the lever, and thus allow the switch contacts to open. The appearance of the instruments is very neat, and made to harmonise with the decorations, and the wiring is concealed in the panelling of the cabins.

Index to Reference Letters on Diagram of Switchboard.

A.	Ammeter.
F.A.	Feeder ammeter.
F.A.P.	" " plugs.
B.V.	Bus-bar voltmeter.
P.V.P.	Paralleling voltmeter plugs.
P.V.	Paralleling voltmeter.
M.T.R.R.	Maximum time-limit and reverse-current relay.
M.T.L.R	" " relay.
S.	Shunt.
S.F.R.	Shunt field regulator.
A.C.B.	Automatic circuit-breaker.
D.F.	Damper fuse.
T.C.	Trip-coils.
R.	Resistance in series with voltmeter.
P.B.	Push-button for short-circuiting voltmeter resistance.

feeder. The shunt trip-coil, however, is operated through a time-limit relay, and takes care of all ordinary overloads, providing a suitable time-limit to give the fuses at other parts of the vessel a chance of operating first.

Four feeders on each board supply the motors for the draught fans: one the engine-room motors, one the engine-room and machinery lighting, and the rest serve the other various lighting and power requirements of the vessel.

FIRE SERVICE.

There is a fire-main on each side of the ship, from which connections are taken to every separate compartment. There are boxes with hydrant and valve in each compartment. In addition there is a system of break-glass fire-alarms, with a drop indicator-box in the chart-room and a drop indicator-box in the engine-room, to notify any outbreak of fire. A Rich's patent fire-indicator is also fitted, situated at the side of the chart-house on the sun deck. From the indicator-box pipes are

The switchboard and exchange apparatus, illustrated in Fig. 95, is contained in a room amidships set apart for the purpose. The central battery system is employed, and the power panel is placed at the top of the switchboard, as shown in the illustration. The distributing frame is of the vertical type, fitted with 120 pairs of fuses in the upper part, and the same number of pairs of arresters and heat-coils below. The space between the fuses and arresters is used as a cross-connecting field. The current is supplied from either of two batteries, each consisting of 13 cells, which are housed close to the switch-room. They are controlled from the board and charged through a lamp resistance direct from the ship's supply, which is at 110 volts.

ship with the nearest land-box. The flexible cable is run underneath the flooring of the landing-stage.

SANITATION.

In carrying out the sanitary work on a ship of the dimensions of the Mauretania many considerations have to be borne in mind. This can be easily understood when one remembers that the passengers and crew equal the population of a small town. The general arrangement of the water-supply system, as well as the question of ventilating soil and waste-pipes, have to be considered from many standpoints, and after that, the best and most serviceable type of fittings with proper connections.

entirely non-concussive, and there is not the slightest jar in any pipe after use. To operate the valve, the handle is pressed which opens the relief-valve B, and allows the water under pressure above the plunger C to escape through the port D. The space above the plunger, it will be noted, is in direct communication with the supply through the opening E, which is fitted with a screw to regulate the supply to the area above the plunger. The pressure being released in the area above the plunger, the latter is lifted by the pressure on its underside, opening the valve and flushing the closet. The valve is closed by the pressure of the water acting on the top of the plunger C, the area on the top being larger than underneath. The rate at which the valve closes is regulated by the screw E, thus allowing any desired amount of water to pass through the closet, and at the same time preventing concussion or water-hammer in the pipes.

In all cases the connections to waste or supply-pipes are made just under the deck, as shown in Fig. 98. The supplies to the closets and lavatories are carried through the deck, and secured by a fly-nut and connected to the main pipe by means of a nut and screwed liner ; a fitting can thus be disconnected without any trouble—an important point when a ship is at sea. Figs. 99 to 101 show a storm-valve, also used with the closet. The patent storm-valve consists of a hinged plate balanced by a weight. When the contents of the closet are discharged, the plate is deflected to a vertical position, thus leaving a perfectly clear outlet. When discharge ceases, the weight raises the plate and closes the valve, and in case there is a back pressure the plate is closed more tightly. This patent obviates the necessity of bending the soil-pipe into a horizontal position, which has to be done when the ordinary storm-valve is used. The new valve can also be placed on soil-pipes at the end of ranges of trough-closets.

A few details of the various fittings may be of interest. The closets in the first and second class are of the wash-down type, but the outlet is flanged, and is 6 in. or 8 in. above the deck. Attached to this outlet is a white-metal box, which encloses the valve—Doulton's patent storm-valve. This, as already explained, allows a perfectly clear discharge of the contents of the pan, while the valve prevents any backflow. It is also accessible for repair without removing the closet. The closet therefore has the cleanliness of the wash-down with a deep seal to the pan, in addition to the advantages of a single-valve pattern. A trouble with many ships' closets is the heaviness of the pull in opening the valve. In this case the valve is placed on a pedestal at the side of the closet attached to the bulkhead, and by pressing a small knob the valve is opened. The action is very easy. As described above, the regulating-screw can be adjusted to give any aftercharge required, so there is thus no need to keep the hand on the valve. The pedestal acts as the supply.

For the third-class passengers a door-action arrangement is used. The valve is made on the same principle as the first and second-class, but is actuated by the opening of the door. The closet is flushed when the door is opened on entrance, and again when the user leaves.

The lavatories are, of course, of various patterns and marbles, onyx and other choice qualities being used in the state and regal rooms. The wastes are concealed, and combine waste and overflow. The action is simple, and the standing-pipe is easily removed. The valves have lever action, and are self-closing and non-concussive. Some lavatories for the crew are made in white vitreous porcelain, enamelled iron, and some in slate. All valves and wastes are made so that the basins fill and discharge quickly.

The baths are cast iron, enamelled inside and out with white vitreous porcelain. This enamel has a smooth, glossy, lasting surface, and equals earthenware for durability, while it is very much lighter in weight and better in appearance. Each first-class bath has a white-metal skeleton spray with shower. Each fitting is governed by a Doulton patent mixing valve (Fig. 102), by means of which the water can be regulated to any temperature by a slight movement of the lever. Cold must be turned on first. This prevents risk of scalding. The supply to the bath enters at the bottom, thus avoiding steam, and is noiseless. The arrangement of this is pretty clearly shown in the sketch. On a handle being turned towards "cold" on a dial, the valve A A is raised, allowing cold water to pass, the hot water being checked by the ring B, which is turned to fit in the

FIG. 95. TELEPHONE SWITCHBOARD.

Calling is done by merely lifting the receiver, which causes a very small opal lamp to light on the switchboard. The two groups of lamps can be seen in Fig. 95, opposite the head-gear of the operator, which is hung at the side of the board. There are no relays for the lamps, as it was found quite practicable for the 24-volt calling-lamps to be worked by the current from the 26-volt battery passing through the instrument when the receiver was lifted. The exchange junction-lines terminate at the board in self-restoring drops. The lines are carried from the board in lead-covered wires to each side of the ship, where they terminate in special boxes, the terminals being platinum-tipped bronze springs. A number of similar boxes are fitted in the landing-stage, containing the terminals of the junction lines from the town exchange. These boxes are distributed so that one of them is accessible wherever the ship is berthed. A length of flexible cable, with terminals at each end in a box containing 10 platinum-tipped studs, connects the

For instance, the trouble arising from concussion in the pipes is serious. Awkward bends are in some cases unavoidable, and loud jars, when valves are closed, are not only objectionable to the passengers, but involve considerable damage to pipes, &c.

In designing the various appliances required on the Mauretania, two important aims were the securing of complete absence of concussion, and a perfect connection between the water and soil-pipes and the fittings. Messrs. Doulton and Co., Limited, Lambeth, who carried out the complete sanitary arrangements, have made a valve that meets these requirements, and the same principle is found in both the flushing-valves for closets and the valves for baths and lavatories. In each case the valve is closed by the pressure, but instead of sharply cutting off the supply when released, it shuts off slowly—the time being adjusted by a regulating-screw. Sections of this valve are given in Figs. 96 and 97 on the next page. Each valve is centre chamber C. On turning the handle further towards "tepid," this ring is raised clear of the chamber, thus allowing the hot water to mix with the cold already flowing. When the handle is turned full to "tepid," the ring D in the outer chamber E comes into proximity with the bottom of the brass seating F, checking to a great extent the flow of cold water, the hot water still flowing freely. The valves are specially arranged so that it is impossible to get more than a certain temperature, in order to prevent scalding. A thermometer is fixed to each valve, so that the bather can at once see the temperature. The shower is in pottery, and the perforated plate can be removed for cleansing. The waste is large, so as to allow the bath to empty quickly. The connections to supply and waste are as before described. The baths for the other class of passengers, and for crew, are of the same material,

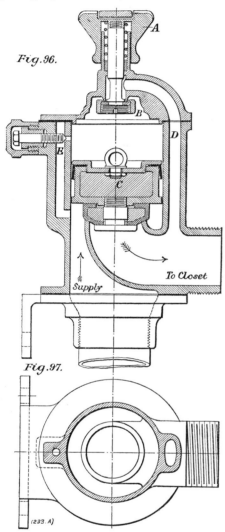

Fig. 96.
Fig. 97.
(233.A)

the only difference being in the size and fittings, some being without showers.

The urinals are of the latest circular-backed pattern, the backs being semi-circular, and made in the finest white glazed fire-clay, so shaped, with a returned rim, that neither urine nor water can come in contact with any joints. The bases discharge into a channel which is covered by a white-metal hinged grating. This grating is removable. The divisions are in marble, varying according to the class. Each range is flushed by an automatic tank connected to spreaders, which cleanse the backs. A separate pipe is carried from the tank to a sparge pipe above the channel, so that every part that may be soiled is cleansed automatically. The urinal is perfectly water-tight, easy to fit, and has very few joints. The urinals for the crew are in vitreous porcelain enamelled iron, and consist of a trough and divisions, but made so as to be fixed clear of the bulkheads.

All the first-class fittings are heavily silver-plated. A number of automatic flush-tanks have been supplied for cleansing lengths of soil-pipe; this is a general practice on shore, but is a new departure in marine work. These tanks are arranged so as to fill at given intervals, and when full the whole contents of the tanks are discharged.

The whole of the sanitary fittings have been manufactured by Messrs. Doulton and Co., Limited, of Lambeth, London, and they have also carried

out the entire fixing. When putting the work in hand they were instructed that the installation was to be as perfect as possible, and to be in advance of anything previously made for ships' use, either at home or abroad. These instructions have been acted upon, and while fully studying the comfort and convenience of the passengers, there is an elaborateness far beyond what has been before supplied to any ships. White metal is used for all piping and castings, and this is heavily silver-plated. In fact, there are few of the most modern hotels that could claim equality with the Mauretania in this respect.

NAVIGATING APPLIANCES.

Everything has been done to make the navigating appliances perfect, and to give the captain on the

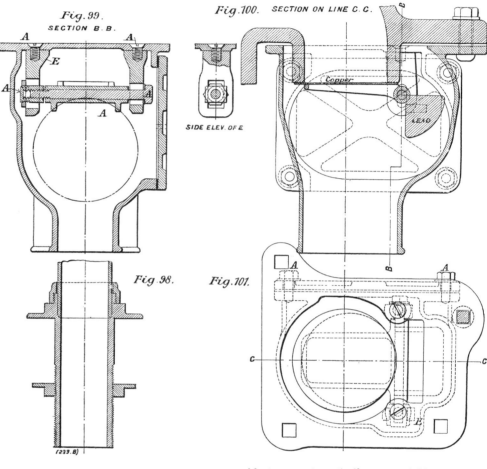

Fig. 99.
SECTION B.B.

Fig. 100. SECTION ON LINE C.C.
Copper
SIDE ELEV. OF E

Fig. 98.
(233.B)

Fig. 101.

Fig. 102.
Dial
To Plunge Bath
Cold Supply
Hot Supply
(222.Z)

bridge complete control over the ship. On the exceptionally large bridge he has telephonic or other communication with every part of the vessel, and tell-tales to indicate that his orders have been carried out, whether in the engine-room, in the steering-room, or at the capstan and anchor stations. The steam steering-gear has been fitted by Messrs.

Brown Brothers and Co., Edinburgh, in a special compartment under the water-line at the rudder-head. It is controlled by the well-known Brown telemotors. An interesting and novel equipment is the electric whistle operator and telegraph, which makes use of electric energy to do the work which formerly devolved on the officer of the watch.

ELECTRIC WHISTLE OPERATOR AND TELEGRAPH.

The "Stellite" electric whistle operator and telegraph, which has also been fitted to the Royal Yachts, is to render more certain signalling and the giving of warnings by whistle from the bridge, and also to relieve the staff on the bridge of the tedious duty of sounding the whistle at short and regular intervals for long periods of time. The instrument combines the function of giving single blasts or automatically-repeated blasts of definite length and at definite intervals, with a telegraph whereby Morse or other code signals may be sounded on the ship's whistle. The action of the whistle is controlled from the bridge, and that of the telegraph from the chart-room or pilot-house.

The apparatus consists of four essential parts, connected together by conductors and on an electric circuit. The whistle is fitted with an operator consisting of a valve worked by an electro-magnet. The working of this magnet is controlled by a combined switch on the bridge, which has three positions—"Off," "On," and "Automatic." A special clock is provided for keeping the contact closed for six seconds in every minute, and, lastly, there is a telegraph key for Morse or other code telegraph work. The operator fitted to the whistle steam-pipe contains a main valve, worked by an auxiliary valve, which in turn is controlled by the electro-magnet. The magnet is placed in a water-tight metal case. A double wire connects from this part of the apparatus to terminals in the clock-case. The combination switch is weather-proof, and from six terminals in it wires are connected to terminals in the clock-case, two of the latter being on a circuit supplied with current from one of the dynamos. The clock and the telegraph key are also connected with these terminals in such a way as to provide the necessary contacts and breaks for working the whistle automatically or as a telegraph. If the switch-handle on the bridge be moved through 90 degrees from the "off" to the "on" position, a distinct blast, of long or short duration, is given, and can be repeated at will. The electrical control is quick and certain in action, and superior to the ordinary hand-lever, especially where, as in this case, the bridge is some distance from the whistle. A hand-lever is, however, provided as a stand-by, but in no way interferes with the action of the electric operator, nor does this apparatus interfere with the hand-lever working.

If the switch be turned through another 90 degrees, the apparatus is set to work automatically, and the clock in the circuit controls the lengths of the blasts and intervals. Once set with the switch over in this position, no further attention need

worm gear to the main windlass engines. These engines are of unusually massive build. The cylinders are 20 in. in diameter, and the stroke is 14 in. Steel, cast or forged, has been largely used in their construction, with the exception of cylinders or side-casings, which are of special close-grained cast-iron.

CABLES AND MOORING-CHAINS.

The mooring-cables, chain-cables, and mooring-bit for the Mauretania were manufactured by Messrs. Brown, Lenox, and Co., Pontypridd,

of any kind, although the load was nearly 90 per cent. above the Admiralty stress.

The mooring-cable is illustrated in Fig. 104, and the mooring-block in Fig. 105. The moorings weigh over 200 tons, and the patent link mooring-anchors 12 tons apiece. The four bridle chains are 720 ft. long, and the main chains are made of square links, each about 4 ft. long, and weigh 4 cwt. apiece. The swivel connection shown in Fig. 104 weighs 4485 lb., and each shackle 711 lb. The links of the buoy pendant are of $4\frac{1}{4}$-in. iron, and weigh 243 lb. apiece,

FIG. 103. CHAIN-CABLE.

FIG. 104. MOORING-CABLE.

FIG. 105. MOORING-BLOCK.

be given to the sounding of the whistle on the part of the staff on duty. When the combination switch is in the "off" position, the telegraph key may be manipulated in the ordinary way, to convey by the sound of the whistle, or even by the cloud of steam issuing therefrom, signals to stations or other vessels. The clock needs winding every four days. This apparatus was supplied by the Electric and Ordnance Accessories Company, Limited, of Birmingham.

CABLE AND ANCHOR GEAR.

As in the case of nearly all large merchant ships, the windlass and capstan-gear are of the well-tried Napier type, manufactured by Messrs. Napier Brothers, Limited, of Glasgow. For the cable-holders, the vertical spindles are 16 in. in diameter, in deck bearings, and with Napier's patent differential brakes, which are exceptionally powerful, being able to hold a load, when riding at anchor in heavy weather, of about 252 tons. The spindles are carried to the shelter-deck, and are connected by

South Wales. A portion of the chain-cable is illustrated by Fig. 103, and the links are $3\frac{3}{4}$ in. in diameter at the smallest part, and $22\frac{1}{4}$ in. in length. The whole cable weighs, with shackles, about 130 tons, the total length being 1900 ft. Each joining shackle weighs $4\frac{1}{2}$ cwt., and the end or anchor shackles $7\frac{1}{2}$ cwt. each. At the end of the cable a huge swivel-piece is inserted, and each weighs $13\frac{1}{2}$ cwt. The end links on the swivel-pieces are made of $4\frac{3}{4}$-in. iron, and the swivel alone weighs $6\frac{1}{4}$ cwt.

The Cunard Company had tests made of three links at Lloyd's proving-house, Netherton, Staffs, and, under the Admiralty strain of 198.8 tons, each link elongated nearly $\frac{1}{4}$ in. The statutory breaking stress of 255.7 tons was then applied, the result being a further elongation of the links by about $\frac{3}{4}$ in. An attempt was made to test the three links to destruction, but the full power of the testing-machine, of 350 tons—one of the most powerful in the country—failed to break the links. There was no sign of fracture or defect

while the end links weigh each 336 lb., being of $5\frac{3}{8}$-in. metal.

CRANES AND HOISTS.

Mention may be made, too, of the cargo-cranes supplied by Messrs. John H. Wilson and Co., Limited, of Sandhills, Liverpool; of four electrically-operated boat-hoisting winches, by Messrs. Laurence, Scott, and Co., Limited, of Norwich; of four deck-cranes, as well as four baggage and mail-hoists, by Messrs. Stothert and Pitt, Limited, of Bath. These appliances, however, correspond exactly with those in the Lusitania, so that there is no need here to repeat the details.

It will thus be recognised that from first to last the ship, so far as Messrs. Swan, Hunter, and Wigham Richardson's work is concerned, is the most complete embodiment of the highest attainments of naval construction, whether regard be had to strength of structure, beauty of decoration, convenience in equipment, or reliability in navigation.

THE CONSTRUCTION OF THE MACHINERY.

THE WORKS OF THE TURBINE MACHINERY CONSTRUCTORS.

Before entering upon a description of the machinery of the Mauretania, it may be interesting to give a short review of the progress of the constructors of the machinery—the Wallsend Slipway and Engineering Company, Limited. This company originated in 1871, under the chairmanship and active management of Mr. Charles Mitchell, of the firm of Sir W. G. Armstrong, Mitchell, and Co., a shipbuilder and engineer, who did much for the development of Tyneside. He had the co-operation of several shipowners, the original idea being to

organise a ship-repairing establishment; and for this purpose slipways were constructed, with repair-shops, which have since been replaced by immense engineering works. Here, as in many other Tyneside concerns, the broad, intelligent policy of Mr. Mitchell is still reflected. The first ship repaired was in 1873, and in the spring of 1874 Mr. William Boyd became managing director, in succession to Mr. C. S. Swan, who began ship-building in the Wallsend yard. The growth of the repairing business induced developments from time to time, the first of these being the erection of a boiler and engine-shop for repair work, and in 1881 extensive new shops were erected.

The manufacture of marine-engines for ships built by other firms in the district was commenced in 1874, and under Mr. Boyd's *régime* the firm gained high repute for economical merchant machinery. Mr. Mitchell continued as chairman of the company until his death in August, 1895, and he was succeeded by Colonel H. F. Swan, C.B., who had been identified with him in the early years of the undertaking. Colonel Swan resigned the chairmanship in June of 1903, when the present chairman, Mr. Thomas Bell, who has been for nearly 14 years a director of the company, was appointed. Mr. Bell has continued the active policy which was initiated in 1897, when a new era began, the directors then

E

being fortunate in enlisting the services of Mr. Andrew Laing, who had been trained on the Clyde, and had been a director and manager of the engineering department of the Fairfield Works. He was associated with Mr. Bryce-Douglas in the design and construction of machinery for a long succession of high-speed merchant ships and warships, and convincing testimony to his ability, as well as to the credit of the Fairfield Works, is afforded by such instances of satisfactory design and manufacture as the Umbria, Etruria, Campania, and Lucania, the predecessors in the Cunard mail service. As to speed, there is no need here to write; their best performances have been set out in Table V. on page 3. In regard to durability, it need only be said that the Etruria has steamed 1,618,000 nautical miles, and the Umbria 1,580,000 nautical miles, or an average of over 70,000 nautical miles per annum, and both have the same engines and boilers as when new. Both are still popular, and do comparatively efficient work even after their twenty-three years' service. The

instructive to notice the advance in the maximum horse-power of any one set of engines, and in the appended table this information is clearly stated.

These facts, combined with the success of the six earlier Cunard liners engined by the Wallsend Works, and the experience of the Cunard Company of Mr. Laing's work, make it easy to understand why the Cunard Company entrusted the firm with the construction of the machinery for the Mauretania. Moreover, Mr. Laing has organised a staff of experienced assistants, including Messrs. Robert Traill, Robert Wallis, Gilbert Campbell, Joseph W. Tocher, Thomas Taylor, Thomas McPherson, John M. Nicholl, John Carr, and William Mathews, with Mr. Matthew Murray as secretary of the company.

The Wallsend Company have, it should be recorded, carried out a large amount of research on the subject of burning liquid fuel in boilers of merchant steamers. Their experience commenced as far back as 1883, but at that time the system was simple and crude. For many years they carried

on a series of experiments with all classes of burners, and finally patented a burner known as the Rusden and Eeles, in which steam is used as the medium for spraying the oil. About 100 vessels have been fitted by the company on this principle. The great objection, however, to the use of steam in spraying the oil is that large evaporating plant has to be fitted to make up for the steam thus lost. To overcome this difficulty, the company a few years ago made exhaustive experiments with the Körting system, wherein the oil is sprayed into the furnace under pressure, by means of pumps, without either steam, compressed air, or other agent. It was found that this plan worked with such success that the company have now finally adopted the system in their general work. Only a few weeks ago a large steamer was completed on this plan, the results obtained on the trial trip being highly satisfactory. Other vessels are now being fitted. This system can be worked in conjunction with either forced or induced draught with economical results.

Fig. 113. The Pattern-Shop at the Wallsend Engineering Works.

Campania and Lucania, which came out in 1893, have steamed—the former 1,042,000 nautical miles, and the latter 1,030,000 nautical miles, or over 80,000 nautical miles per annum. Up till recently they were the fastest British ships on the Atlantic.

In view of his training and experience it was only natural that Mr. Laing should pursue a policy of development, not only in the organisation and equipment of the Wallsend Works, but also in the size and importance of the work carried out. The works during his *régime* have been largely reconstructed, and the area under roof has in ten years been increased by 86 per cent.—from 133,000 square feet to 250,000 square feet. The highest class of work has been undertaken, of which the Mauretania is so far the culminating point. Mr. Laing has also brought the works to a prominent place in regard to warship machinery, and the firm have now in hand, amongst other work, the turbine machinery for one of the new battleships of the Dreadnought type—H.M.S. Superb. As to the producing capacity, we have from our annual returns prepared a statement showing the output in the ten years prior to Mr. Laing's appointment, and in the ten years subsequent to his taking over the management. From this table it will be seen that the total for the past ten years is much more than double that of the preceding ten years, and that the average is over 59,000 indicated horse-power, as compared with 26,000 indicated horse-power. It is also

TABLE XII.—*Illustrating Progress of Wallsend Slipway and Engineering Works.*

Year.	Total Indicated Horse-Power for the Year.	Average Indicated Horse-Power of Each Set of Engines.	Maximum Indicated Horse-Power of any One Set of Engines.	Remarks.
1887	17,750	1200	2,925	
1888	23,250	1100	2,150	
1889	39,750	1420	2,260	
1890	40,170	1550	3,360	
1891	34,220	1500	3,300	
1892	25,700	1850	4,500	
1893	16,640	1850	3,000	
1894	21,250	1125	2,500	
1895	29,260	1725	3,000	
1896	13,460	1350	2,800	
	261,450			
1897	22,675	1625	5,000	
1898	68,100	4000	11,500	Inc. Russian ice-breaker Ermack.
1899	67,600	3400	12,000	Including R.M.S. Ivernia.
1900	51,750	2200	5,000	„ H.M.S. Espiegle.
1901	46,650	2350	4,500	„ H.M.S. Odin.
1902	69,150	3850	12,500	„ H.M.S. Challenger and R.M.S. Carpathia.
1903	42,360	2500	6,600	Including R.M.S. Slavonic.
1904	41,400	2600	6,000	
1905	66,800	3200	23,5·0	Including H.M.S. Warrior.
1906	115,500	8250	70,000	„ R.M.S. Mauretania.
	591,985			

It was also found, after considerable experience, that one of the great drawbacks in connection with the burning of liquid fuel was the difficulty in obtaining the oil free from water. In order to remove the water numerous experiments were carried out, so as to arrive at a system which would separate the water from the oil without in any way interfering with the supply to the burners. Finally, the Flannery-Boyd patent system of settling-tanks was invented, and such tanks are fitted so that while the oil is being supplied to the burners from one set of tanks, others are used to separate the water from the oil.

The Wallsend Slipway and Engineering Works cover an area of about 25 acres, being on the north bank of the Tyne, with a river frontage of about 1200 ft. The general view of the works, which we give on Plate XXXV., affords indication of their extent and importance. On the land side there is the North-Eastern Railway, from which there are extensive sidings into the works, so that direct communication is established with all parts of the country. On the east side—that to the right of our engraving—there runs the Willington Gut, which has been dredged and widened, and alongside is a jetty of 1000 ft. in length, which affords splendid berthage for large ships.

Almost every department has been reconstructed, including the offices, as the higher class of work done required a much larger designing and drawing staff than formerly.

The offices are divided into two parts, the one a two-story building, with basement, 110 ft. long by 60 ft. wide, accommodating the commercial department, estimating department, tracing-office, board-room, and private rooms. The other part is a one-story building, with basement. On the ground-floor is the drawing-office, in four bays, each 60 ft. long and 22 ft. wide, running from east to west, with weaving-shed roof, so that all light is from the north. The splendid light got by this construction immediately attracts attention when one enters the building, and this and the general arrangement are well shown in the view on Plate XV., Fig. 111. At the south-west corner a part is screened

Plate XV. On this same Plate an illustration of the tracer's-room is published (Fig. 112).

As to the various shops where the Mauretania machinery has been constructed, we published a few years ago a description of the equipment of the establishment.* Our narrative of the building of the boilers, turbines, &c., will involve reference to many of the important machine-tools. It is, however, interesting to note the leading particulars of the various shops. We may refer first to the pattern-shop, illustrated on the opposite page, Fig. 113. It is a separate single-story building, 180 ft. long by 70 ft. wide, in two bays, built of steel framing. The roof is entirely of glass, while the sides and ends are covered with corrugated sheet-iron. At the end of one bay is the

5 cwt.), their length being 27 ft. 10 in., their width 10 ft. 9½ in., and the thickness 1$\frac{21}{64}$ in. ; that the total weight of the larger boilers, without mountings or water, is about 100 tons each, and that the average output of the works is three normal-sized boilers per fortnight. Views of the boiler machine-shops are given on Plate XVI. In the boiler-shop no new machinery was required to undertake the work on the Mauretania. Amongst the principal machines in this department may be mentioned the plate-edge planing-machine by Messrs. Hugh Smith and Co., of Glasgow, with a stroke of 35 ft. 6 in. ; vertical plate-bending rolls, by Messrs. T. Shanks and Co., of Johnstone, capable of dealing with plates up to 12 ft. 6 in. wide and an hydraulic riveting-machine, with a 12-ft. gap, by Messrs. Hugh Smith and Co., Glasgow.

The erecting-shop and machine-shop consist of two bays. The machine-shop bay is 430 ft. long by 75 ft. wide, and the erecting-shop bay, which is quite new, is 640 ft. long by 60 ft. wide, the top of the crane-rails being 43 ft. above the floor-level, and the height above the rails to the underside of the roof being 8 ft. In the machine-shop bay are three overhead travelling-cranes, besides numerous light hydraulic cranes on girder columns for serving the machines. In the erecting-shop bay there is one 30-ton and two 65-ton electric travelling-cranes, also three 7-ton and one 3-ton hydraulic cranes fixed to columns supporting the travelling-crane rail-girders. The turbine-shop is illustrated by Fig. 108 on Plate XXXV.

Reference need only be made to the heavy machines used in the construction of the turbines of the Mauretania. The lathe in which the rotors were turned was made by Sir W. G. Armstrong, Whitworth, and Co., Limited, Manchester, and is capable of taking in work up to 18 ft. diameter by 50 ft. long. The turbine-casings were bored and grooved in a circular planing-machine by the same makers, the table of this machine being 20 ft. in diameter, and the available height for work 13 ft. The horizontal joints of the casings were machined in a vertical and horizontal planer, by Messrs. T. Shanks and Co., Johnstone, which is capable of covering a face 25 ft. by 23 ft. These machine-tools are illustrated in connection with the work on turbine and rotor-casings on Plates XX. and XXI.

The iron-foundry is 210 ft. by 120 ft., and comprises a centre bay, with a lean-to annexe. The centre bay is 52 ft. wide, and in this are the overhead travelling cranes, capable of dealing with the heaviest weights. Castings up to 30 tons are made here, while the annexes are utilised for the smaller castings, and are well supplied with hydraulic and hand-power cranes fixed to the main columns of the building. There are two cupolas, the blast for which is supplied by a Roots blower driven by a variable-speed three-phase motor. There are also a number of core-drying stoves ranged along one side of the building, and opening into the foundry.

The brass-foundry and coppersmith's shop is 120 ft. by 70 ft. wide. In the brass-foundry are two overhead travelling-cranes, and at one end there is a pit capable of taking in long shaft-liners. The brass-furnaces and core-drying stoves are ranged along one side. In the coppersmith's shop there are the usual machines necessary for this kind of work, prominent amongst these being two hydraulic bending presses for copper pipes. The blacksmith's shop is 160 ft. by 75 ft., and alongside it is the plumber's shop, 160 ft. by 40 ft., and both of these are well equipped with tools and machinery necessary for carrying on those branches of the business.

For repair work, which is of an extensive nature, there is a graving dock 540 ft. long and 66 ft. wide at the entrance, the depth of water over the sill at ordinary spring tides being 25 ft. The pumping machinery of the dock consists of two 36-in. centrifugal pumps. There are also two slipways, each 1000 ft. in length, and capable of dealing with vessels up to 270 ft. long and 2400 tons register. Between the slipways and the graving dock is the shipyard shed, 220 ft. by 40 ft., equipped with modern machine-tools and other appliances, besides bending-slabs, furnaces, &c.

The whole of the machinery in the works is driven by three-phase electric-motors, the smaller machines in the shops being driven in groups, and the larger machines independently. A large air-compressing plant forms part of the equipment of the works, with mains through all the shops and leading to every part of the yard.

SECTION LOOKING FORWARD ON FRAME 167

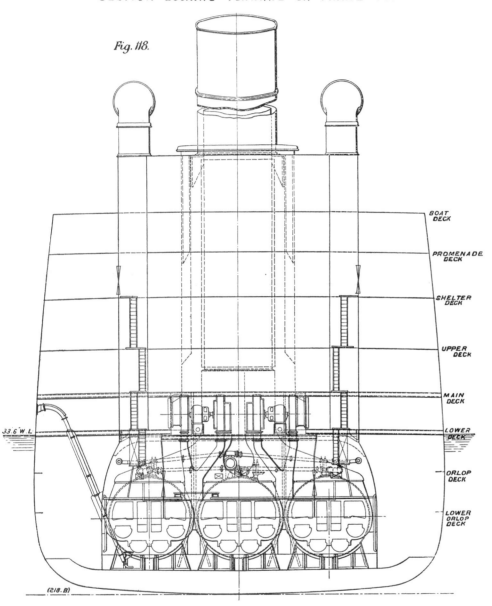

Fig. 118.

off as a service-room, from which all drawings, &c., that may be required by the draughtsmen are supplied. This service-room is in direct communication with the fireproof safe, where all drawings and tracings are stored. Of this safe, situated in the basement of the building, an illustration is given on Plate XV., Fig. 110. The arrangement is, as shown, very convenient. The floor space, of 44 ft. by 30 ft., is almost entirely covered with racks for tubes containing the tracings or negatives for sun-prints, or with drawer-stands ; and each set of machinery has a drawer and negative tube designated by the contract number. In the basement there is also a 50-ton testing-machine, of the latest design, by Messrs. Crow, Harvey, and Co., Glasgow. The photographic department is also in the basement, and here the company have one of Messrs. J. Halden and Co.'s continuous photo-copying machines, of the double pattern, copying two tracings at one time, and a continuous combined washer and electric dryer for taking the prints when they leave the copying-machine. A view of this department is given in Fig. 109 on

wood-working machinery, conveniently situated as regards the wood-yard, and along one side are the turning-lathes. Adjoining the pattern-shop is a building 90 ft. by 50 ft., and in this most of the valuable patterns are stored.

The boiler-shop, which is well shown in the various engravings of the Mauretania boilers, is in four bays, two of which are 260 ft. long, one 310 ft. long, and one 330 ft. long, giving a collective width of 220 ft. The bay which is 330 ft. long is 75 ft. wide, with a height of 60 ft. to crane-rails, with two overhead travelling-cranes of 70 and 100 tons lifting capacity respectively. The smaller bays are used for the machining and preparing of the plates, the final assembling of the boilers being done in the large bay. It may suffice in the way of description of the machine-tools if we state that the plates of the boilers of the Mauretania were for double-ended boilers 37 ft. 9 in. long, 7 ft. 8 in. wide, and 1$\frac{21}{64}$ in. thick, weighing 7 tons 3 cwt.; that for single-ended boilers the plates were heavier (7 tons

---

* See Engineering, vol. lxxiv., page 695.

THE ARRANGEMENT OF THE PROPELLING MACHINERY.

The plans and sections on the two-page Plates, XXXVI., XXXVII., and XXXVIII., on Plate XVII., and on the preceding page, afford a clear idea of the general arrangement of the propelling machinery in the ship. It is, however, exceedingly difficult to convey, with the assistance of drawings alone, an adequate idea of the immensity of the machinery. It must be borne in mind that the height from the platform-level to the top of the engine-room skylight is 79 ft. The reader will further be assisted by the photographs we reproduce. An explanation of these general drawings will form a convenient preface to the fuller description of the important units and of the system of constructing these. As shown by the engravings on Plate XXXVI. and on page 27, the boilers are arranged in four rooms. The forward, or No. 1 boiler-room, has five double-ended and two single-ended boilers, and in the others there are six double-ended boilers. This arrangement forward became necessary owing to the fining of the ship's lines. In No. 1 boiler-room there is on each side forward a ballast-pump, made by Messrs. Carruthers, of Glasgow. These pumps are of the duplex type. On the starboard side also is the auxiliary feed and ash-ejector pump, whilst on the port side, in the corresponding position, there is placed a refrigerating-pump. The auxiliary machinery in No. 2 boiler-room consists of an auxiliary feed and ash-ejector pump of the duplex type, made by Messrs. G. and J. Weir, and an auxiliary feed-pump, also by Messrs. Weir, and of the same capacity as the main feed-pumps in the engine-room. These pumps are placed at the after bulkhead of No. 2 room. In No. 3 boiler compartment there is the same arrangement of pumps at this bulkhead on the forward side, the bulkhead in this case being suitably recessed to receive these. In No. 4 boiler-room, at the aft bulkhead, is placed an auxiliary feed and ash-ejector pump. In each boiler compartment there are two of See's ash-ejectors and two of Crompton's ash-hoists. All the ash-ejector pumps are of the same capacity, and all pumps in the boiler-room spaces are cased in to prevent access of dust.

Adopting still the forward-to-aft order, we first review the arrangement of machinery in the main engine-room, as illustrated by the views on Plate XXXVII., Figs. 119 and 120, and by Figs. 124 and 125 on Plate XVII. It will be seen that there are four shafts, the two wing shafts being driven by the high-pressure turbines, and the two inner shafts by the low-pressure turbines, astern turbines being also fitted on the latter shafts. There is a longitudinal bulkhead between each high-pressure turbine and the proximate low-pressure turbine. Thus there are three turbine compartments, those on the port and starboard side respectively, having the high-pressure turbines, with a central room containing the two low-pressure and astern turbines. In each turbine-room there are ingeniously-disposed pumps and other auxiliary engines in convenient places at various heights. On the forward turbine-room bulkhead there are the main feed-pumps, one set in each high-pressure turbine-room—those at the sides—and two sets in the low-pressure turbine-room—that in the centre of the ship. There are two sets of evaporator machinery—one for making up the boiler-feed, and the other for ship purposes generally—at the forward end of each high-pressure turbine-room. Aft of this, in the port room, are placed the fresh and condensed-water pumps, and in the corresponding place in the starboard room a refrigerating pump. The water-service pumps, two in number, are arranged in the centre of the ship between the astern turbines in the low-pressure turbine-room; these pumps are of the duplex type and were made by Messrs. Carruthers, of Glasgow. Aft of these are the fire and sanitary pumps. The six oil-pumps are also in the centre of the ship between the low-pressure and astern thrust-blocks. These are placed well below the floor-level on the turbine-seating, a well being formed in the floor for access to them. The four hotwell pumps are located at the aft bulkhead in the low-pressure room, the bulkhead being recessed at this place to receive them. The four bilge-pumps are erected against the longitudinal bulkhead at the wings of the low-pressure room. These pumps are of the single-cylinder double-acting type, and made by Messrs. G. and J. Weir.

The two main condensers are situated in a separate compartment aft of the low-pressure turbine-room, and abaft of this, in two compartments separated by a centre longitudinal bulkhead, are the auxiliaries for the main condensers, the circulating pumps being placed in the wings in each compartment, and the wet and dry-air pumps against each side of the longitudinal bulkhead. In the starboard room there is, in addition, a duplex pump for supplying water to the turbo-oil-coolers. Above these compartments, on a flat at the level of the orlop deck, are the four turbo-generators, two in each of the rooms, which are divided by a fore-and-aft bulkhead.

In rooms aft of the high-pressure-turbine rooms in the wings of the ship, and over the high-pressure-turbine shafts, there are on the starboard side the auxiliary condensers, with all their auxiliaries—air and circulating pumps, the surface heaters, and the main and auxiliary feed-filters, whilst in the port room there are the Stone-Lloyd pumps for operating the mechanism of the water-tight doors.

On Table XIII. on this page we give a complete list of the auxiliary engines in connection with the propulsion of the ship.

TABLE XIII.—List of Steam Auxiliaries.

Name of Pump.	Number	Makers.	Type of Pump.	Size of Steam-Cylinders.	Size of Water-Cylinders.	Stroke of Pump.	Position in Ship.
Main feed-pumps ..	4 pairs	G. and J. Weir, Limited	Single-cylinder double-acting	Two 18 in.	Two 13½ in.	30 in.	Forward engine-room bulkhead high-pressure and low-pressure-rooms.
Auxiliary feed-pumps	2 pairs	G. and J. Weir, Limited	Single-cylinder double-acting	Two 18 in.	Two 13½ in.	30 in.	1 pair aft bulkhead of No 2 boiler-room; 1 pair forward bulkhead of No. 3 boiler-room.
Auxiliary feed and ash-ejector	4	G. and J. Weir, Limited	Duplex	Two 14 in.	Two 10 in.	14 in.	One in each boiler-room.
Hotwell pumps .	4	G. and J. Weir, Limited	Single-cylinder double-acting	One 12½ in.	One 14½ in.	30 in.	Aft end of low-pressure turbine-room.
Wet-air pumps ..	4 twin	G. and J. Weir, Limited	Beam, double-cylinder	Two 14 in.	Two 40 in.	24 in.	Auxiliary machinery-room.
Dry-air pumps.. ..	4 twin	G. and J. Weir, Limited	Quick revolution	Two 7 in.	Two 24 in.	7 in.	Auxiliary machinery-room.
Main circulating-pump	2 sets	W. H. Allen, Son, and Co., Limited	Quick revolution	Two 18 in.	Four impellers, 42 in. diam.	10 in.	Auxiliary machinery-room.
Auxiliary circulating-pump	2	W. H. Allen, Son, and Co., Limited	Quick revolution	One 7 in.	One impeller, 36 in. diam.	6 in.	Auxiliary condenser-room.
Auxiliary air-pumps ..	2	G. and J. Weir, Limited	Single-cylinder single-acting	One 10 in.	One 22 in.	12 in.	Auxiliary condenser room.
Oil-pumps	6	G. and J. Weir, Limited	Single-cylinder double-acting	One 7 in.	One 8½ in.	15 in.	Low-pressure-turbine room.
Water service pumps	2	J. H. Carruthers and Co.	Duplex	Two 7½ in.	Two 10 in.	12 in.	Low-pressure turbine room.
Turbo-oil-cooler; water service pump	1	Clarke, Chapman, and Co., Limited	Duplex	Two 2½ in.	Two 2½ in.	3½ in.	Auxiliary - machinery room (starboard).
Wash-deck and fire-pump	1	G. and J. Weir, Limited	Duplex	Two 12 in.	Two 10 in.	10 in.	Low-pressure turbine room.
Sanitary pumps ..	2	G. and J. Weir, Limited	Duplex	Two 12 in.	Two 10 in.	10 in.	Low-pressure-turbine room.
Bilge-pumps	4	G. and J. Weir, Limited	Single-cylinder double-acting	One 8 in.	One 10 in.	21 in.	Low-pressure-turbine room (wings).
Ballast-pumps	2	J. H. Carruthers and Co.	Duplex	Two 8 in.	Two 10 in.	10 in.	Forward end of No. 1 boiler-room.
Fresh and condensed water pumps	2	J. H. Carruthers and Co.	Duplex	Two 6 in.	Two 6 in.	6 in.	Port high-pressure-turbine room.
Refrigerating pump ..	2	Liverpool Engineering Company	Duplex	Two 6 in.	Two 7½ in.	6 in.	No. 1 boiler-room and starboard high-pressure-turbine room
Stone-Lloyd	2	J Stone and Co.	Duplex	Two 15 in	Two 6 in.	15 in.	Port auxiliary condenser-room
Bulkhead valve; Brown's engine	2	Brown Brothers	Single-cylinder	One 10 in.	..	12 in.	Forward low-pressure-turbine room bulkhead
Manœuvring valve; Brown's engine	2	Brown Brothers	Single-cylinder	One 12 in.	..	15 in.	Low-pressure-turbine room longitudinal bulkhead.
Evaporator feed-pump	2	Liverpool Engineering Company	Duplex	Two 5 in.	Two 5 in.	6 in.	High-pressure-turbine rooms.
Evaporator brine ,,	2	Liverpool Engineering Company	Single-cylinder double-acting	One 4 in.	One 4½ in.	6 in.	High-pressure-turbine rooms.
Distiller circulating pumps	2	Liverpool Engineering Company	Duplex	Two 8 in.	Two 9 in.	8 in.	High-pressure-turbine rooms.

THE MAIN TURBINES.

As we have already stated, there are six turbines: two high-pressure and two low pressure for going ahead, and two high-pressure for going astern. The two high-pressure ahead turbines are, as already explained, placed in the wings of the ship, while the two low-pressure ahead, and the high-pressure astern turbines, are connected to the inner shafts. As shown on the plan, Fig. 120 on Plate XXXVII., the low-pressure shafts are at 9 ft. 6 in. centres from the middle line of the ship, while the high-pressure shafts are 27 ft. from the middle line of the ship, so that the distance between the high-pressure and the low-pressure shafts is 17 ft. 6 in. It will be noted that, as seen in plan, the shafts are parallel with the middle line of the ship, whereas, as shown in the elevation, Fig. 119, they are at a slight angle to the level of the keel, the rake in elevation in the case of the low-pressure turbine being about $\frac{2}{10}$ in. per foot, and in the high-pressure turbine rather less than $\frac{1}{2}$ in. per foot. The high-pressure turbines, as shown in the plans and sections, are in advance of the low-pressure, the centre of the former being about 20 ft. forward of the centre of the latter, while the astern turbines are still further forward, the intervening space being about 10 ft., and within this is located, on the shaft, the thrust-blocks. This arrangement of turbines, it will at once be recognised, reduces to the minimum the length of the steam-pipe connection between the exhaust end of the high-pressure turbine and the steam inlet of the low-pressure turbine. Moreover, it facilitates the disposition of the auxiliary machinery in the engine-room; but it will be understood that, although the high-pressure and low-pressure ahead turbines alternate in the longitudinal line, they do not at any point overlap. As to the length of shaft, that can readily be gauged from the plan and section. The centres of the outer propellers are 78 ft. 11 in. forward of the inner propellers, the two inner propellers being 12 ft. 10 in. in advance of the aft perpendicular. This location of the propellers was determined after very considerable experiment, as has already been described.

ROTORS AND CASINGS.

In the construction of the turbines a different method was adopted from the procedure followed in connection with the Lusitania. For the Mauretania the discs and gudgeons, as well as the shaft and drums, were constructed of Whitworth fluid-pressed steel, which, as is well known, gives a most reliable and homogeneous metal. With the object of getting the maximum strength and rigidity with a minimum weight, it was finally settled that there should be as few parts as possible, and that all stiffeners should be solid, and form part of the drums, so as to avoid any distortion or straining when heating up or cooling down, and with this object, together with that of securing a truly-balanced drum, all of them were machined both inside and outside, as well as all the ribs and stiffeners. It will interest our readers to know that when all the three large low-pressure drums were screwed together, and the gudgeons and discs bolted in and tried in the lathe, the combination was found to be perfectly true.

As a consequence of this precision and homogeneity there was no necessity for testing the balance by spinning the turbines in the shops after construction. The various parts were fitted up in the ship, where the first spin under steam was undertaken little more than a week before the vessel proceeded to sea, when it was found that all the turbines were absolutely true in balance. This bold step has afforded a splendid proof of the

pressure rotor complete is over 72 tons, of the low-pressure rotor 126 tons, and of the astern rotor 60 tons. Views of the turbines completed are given on Plate XVIII., and on the next page.

The rotors are built up of the usual units, with a spindle for each end, on which there were secured double discs coupled together by bolts, to which, again, there was bolted the drum. In order to facilitate the connection of the discs, the shaft at

pressure and low-pressure rotors, and of two lengths in the case of the astern rotors. The following was the mode of manufacture of the enormous low-pressure drums, which were made from 120 tons of a special quality of steel from Siemens-Whitworth furnaces, run into an ingot mould 6 ft. in diameter, and whilst quite liquid subjected to an hydraulic pressure of 12,000 tons. After the ingot had cooled down it was parted off,

Fig. 126.

Fig. 127.

Figs. 126 and 127. Castings for Turbine-Casings.

character of the Whitworth metal, and of the accurate workmanship. This is the more pronounced when the dimensions are taken into consideration. The high-pressure drum is 96 in. in diameter, with blades ranging from about 2½ in. to about 12 in. long, while the low-pressure drum is 140 in. in diameter, with blades ranging from about 8 in. to 22 in., and the astern drum is 104 in. in diameter, with blades ranging from about 2 in. up to 8 in. In all three instances there are eight stages of expansion. Perhaps, however, a better idea can be formed of the magnitude of the work when it is stated that the total weight of the high-

this point was made slightly conical; this point also was considerably larger than at the bearings or in the intermediate length. The greatest diameter in the case of the high-pressure turbine is 3 ft., in the case of the low-pressure turbine 4 ft. 4 in., and of the astern turbine 3 ft. 3 in. In all cases the shafting is hollow. The over-all length of the turbine rotors, including the bearings, is, in the case of the high-pressure turbine 45 ft. 8 in., of the low-pressure turbine 48 ft. 1⅞ in., and of the astern turbine 30 ft. 1¼ in.

The drum, which was bolted to the discs, was made up in three lengths in the case of the high-

and then bored for hollow forging and enlarged to about double its original diameter, with the flanges and stiffening ribs forged thereon. The next operation was the rough turning and boring all over, after which each drum was thoroughly annealed, so as to remove all internal stress, and thus avoid any tendency to distortion. The drums were then fine-bored, turned, screwed, and shrunk together, with the results previously mentioned, and finally, owing to their enormous size, shipped by special steamer, viâ the Manchester Ship Canal, to the Tyne.

The metal of the finished drums varied in thickness from $1\frac{7}{8}$ in. to $2\frac{1}{16}$ in., but at the point of junction it was almost trebled in thickness to form an internal flange where the parts were bolted together, and here the buttress thread was turned so that the parts could be screwed together at the flange preparatory to the fixing of the bolts. The connections were made while the metal was hot. The buttress thread obviates any possibility of the metal opening out at the outer points of connection during contraction.

The turbine-casings, illustrated on the preceding page, are of cast iron, and were made by Messrs. Fullerton, Hodgart, and Barclay, Limited, Paisley. In the case of the largest piece, which weighed over 35 tons, there were upwards of 100 pieces of mould and cores, each of which had to be adjusted and fixed in its exact position. The

Works a number of experiments in order to test the various methods of rooting, binding, and shrouding the blades. Early in turbine work he became a strong advocate of the segmental method of building up the blades, alike for rotors and casings, realising that this means afforded at least equal security and accuracy with the separate system of blading, at the same time enabling the work of completing the turbines to be done much more rapidly, because the segmental sections could be built up contemporaneously with the manufacture and machining of the rotor and casing. Indeed, in the case of the Mauretania's turbines, one of the turbines was completely bladed in 14 days; and when it is remembered that the total number of blades in this rotor was 50,000, it will be recognised that the system, from the point of view

139. The Willans and Robinson arrangement commended itself for the roots, but the Parsons method of binding the blades was adopted. It has been urged by some that the bending of part of the blade over the base-plate at the root, as shown on the plan in Fig. 139, tended to punish the metal; but tests were made to ascertain the tensile strength of the metal before and after the stamping to the bent form, and these tests gave results which were quite satisfactory. Vibration tests were also carried out to test the effect of the various methods of fixing the blade-roots.

Having fixed upon the system to be adopted, the Wallsend Slipway and Engineering Company secured special machinery for carrying out the various operations, and they have now one of the best-equipped blading departments in the country,

FIG. 129. THE TURBINES IN THE WALLSEND ENGINEERING SHOPS, WITH HIGH-PRESSURE TURBINE IN FOREGROUND.

iron used was of various selected brands, re-melted into pigs to make sure of it being homogeneous; test-bars were cast on every casting, and tested considerably above Admiralty requirements. Each of the castings, after being taken out of the mould, cleaned and fettled, was put into an annealing stove, and so re-heated up to from 800 deg. to 900 deg. Fahr., at which heat it was kept for 24 hours; afterwards it was allowed to cool slowly, and only taken out of the annealing furnace when quite cold. This, besides annealing the castings, had the effect of taking away any strains set up during the contraction of the metal after being cast. It is very creditable to the workmen employed upon these castings that not one of the large moulds was defective in any way.

The bladed portion was made separate from the ends. These latter are in two pieces, with a central joint. The bottom portions of the steam and exhaust ends are cast in one with the bearing stools, and the thickness of metal varies from $1\frac{3}{4}$ in. to $2\frac{5}{8}$ in. The portions of the casings which carry the blades were cast separately from the steam and exhaust ends, and these parts were fitted together and attached to the ends with a circumferential joint. The usual longitudinal division was made to enable the casing to be lifted for the examination of the rotor. The metal in the casing is about $2\frac{5}{8}$ in. thick, and, as shown in the various drawings and photographs reproduced (see Plates XVIII. and XIX.), it is well ribbed. The bolts used were formed of silicon steel of a tensile strength of from 34 to 37 tons per square inch.

BLADING EXPERIMENTS AND MANUFACTURE.

The subject of the blading of the turbines has received equal, if not greater, consideration than the forgings for the rotors and the castings for the casings, and in the initial stages of the work Mr. Laing had carried out at the Wallsend Engineering

FIGS. 136 TO 139. SYSTEMS OF BLADING TESTED.

of time, confers a distinct advantage. A segment and a complete ring of blades are illustrated on Plate XXIII.

The question which remained to be determined had reference to the best system, and quite three years ago a series of experiments were entered upon in order to test various possible systems of segmental blading. In view of the deep packing-pieces required for the larger blades, different methods of side caulking for securing the roots of the blades were tested, and the detail drawings reproduced above are, from this point of view, interesting. These are more or less self-explanatory. There was devised a system of stringing the blades at their roots, along with the distance-pieces, in combination with a continuous shroud at the tips (Fig. 137). The Willans and Robinson system was also tested, and two other systems of blading, as illustrated by Figs. 138 and

whether regard be had to independent blading, to the Willans and Robinson system, or to the later Parsons root system. On Plate XXII. we reproduce, in Fig. 141, an engraving showing part of this department. The blades are delivered in rolled bars, and are cut to length in one of several Taylor and Challen stamping-presses. Where the Willans and Robinson system is to be adopted a similar tool stamps the root of each blade to form the right angle, shown on the plan in Fig. 139, for insertion into the segmental root-plate. A corresponding machine makes the indent for the Parsons binding-strip near the tip of the blade, while a small milling-machine fines the point of the blade to that gouge-pointed shape which is now universally adopted in order to obviate any effect from the seizure of the blade against the proximate surface when running. The blading adopted in the Willans and Robinson system necessitated the construction of an ingenious tool which mills out the groove for each blade at the correct position in the foundation plate of the segment. The blades are then assembled and secured to these root-blades.

With the Parsons system of root-fixing, adopted for the machinery of the British battleship Superb, now being made at the Wallsend Engineering Works, the system of manufacture is only slightly different. The blades are similarly cut to length, the indent made where required for binding, and small tools used for boring the hole, by means of which the blades are strung together on wire along with distance-wedges. The wedges which, on plan, take the curves corresponding to the blade, are similarly cut to length and bored. For the assembling of the blades and distance-wedges, castings are made to correspond to part of the circumference of the rotor or the casing, and these form cheeks, which are bolted together with a distance-piece, corresponding to a groove in the rotor or casing. In building up one segment or length of blading, the wire is passed through the hole in one blade and secured; distance wedge and blade are alternately strung and tightened up in the groove between the cheeks by means of a caulking tool ingeniously formed with a groove on the lower side to fit over the wire. The stringing completed, the blades are trued up in the vertical line. The next operation is the insertion of the binding wire, after which the lacing is put on around the binding wire and blades with silver solder heated by gas blow-pipes. The rapidity with which the work is done results as much from the deftness of the operators, due to experience, as from the admirable special appliances devised for each operation. To ensure experience each man carries out one operation, and thus cutting, drilling, lacing and caulking, trueing, binding, and soldering are each done by separate workmen. The segments are finally filed up to remove trimming, &c., and are then ready to be inserted in the rotor or casing. This, as we have already indicated, may be rapidly done. The segments, being numbered according to their exact position in the turbine, are assembled and caulked into the grooves, first with wooden mallets, and later with special caulking tools, so formed that they can be inserted between the blades to abut on the caulking-piece.

GLANDS, BEARINGS, THRUST-BLOCKS, SHAFTING, &c.

The turbine-glands surround the spindle where it leaves the turbine-casing in order to obviate, in the case of the high-pressure turbine, the leakage of steam from the casing, and in the case of the low-pressure turbine the leakage of air from the atmosphere into the casing and thence to the condenser. The glands are of cast iron, with a horizontal joint, and are bolted to the gland recess at the casing ends. The packing is of the point or V type, with very small clearance, with the addition of rings of steam-pockets. There are at the outer ends Ramsbottom rings of "Ajax" bronze. In the case of the high-pressure gland there is one steam-pocket either, to take reduced steam or to leak off to the condenser, as the conditions of running may require. In the case of the low-pressure and astern glands, there are two steam pockets: the inner one, arranged to leak off to the end of the third expansion of the low-pressure turbine, the other to admit reduced steam at sufficient pressure to preclude the passage of air.

The bearings for all the turbines are of cast iron lined with white metal on their running surfaces. The outer wall is in the form of a sphere, which works in a dished pedestal, in order to ensure an equal pressure upon all parts of the length, notwithstanding any possible deflection of the shaft. The bearings are arranged for internal water circulation; the bearing cap is also of cast iron, but has no water circulation. At the centre of each bearing there is fitted a safety strip of "Ajax" bronze $\frac{3}{16}$ in. below the white metal. This was fitted so that if the white metal by any chance gets heated and runs, the rotor will rest on the safety strip, and the blades on the rotor will still be kept clear of the casing, while at the same time the casing blades will not rub against the rotor surface.

The thrust-block in the case of the high-pressure turbine is at the forward end, while, as we have already indicated, it is, in the case of the inner shafts, between the low-pressure ahead and the astern turbines. The thrust-block is of cast iron, with a bolted steel bush for holding the thrust-rings; these latter are of gun-metal, with white metal on the rubbing face. The top portion of the thrust-block takes the steam thrust, and the bottom portion the propeller thrust. The block in all cases is on a sole-plate of its own, and can be moved in a fore-and-aft direction for the purpose of adjustment by means of powerful bolts. The upper portion, which, as we have said, takes the steam thrust, can be moved relatively to the under portion; this allows for the adjustment of running clearances in the thrust-rings. The thrust-shaft is bolted on to the main turbine-shaft by the usual couplings and bolts.

For adjusting the dummies, which are of the face type, for the high-pressure and low-pressure turbines, and which run with very fine clearances in an axial direction, the whole block is moved either way to give the necessary clearance. The dummies in the astern turbine are of the radial type, so that the lateral adjustment of the low-pressure dummy does not affect the clearance of the dummy in the astern turbine. Midway along the dummy there is a pocket formed, which is connected by a pipe to one of the succeeding expansions. In the event of the pressure in this pocket being greater than in the expansion to which it is connected, a portion of the steam is allowed to leak into the expansion, the remainder escaping to the exhaust.

At the casing ends there are fitted micrometer gauges, which enable the exact clearance of the dummies to be ascertained while running.

The line shafting is 20 in. external diameter and 10 in. internal diameter; the maximum length of any one piece is 23 ft., and all is of 28 to 32-ton steel. All the shafting was made by Sir W. G. Armstrong, Whitworth, and Co. The couplings are 35 in. in diameter by $4\frac{3}{4}$ in. thick, and are coupled together by tapered bolts having hexagon heads. The plummer-blocks are of cast iron, lined with white metal on the bearing surfaces, and are arranged for internal water service on the bottom. Ordinary syphon lubrication is fitted, as is also external water service.

The propeller-shafts are all 30 ft. $1\frac{5}{8}$ in. long and $22\frac{1}{4}$ in. in external diameter, with a 10-in.-diameter hole. The propeller-shaft liner is of gun-metal, in one piece, the diameter over the liner being $24\frac{3}{4}$ in. A view in the shaft tunnel is given on Plate XXIX.

The stern-tube is of cast iron, the minimum thickness of metal being 3 in.; the forward and after bushes are of gun-metal, fitted with lignum-vitæ strips. Each propeller-boss is of cast steel. The three blades are of manganese-bronze, and are attached to the boss with high-tensile steel studs and manganese-bronze nuts.

There is a set of turning-gear to each line of shafting, placed, in the case of the outer shafts, at the aft end of the high-pressure turbine, and in the case of the inner shafts at the aft end of the low-pressure turbine. The gear consists of an electric motor of 30 brake horse-power, capable of taking double the load at starting. The drive from the motor is by a Hans Renold chain, which works on to a wheel keyed on the first-motion worm, the worm-wheel of which is again keyed on the second-motion worm-shaft, which is vertical, and gears into the gun-metal worm-wheel on the turbine shafting. The bracket which carries the first and second-motion worms rests on a machine-bed, and can be moved in and out of gear by means of a screw. The gear is arranged to make one complete revolution of the shafting in $8\frac{1}{2}$ minutes, and the motors are interchangeable with the lifting-gear motors.

Forced lubrication is applied to the main bearings, and there are six of Weir's pumps fitted in the centre engine-room between the low-pressure ahead and the astern turbines, to maintain the pressure. Four of these suffice for the duty, so that two are stand-by pumps. The sections are cross-connected, so that any pump can draw from either set of oil-drain tanks, port or starboard. The oil can be supplied to the bearings either by the pumps direct or from an overhead gravitation system. In the discharge from the pump an oil-cooler is interposed on one of the upper platforms near to a downcast ventilator. There are two pipes to each bearing and thrust, one from the overhead tank and the other from the pump direct. The pressure due to gravity from the tank is from 5 lb. to 10 lb. per square inch. There are four large tanks for reserve oil, and on the end of each bearing there is an oil save-all. The drains from the latter are taken into the drain-tanks below the astern turbines. In the case of the high-pressure steam ends and the low-pressure-steam ends the drains are led into the casing ends below the bearings. The casing end forms part of the same casting as the steam end of the turbines, and it is consequently important to maintain an equable temperature throughout the casting, so that there may be the minimum of variation consequent upon unequal expansion. The outlet for the oil in the casing is therefore at a high level, to ensure that there will always be in the casing a large gathering of oil, which is at about the same temperature as the shaft, within the bearing. There is thus the minimum effect upon the dummy clearances due to unequal expansion in the whole bearing. Sight-glasses are fitted in the drain-pipes from each bearing, enabling the engineer to see the amount of oil which is passing through.

THE TURBINE LIFTING-GEAR.

There are six sets of lifting-gear, one for each turbine, and for each set there is a 30-brake-horse-power motor, capable of taking double load at starting, interchangeable with the turning-gear motors. The general arrangement of the lifting mechanism is well shown on the plans and sections on Plates XVII. and XXXIII. On the motor-shaft there is keyed a spur-pinion, gearing into a spur-wheel on a shaft which runs the full length of the turbine, but at a considerable height above it. From each end of this shaft there is driven, by a Hans Renold chain, a wheel keyed on the worm-shaft of the main lifting-gear bracket. This worm-shaft drives a gun-metal worm-wheel, supported on ball-bearings, and forming the nut in which the lifting-screws work. The lifting-screws, one at each end, are 7 in. in diameter and $1\frac{3}{4}$ in. pitch. The main lifting-gear brackets are bolted down to strong beams running between the longitudinal bulkhead and the casing side at the main-deck level. The columns for guiding the casings and rotors are 7 in. in diameter. They are bolted to the turbine-casing, and, where practicable, extend to the underside of the lifting-beams, or to deck-beams. In cases where it is not possible to carry these columns up to beams, owing to interference with the main turbine connections, they are stopped short and braced at the top by stays running across to the longitudinal bulkhead. There are two columns at each end of the turbine, and guide-brackets on the casing embrace these columns, as does also the cast-steel crosshead connected to the main lifting-screws. In lifting a casing the ends of the steel crosshead engage the underside of the guide-brackets, and when the casing has been lifted the requisite height, forged steel columns are inserted between the top and bottom horizontal flanges of same. This prevents the casing coming down, but leaves the crosshead free to return and lift the rotor. For lifting the rotor a cast-steel strap lined with white metal is slung round under the shaft between the bearing and the gland, and the crosshead is lowered until it comes in contact with the top of the shaft. Bolts are then passed through the crosshead and these screw into the strap; the rotor can then be lifted.

This gear can also be used for turning out a main bearing as follows:—A strap is bolted round the lifting column, which prevents the cross-head coming quite down on to the shaft; the bolts previously referred to raise the steel strap, and hence the shaft. A forged steel strap is bolted over the shaft to the bearing. The shaft is then turned round by the turning-gear. As the weight of the shaft is taken on the cast-steel strap, the friction between the strap bolted to the bearing and the shaft is sufficient to turn out the bottom half of the bearing; the steel strap meanwhile acts as a bearing, and being lined with white metal, prevents injury to the shaft at this place.

Preparatory to the lifting of the high-pressure turbine casing and rotor, the exhaust branch is carried aft on a special trolley. The steam-strainer is also, by a trolley, swung into the wings of the ship, and by means of chain-blocks the rotor bearings are raised a sufficient height to clear the lifted position of the rotor-spindle. The casing and rotor are now ready for lifting. The high-pressure casing has to be lifted through 4 ft. 10 in., and the time taken in the operation is 15 minutes.

In the lifting of the low-pressure casing and rotor it is necessary, first, to dispose of the upper portion of the steam-inlet branch, which is slung on a beam under the main deck, the lower portion being swung round to rest on the casing. The cast-iron portion of the main exhaust branch is dismantled, the forward part being placed flat on the casing, whilst the other three parts are carried in slings at the sides and aft of the turbine. The rotor bearings, by means of chain-blocks, are lifted sufficient to clear the shaft when in its lifted position. The low-pressure casing and rotor are then ready for lifting. The time taken to lift this casing is 20 minutes.

In the astern casing the exhaust-pipe has to be first raised sufficiently to clear the lifted position of the casing. This is done by having the exhaust-pipes hinged a certain distance along, and by taking out a wedge-piece between the pipe and the exhaust branch the pipe is free to be swung up, and hung from the underside of the main deck. The strainer is moved along the casing to clear the exhaust-pipe, and the rotor bearings,

speed, the gear would close both of the stop-valves on the bulkhead. In order that either valve may control the machinery in both engine-rooms, there is a cross-connection.

Here there may be properly introduced a description of the governor-gear, and its connection with these main valves. This governor-gear, which is of the Aspinall type, is driven off the forward end of each line of main shafting through a worm and worm-wheel keyed to the shaft at right angles to the main shaft, and from one end of this is taken the crank and connecting-rod for driving the lever carrying the Aspinall governor, while from the other end there is taken the drive for the tachometers. The governor makes half the number of revolutions of the turbine. In the event of excessive speed, the pawls on the Aspinall governor come into contact with the trip-lever, which is connected to the horizontal

bine is usually thrown completely out of action. Thus, in going out of harbour or entering port, where there are frequent changes in the direction of rotation of the propellers, the centre shafts only are used, and on such occasions the manœuvring valve, which does all the work, is therefore of very considerable importance, and its operating mechanism of great interest. It has an 18-in. inlet, and consists of double valves fitted with the Bevis-Gibson disc.* The feature of this disc is that in order to overcome the play which sometimes arises in equilibrium valves, due to unequal expansion between the valve and the valve-casing, the upper valve is fitted with a light disc, secured to the round body by a junk-ring, while the lower valve has the ordinary mitre face. The valve when closed rests on the mitre face, and the steam acting on the light disc keeps it down to the face and makes a steam-tight joint. One of the two valves controls

Fig. 144. Starting and Manœuvring Gear.

by means of chain-blocks, are lifted a sufficient height to clear the shaft. The astern casing and rotor are then ready for lifting.

THE STEAM DISTRIBUTION AND VALVES IN THE TURBINE-ROOMS.

Of equal interest is the arrangement for the distribution and control of the steam through the successive turbines, and especially the arrangement made to ensure rapid manipulation of the valves, so as to secure quick manœuvring of the ship. In this connection we confine ourselves to the arrangement within the turbine-machinery rooms, leaving the boiler equipment until a later period. As shown in the drawings of the general arrangement of the main machinery on Plate XXXVII., there are two lines of main steam-pipes entering the engine-rooms, the two forward boiler-rooms being connected to the port main steam-pipe, and the two aft boiler-rooms to the starboard main steam-pipe. These pipes are 24 in. in diameter, and made of lap-welded wrought iron, with screwed-on wrought-iron flanges. In these two pipes on the engine-room side of the bulkhead are placed the stop-valves, which are operated by a Brown steam and hydraulic engine. This engine can also be operated by hand. It is connected to the governor-gear by shafting common to both valves and to all four turbines, so that if any one of the turbines exceeds a predetermined

shaft extending across the engine-room, and actuates, through a lever, the valves of the Brown engine for the main steam-valves. Between the trip-lever of each turbine governing-gear and the shaft across the engine-room is a slotted end, so that in the event of any one turbine exceeding the speed, it would operate the shaft controlling the stop-valve without disturbing the governor-gear of any of the other turbines. By a similar means the Brown engine can be set in motion to open the main valve without being connected to the governor-gear of the turbine which had exceeded the speed limit. The slot in this case is formed in the rod, which is connected to the hand-lever of the Brown engine. Owing to the cross-connection both valves may be closed in the emergency described, but either may be opened by hand, enabling the steam to pass to any of the twin sets of turbines.

The steam, after passing through the main valve, enters a separator of the spiral type, from which the water is drained, either through a trap or straight into the hot-well. Steam from this separator passes either through the high-pressure regulating valve, which, like the main steam-valves, is of the equilibrium type, or to a manœuvring shut-off valve, which is of the piston balanced type, and thence to the manœuvring valve of the equilibrium type.

This last valve, as its name suggests, is only used for manœuvring, when the high-pressure tur-

the admission of the steam to the low-pressure turbine for going ahead when manœuvring, and the other regulates the steam supply to the astern turbine on the same shaft.

The valve-operating mechanism had, therefore, to be arranged to ensure that both valves could not be opened simultaneously, but that both valves might be closed at the same time. On the opposite page is a drawing illustrating the mechanism of the valves. It will be seen that on the end of the valve-spindle there is a lever connecting with both spindles. From the centre of this lever there is a spring compressed between the valve-casing and the lever, which tends to keep both valves closed. Mounted on each valve-spindle at a higher point is a sliding-block, which is connected by links to a common lever fulcrummed in the centre. This lever is attached to the Brown steam and hydraulic engine used for actuating the gear. When the engine moves, it acts, through the fulcrum lever, to lift one of the sliding-blocks until it comes into contact with a shoulder on one spindle, whereby one of the valves is opened. The other end of the fulcrumed lever, being depressed, pulls the block attached to it downwards, and as the latter rides loosely on the spindle, this valve is not affected. The return stroke of the engine brings the fulcrumed lever to the horizontal position, pulling

* See Proceedings of the North-East Coast Institution of Engineers and Shipbuilders, 1902.

the block down the spindle. At the same time the spring closes the valve.

This manœuvring valve is worked from the starting-pedestal (of which an engraving is given on the opposite page, Fig. 144) by the inner wheel shown. This wheel works, through mitre-wheels, spindles terminating in the screw which operates the valve of the Brown engine. When the piston is in mid-position, both valves are closed ; the forward stroke opens the valve which admits steam to the astern turbine, and the backward stroke operates the ahead valve. Through one of the sliding-blocks already described there is driven a connecting-rod which shows on the starting pedestal the position of the manœuvring valve. In the event of the Brown engine breaking down,

to the body in order to reduce friction as much as possible. The port rests on two gun-metal rollers, which run on a machined gun-metal path, the rollers being fitted with roller-bearings.

The mechanism for operating the valve is also illustrated on Plate XXIV. There is a special electric motor mounted on a bracket secured to the valve casting. The motor spindle is supported at its outer end on a corresponding bracket, and has upon it worms gearing into worm-wheels keyed on the screwed forged-bronze spindles for opening and closing the valves. These are supported by gun-metal tubes to prevent sagging. There is also a bevel gear for operating the valve by hand. On the mitre shaft there is a small spur-wheel geared into a larger wheel, the spindle of which latter is

outlet—31 square feet—the valve can be closed within two minutes. In the case of the 60-in. valve, which controls the exhaust from the high-pressure turbine to the condenser direct, where the exhaust area is 20 square feet, the mechanism is exactly the same, the only difference being that the valve has one instead of two spindles for opening and closing it. At the starting pedestal there is an index fitted to show the action of the valve after the actuating lever has been manipulated.

The exhaust-pipe from the high-pressure turbines passes through the longitudinal bulkhead dividing the engine-rooms, and copper expansion-pieces are fitted at this point, as illustrated in Figs. 161 and 162, below. In order further to avoid a steam-pipe connection to the ship-work a steel frame is fitted in

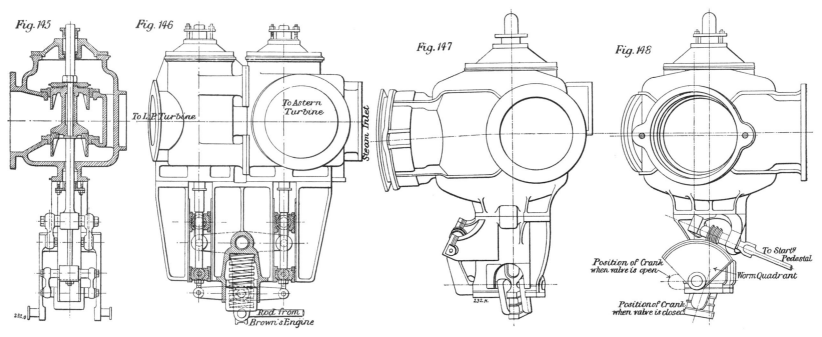

FIGS. 145 AND 146. MANŒUVRING VALVE AND ACTUATING GEAR.   FIGS. 147 AND 148. HIGH-PRESSURE REGULATING GEAR AND OPERATING GEAR.

there is a hand-pump at the starting pedestal which enables the manœuvring valves to be opened and closed by water pressure in the Brown engine.

In ocean steaming, however, this manœuvring valve will not be in operation, the steam from the separator passing to the high-pressure regulating-valves (Figs. 147 and 148). This is a 24-in. valve, made of cast steel, and is operated by hand-gear through the larger wheel on the starting pedestal. The gear, although operated by hand, is of very powerful type, and consists of a worm and worm quadrant keyed to a crank-shaft, with a rod connecting to the valve-spindle. The arrangement is such that the valve is just closing when the crank is near the dead centre, so that a very powerful closing effort is developed. The arrangement has also this advantage—that it takes a very small number of turns to open the valve : from full-open to full-closed, about 12½ turns of the hand-wheel. Besides being opened from the starting pedestal, this high-pressure regulating-valve has also an auxiliary hand-gear in the high-pressure-turbine room, which operates the same spindle through bevel-gear.

The area of the exhaust port from the high-pressure turbine is about 31 square feet, and connections have been formed so that the high-pressure turbine may exhaust either to the low-pressure turbine or direct to the condenser. These connections are controlled by valves, the exhaust-valve to the low-pressure turbine being of the sluice type, 75 in. in diameter, and the exhaust-valve from the high-pressure to the condenser direct of the same type, and 60 in. in diameter. Generally the two valves are of the same design, and similar in their operation. On Plate XXIV. we illustrate the 75-in. sluice-valve, which was constructed by Messrs. Glenfield and Kennedy, Limited, of Kilmarnock. The valve was made for a working pressure of 30 lb. to the square inch, and the body was cast in halves, which were afterwards machined and bolted together. The actual valve or port is of circular box form, the face of which is of gun-metal of heavy section, attached by gun-metal pins. A similar ring is fixed

FIGS. 161 AND 162. EXPANSION PIECES FOR STEAM-PIPES THROUGH BULKHEADS.

screwed with a fine thread, on which travels a nut, the latter at the end of the travel coming in contact with a link for throwing the motor switches out.

These valves also are operated from the starting pedestal ; the levers for this purpose are the two outer ones from the centre line of the ship, as shown in the photograph reproduced on the opposite page. Notwithstanding the great area of the

the bulkhead, having a sliding-piece with suitable packing, as illustrated, which accommodates any movement, vertical or horizontal, in the steam-pipe due to expansion or contraction, and at the same time precludes any slight vibration of the bulkhead affecting the exhaust connections. In the exhaust, direct into the main condensers from the high-pressure turbine, similar connections are made where the pipe passes through the bulkhead. The exhaust from the high-pressure turbines passes into the main exhaust-pipe from the astern turbine, which is 6 ft. 3 in. in diameter, and joins the main exhaust from the low-pressure ahead turbine, which latter is connected direct to the condenser.

The main exhaust trunk is a rectangular box built up of four plates with flanges, and well stayed internally, as shown in the photograph reproduced in Plate XXV. This construction was adopted as it enabled the trunk to be taken to pieces easily, to allow the turbine-casing under it to be lifted close up to the bend of the exhaust connection into the condenser. The bend is of steel plates riveted, and to this bend the astern exhaust is connected. Some idea is suggested of the size of this exhaust by the engravings on Plate XXVI., and the opening, it may be said, is 10 ft. 6 in. by 15 ft. 6 in. Copper expansion-pieces are fitted between the exhaust-bend and the sliding-plate on the transverse bulkheads which separate the engine-room from the condenser-room. This expansion connection allows for vertical rise, or athwartship play, due either to expansion or vibration of the ship's structure. On the after side of this plate there is another copper expansion-piece, connecting to the exhaust branch of the main condenser.

At the steam inlet on each turbine there is a strainer, the body of which is of cast steel fitted with a cartridge of perforated brass.

To enable the pressure in the successive stages of expansion within each turbine to be ascertained gauges have been fitted on all turbines ; but instead of a separate gauge being adopted for each stage of expansion, there are only two in each turbine, each fitted with a three or a four-way cock, so that by

F

CIRCULATING PUMPS FOR MAIN CONDENSERS.

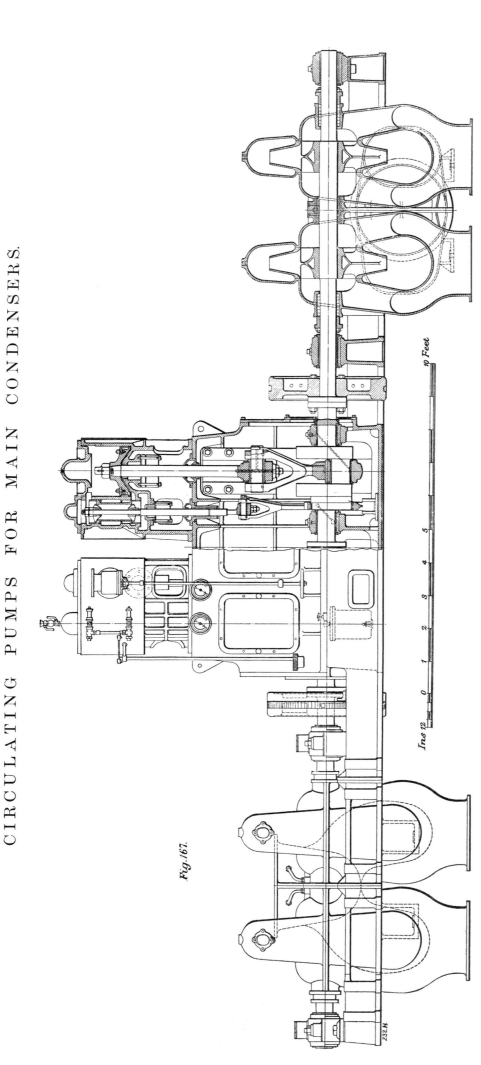

Fig. 167.

Ins 12   0   1   2   3   4   5   10 Feet

232H

turning a handle the pressure at each stage of expansion can be indicated on the gauge-dial.

THE CONDENSING PLANT: FROM EXHAUST STEAM TO FEED WATER.

There are two main condensers fitted in a separate compartment abaft the main turbine-rooms. The cooling surface in each is about 41,500 square feet. As shown in the engravings on Plate XXVI. the shell of each condenser is built up of steel plates, with gun-metal ends, while sight-holes and examination-doors are fitted. The tube-plates, which were made by Messrs. Vivian and Sons, are of unusual size. The tubes are ¾ in. in external diameter, and 18 W.G. thick. Each condenser is fitted with the Harris Anderson patent condensertube protector, already described in ENGINEERING, vol. lxxxi., page 380. The circulating-water inlets, of which there are two in each condenser, are 32 in. in diameter. The water is directed to pass through the lower nest of tubes, and returns through the upper nest, where it is discharged overboard through large gun-metal valves on the ship's skin.

The main circulating pumping-plant, supplied by Messrs. W. H. Allen, Son, and Co., Limited,

Bedford, is, up to the time of writing, the largest plant of its type afloat, and consists of four of Messrs. Allen's single - cylinder high - speed forced-lubrication engines and eight of their well-known "Conqueror" type of centrifugal pumps. These pumps are arranged in pairs, each pair having a suction branch 22 in. in diameter, and uniting into one common discharge branch 32 in. in diameter. The engines are arranged in duplicate, so that the main pumping machinery consists of two sets, each set with two single-cylinder engines driving two pairs of pumps. These arrangements are all shown on the part section and part elevation above (Fig. 167), from which it will be seen that by means of a loose coupling the engines can be coupled together if so desired. Weights have been provided whereby counterbalancing has been carried out to a remarkable degree of accuracy.

The cylinder and valve-chest are in one casting, the metal being of a specially tough and close-grained quality. The diameter of each cylinder is 18 in. with a 10-in. stroke, and each engine is capable of developing 350 brake horse power when running at 300 revolutions per minute, being supplied with steam at the stop-valve of 160 lb. pressure per square inch, and exhausting against a back pres-

sure of 10 lb. per square inch. The distribution of the steam is effected by means of piston-valves. The cylinder casting is well insulated with silicate cotton, the whole being covered with burnished sheet-steel, and supplied with the necessary draincocks and relief-valves.

Between the cylinder and trunk is a substantial distance-piece, which is cast solid with the cylinder at the bottom end, and by means of which the cylinder is bolted to the trunk. This distance-piece is provided with ample openings, enabling easy access to be made to the stuffing-boxes and glands of the rods, all of which are packed with metallic packing of the United States type. The cast-iron trunk upon which the cylinders are bolted is machined at the top and bottom flanges, and carries the guide-faces for the cross-heads, these faces being machined square with the top of the trunk. As will be seen, this trunk is fitted with three doors, which can be removed for inspection and for making any necessary adjustments to the working parts, and also with bosses and removable caps for fixing in the gear for indicating the engines. Where the rods pass through the trunk special glands of Messrs. Allen's own design are provided; these oil-glands are the outcome of experience and numerous tests, and are so arranged that it is

impossible for oil to work up from the crankchamber into the cylinder, or for water to find its way down to the crank-chamber. The bottom flanges of the trunk are bolted to a cast-iron boxsection bed-plate, in which are arranged the oilreservoirs, filters, pipes, and oil-pumps, each of these being in duplicate. The oil is forced through the system of pipes to all the working parts and bearing surfaces by means of a valveless pump driven from the engine eccentric.

To still further ensure the easy manipulation of these engines the steam and oil pressure-gauges and levers for the stop-valves and for regulating the drain-cocks are all fixed at the front of the engine-trunk, while close at hand on the bed-plate are placed the valves for regulating the oil pressure. Cast at each end of the bed-plate is an extension, which is bolted to a similar extension of the pumpcasing. This extension carries an outer bearing for the pump-spindle, and also the barring gear for each fly-wheel. Tachometers are fitted to each engine.

The main pump-casings and impellers are of gunmetal, the casings being 1⁹⁄₁₆ in. thick, and the diameter of the impellers 42 in. The pump-spindle is of forged bronze, carried in bearings external to the pump-casing; where it passes through the casing, stuffing-boxes are provided with gun-metal glands and adequate oiling arrangements.

The main air-pump installation consists of four sets of wet-air pumps, and four sets of dry-air pumps. The wet-air pumps, made by Messrs. G. and J. Weir, Limited, are of the beam twin type, each set having two steam-cylinders, and two pump-barrels. Two sets of pumps draw from each condenser. The dry-air pumps, also made by Messrs. G. and J. Weir, are of the twin enclosed type, there being two steam-cylinders and two pump valves in each set. Two sets of both wet and dry-air pumps draw from each condenser. A section of the dry-air pumps is given in Fig. 168, annexed. These dry-air pumps have 7-in. steam cylinders with piston valves, and 24-in. air cylinders adapted for a 7-in. stroke. The air-chambers, of gun-

discharge sides. Each pump is also fitted with a direct steam connection. The water is drawn by these pumps from the hotwell tanks, and is discharged through the main-feed filters, made by the Harris Patent Filter Company, and already fully illustrated and described in ENGINEERING of August 2 last, page 161. From the filters the water passes through the surface feed-heater, made by Messrs. G. and J. Weir. In this heater the water enters at the bottom and passes through the tubes, which are vertical, the exhaust from the auxiliaries being circulated on the outside of the tubes. The exhaust steam therefore gives up to the feed-water its heat. In so doing it is condensed, and returns as water to the hotwell tanks. All the auxiliaries, with the exception of the turbine-generators, exhaust into this heater. This surface-

Weir, and are of the duplex type. They are connected to either range of feed-discharge pipes, as are also the two sets of auxiliary feed-pumps in the boiler-rooms. The distributing valves for the boilers are placed on the bulkheads at a convenient position in each stokehold.

THE BOILERS.

There are twenty-three double-ended boilers and two single-ended boilers, the collective firegrate area being about 4060 square feet, and the heating surface about 159,000 square feet. In each double-ended boiler there are eight furnaces, and in each single-ended boiler four furnaces, thus making 192 furnaces in all. These furnaces are of the Morison suspension type, and were made by the Leeds

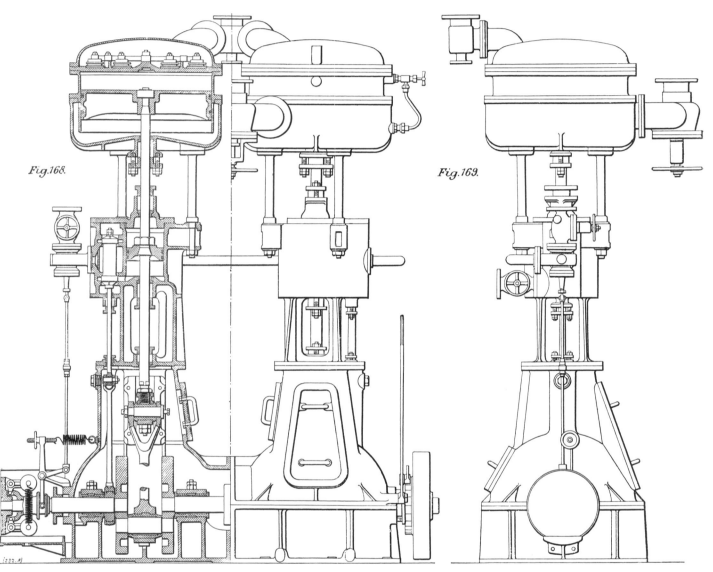

FIGS. 168 AND 169. DRY-AIR PUMPS FOR MAIN CONDENSERS.

metal, are above the steam cylinder, and the air passes into the barrel above the buckets through round openings, and is forced through the head-valves on the up-stroke of the pump. Increase of temperature is checked by a small supply of circulating water which passes through the air chamber.

Two hotwell tanks are situated under the main condensers, and are arranged to be worked together or independently. Four hotwell pumps by Messrs. Weir are placed at the after end of the low-pressure room, and are thus in close proximity to the hotwell tanks from which they draw. The arrangement is such that any pump can draw from any tank, and any pump can discharge to either heater on the port or starboard side. The steam supply to the pumps is controlled by a float in each hotwell tank, which operates a control-cock taking the steam from the auxiliary range. The outlet from this cock passes on to another control-cock regulated by the float in the direct-contact heater. The outlet from this cock is connected to the steam-inlet valve on the pumps. The pumps are thus controlled on both the suction and

heater was fitted so that full advantage could be taken of the heat in the exhaust without the disadvantage of oil being admitted into the feed system. The feed-water then passes either to the direct-contact feed-heater, or direct to the feed-pumps in the boiler-room.

The exhaust from the turbo-generators passes into the direct-contact heater, as does also the vapour from the feed-make-up evaporators. The direct-contact heaters—two in number—are also by Messrs. G. and J. Weir, and are of their usual type, the exhaust steam mixing directly with the feed-water, and thus further raising its temperature.

The water next passes to the feed-pump suctions in the engine and boiler-rooms, and is discharged into the main-feed ranges. There are four sets of main-feed pumps in the engine-room, and the feed-discharge pipes are so arranged that each boiler-room can be fed by one of these pumps through an independent pipe. The auxiliary-feed and ash-ejector pumps, of which there are four—one in each boiler-room—were made by Messrs. G. and J.

Forge Company. There is a separate combustion-chamber to each furnace, and the construction of these and of the boiler-shells is well shown in the engravings on Plate XXVII. The boiler shell-plates and stays are of high-tensile silicon steel of from 36 to 40 tons per square inch, supplied by Messrs. J. Spencer and Sons, Newburn.

Appended are the average tests of the shell-plates and butt-straps which are supplied for the boilers of the Mauretania :—

Shell-Plates :

Tensile strength ...	...	36.937 tons per sq in.
Elongation ...	...	20.905 per cent. in 10 in.
Elastic limit ...	...	21.85 tons per sq. in.

Butt-Straps :

Tensile strength ...	...	37.122 tons per sq. in.
Elongation	...	21.27 per cent. in 10 in.
Elastic limit ...	...	21.38 tons per sq. in.

Silicon steel was adopted after considerable experimental work, undertaken by the makers in order to satisfy the requirements of the Board of Trade, Lloyd's, and other registry societies. The result was to greatly reduce the weight of the boilers. The front and back ends are, however, of ordinary mild steel. The uptakes are of the usual construction, built of steel plate, there being an inner and an outer casing, with an air space between. The boilers are fitted throughout with Silley's patent

from 225 to 450 revolutions per minute. No-voltage and overload automatic releases are fitted to these controllers, giving complete protection to the motors under all conditions. When running at the lowest speed the approximate output of air

cubic feet of air per minute against a water pressure of 1 in. when running at a speed of 900 revolutions per minute. The discs for these fans are also of special brass sheeting. The motors are of the four-pole series-wound type, and are each cap-

FIG. 172. UPTAKE FOR SIX BOILERS.

air-tight smoke-box door. As will be seen from the illustrations already mentioned, the uptakes are divided, forming a passage-way, which allow the whole of the main steam and auxiliary pipes and feed-pipes to be carried through the centre of the ship. With the exception of the steam stop-valves, which are of cast steel, all the mountings are made of gun-metal, the usual feed-check, scum, and blow-down valves being fitted. The uptakes are illustrated on the present page and on the two-page Plate CI., on which also is given an engraving of the completed boilers in the Wallsend boiler-erecting shop.

There are four funnels, one from each boiler-room. They are elliptical in cross-section, and measure externally 23 ft. 7 in. by 16 ft. 7 in. ; the height from the base line of the ship is 153 ft. On Plate XXVIII. there is an illustration of the funnels in the erecting-yard at the Wallsend Works, and on the same plate an engraving from a photograph of one of the stokeholds.

Howden's system of draught is fitted, the fans being electrically driven. These fans, thirty-two in number, were made by Messrs. W. H. Allen, Son, and Co., and are arranged in pairs, each pair being driven by a motor, also made by Messrs. W. H. Allen, Son, and Co. The fan-impellers are of the single-inlet type, being 66 in. in diameter, and each capable of delivering 33,000 cubic feet of air per minute against a water pressure of $3\frac{1}{2}$ in. on the discharge side when running at 450 revolutions per minute. These impellers are made of brass-plate of special composition to resist corrosion, the bosses being of steel. The motors, of which there are sixteen, are of the four-pole continuous-current type, completely enclosed, and are each capable of developing 50 brake horse-power at a speed of 450 revolutions per minute when supplied with current at a pressure of 110 volts. Owing to the somewhat high temperature in which these motors have to work, a very ingenious arrangement is provided whereby they may be cooled. Situated between the motor at the commutator end and one of the 66-in. fans is an auxiliary fan with separate casing, the disc being 48 in. in diameter, and made of sheet brass. The discharge is connected to the underside of the motor end-plate, the air being circulated round the commutator and armature, and leaving at the upper opposite end. Each fan is provided with a water-gauge and tachometer. Figs. 176 and 177 on the opposite page show sections of motor and fan. The controllers for these motors are also of Messrs. Allen's manufacture, and are capable of regulating the speed in equal increments by field variation

from each fan is 17,000 cubic feet per minute against a water pressure of 1 in.

The fan-room is well ventilated by eight of Messrs. Allen's single-inlet fans, 21 in. in diameter. Each fan is driven by a motor of the totally-enclosed type, and is capable of delivering 1000

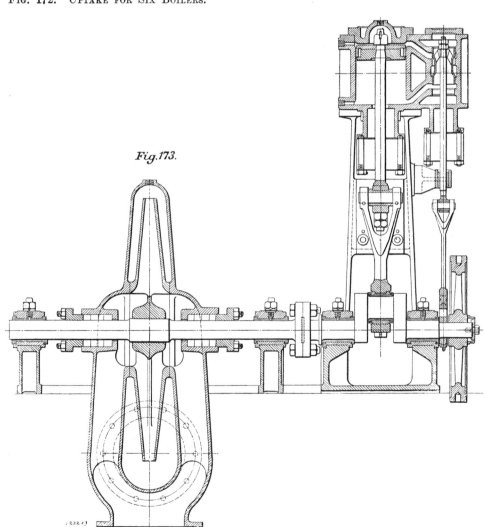

FIG. 173. THE CIRCULATING PUMPS FOR THE AUXILIARY CONDENSERS.

able of developing normally an output of 5 horse-power when supplied with current at a pressure of 110 volts and running at a speed of 900 revolutions per minute. Each motor is supplied with a controlling panel consisting of a double-pole quick-break switch, tubular fuses, and starting and regulating

ELECTRICALLY-DRIVEN FANS FOR BOILER DRAUGHT

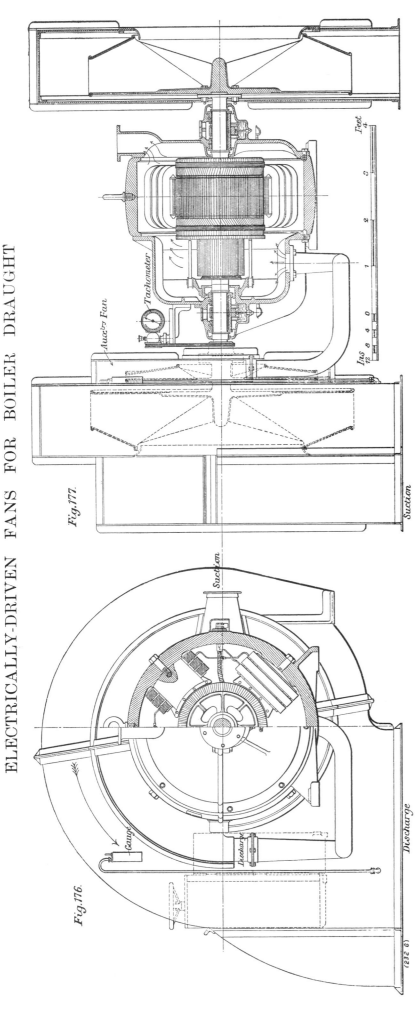

Fig. 176.

Fig. 177.

resistances, the whole being self-contained and mounted upon a panel suitable for erection on the bulkhead. As shown in the boiler-room elevation, the air-trunk shafts are fitted with cowls of the ordinary type.

There are eight See's ash-ejectors fitted, two in each boiler-room, placed at the forward and after end; eight Crompton's ash-hoists are also fitted; these are placed at the wings in the middle of the rooms, two to each room.

In all boiler-rooms the bunkers are at the side, but in addition there is forward of No. 1 boiler-room an athwartship reserve bunker.

AUXILIARY CONDENSERS AND MISCELLANEOUS PUMPS.

There are two auxiliary condensers of the Morison "Contraflo" type, which have already been fully illustrated and described in ENGINEERING, vol. lxxx., pages 471 and 475. As in the main condensers, the tubes are $\frac{3}{8}$ in. in external diameter by 18 W.G. thick. These condensers are capable of dealing with the exhaust from all auxiliaries and with the turbo-generator exhaust, when it is not utilised for the surface or direct-contact heaters. The auxiliary circulating pumps, one for each condenser, were made by Messrs. W. H. Allen, Son, and Co., Limited, Bedford; they are of the single-cylinder open type (Fig. 173, page 36). The cylinder is in each case 7 in. in diameter, with a 10-in. stroke, and is direct-coupled to a gun-metal centrifugal pump with suction and delivery branches 10 in. in diameter. The pump-spindle is of forged bronze, carried in bearings external to the pump-casing, an arrangement similar to the main sets. The disc is of gun-metal, 36 in. in diameter.

The auxiliary air-pump is by Messrs. G. and J. Weir, single-acting, and known as their "Mono-type." There is one for each condenser. The auxiliary air-pump discharges the water through a Harris auxiliary feed-filter, and from thence the water passes to the hotwell tanks.

EVAPORATING PLANT.

The evaporating plant was made by the Liverpool Engineering and Condenser Company, Limited, there being two complete sets for the ship. Each set consists of one evaporator for the production of distilled water, and two for feed-make-up purposes, the two latter being arranged to work compound or single effect. The evaporator shells are of rolled naval brass, the ends being of gun-metal. There are to each set of these evaporators two distilling condensers, the shells of which are of galvanised steel.

In connection with each set of evaporators there are the following pumps:—One brine-pump of the single-cylinder double-acting type; one evaporator feed-pump of the duplex type, and one circulating pump for the distilling condensers, also of the duplex type; all of which were made by the Liverpool Engineering Company.

THE VENTILATION OF ENGINE AND BOILER-ROOMS.

For ventilating the engine-room there are ten 21-in. Sirocco fans, fixed to ventilators in which a louvre is arranged, so that the fans can draw from the upper portion of the ventilator and discharge to the lower portion. Under go-ahead conditions, however, these fans are not in use, the louvres being then opened and natural draught resorted to. For discharging heated air from a portion of the machinery spaces, where natural circulation is deficient, there are six 30-in. Sirocco fans fitted. These discharge the heated air up the engine casings and upcasts. Four 15-in. Sirocco fans are also fitted for drawing the heated air from below the engine-room floors. These also discharge into the engine casing.

As before mentioned, for ventilating the boiler-rooms the air from the downcast trunks at the wings of the boiler-rooms is induced, by means of screens, to pass across the stoking-platform before going to the inlets of the forced-draught fans, the heated air from the boiler-tops passing up the funnel casing.

ELECTRIC MOTORS.

The turning and lifting-gear motors for turbines, to which reference has already been made, are of the 4-pole semi-enclosed reversible type, compound-wound, arranged to give a starting torque of twice the normal, the necessary controllers for operating these motors being placed close to them.

TABLE XIV.—*Particulars of Electric Motors in Machinery Spaces.*

Motor.	Brake Horse-Power.	No. Off.	Maker.	Position in Ship.
Turning gear ...	30	4	Lancashire Dynamo & Motor Co.	Aft end of H.P. and L.P. turbine rooms
Lifting ,, ...	30	6	,,	At main deck level
75-in. sluice valve ,,	12	2	,,	On valve
60-in. ,, ,,	12	2	W. H. Allen, Son & Co., Limited	,,
Stokehold fans ...	50	16	,,	In fan-rooms
Fan-room ventilating fans	5	8	,,	,,
Engine-room ventilating fans	4	10	Lancashire Dynamo & Motor Co.	On ventilators
,, ,,	25	6	,,	Main and lower deck levels
,, ,,	1	4	,,	Main deck level

The 1-brake-horse-power and the 4-brake-horse-power ventilating-fan motors are of the shunt-wound semi-enclosed type, starting and speed-regulating rheostats, with automatic no-load and overload release quick break. The main switch and fuses of the Universal type are fitted. The 25-brake-horse-power ventilating fans are of the shunt-wound semi-enclosed type, fitted with controllers consisting of starters, interlocked shunt speed-regulators and double-pole switches, the switch gear being mounted on enamelled slate slabs fixed in a ventilated iron case having a hinge door for access, the operating handle alone being exposed.

The sluice-valve motors are of the semi-enclosed compound-wound type and are reversible; the controllers for operating them are placed inside the starting-pedestal.

Table XIV. on the preceding page gives a list of the motors in the machinery department.

AUXILIARY PUMPS.

The fire-pump was made by Messrs. G. and J. Weir, and is of the duplex type. The sanitary pumps, of which there are two, are also by Messrs. Weir, and are of the same type and size as the fire-pumps. They are illustrated in Fig. 178, annexed, and the dimensions are given in the table of auxiliary machinery on page 28. The fresh-water and condensed-water pumps are of the duplex type, and were made by Messrs. Carruthers, of Glasgow. Both pumps are arranged to draw from the fresh-water tanks aft, and also from the reserve fresh-water tanks in the double bottom. The fresh-water pump discharges through a filter, and from there the water is directed forward, aft, or amidships. The condensed-water pump also discharges forward or amidships, but can also discharge to the hotwell for feed-make-up purposes.

THE MACHINERY IN THE SHIP.

The engravings on Plates XXV. to XXXII. are from photographs of the machinery, and these not only afford some indication of the immense units in the ship, but suggest the great thought and experience which were involved in the disposition of the mechanism, in order to ensure, as far as possible, accessibility and supervision. The view, Fig. 179 on Plate XXIX., shows the starting-platform looking towards the port side. A view of the various wheels, levers, and gauges appears on page 32, but, as it was taken in the shop, it does not adequately convey the exact state of the case. This starting-platform is on the turbine-room level, and the engineer has in front an inner wheel, shown to the left, for working the manœuvring valves, an outer wheel for the main high-pressure regulating-valve, and beyond, although not seen in the photograph, are the levers for the sluice-valves, &c. The gauges record the pressures, vacuum, &c., and the larger dial shown is for indicating approximately the revolutions.

As this is the alpha of the machinery, so the photograph on the same plate, Fig. 180, is the omega, since it shows the shaft alleyway with the propeller shaft. This view illustrates also the boss-ing out of the ship. The line shaft is 26 in. in ex-ternal diameter and 10 in. in internal diameter, the couplings, well shown in the engraving, being 35 in. in diameter by 4¾ in. thick. It will be noted that the bearings are of great length.

On Plate XXX. there is a view of the turbo-generators, which are described on page 20. The turbines are of the high-pressure type, and exhaust into Weir's direct-contact heater. There are four sets, two of which are included in our engravings, while beyond may be seen one of the switchboards, of which a description is given on page 21. To the left of the engraving are shown the tops of the steam-cylinders of the circulating-pumps.

The other view on Plate XXX. is from a photo-graph taken at the after end of the low-pressure turbine-room looking athwart the ship. To the right is the bulkhead separating the turbine-room from the condenser-room, and in the distance the longitudinal bulkhead dividing the high-pressure from the low-pressure-turbine room. To the left is the connection between the exhaust port of the low-pressure and the exhaust bend into the main condenser. When it is desired to raise the rotor of the low-pressure turbine, this cast-iron portion of the exhaust is dismantled, the forward part being placed flat on the casing, while the other three parts are held in slings abaft the turbine. The bottom platform is over the shaft rotated by the

low-pressure turbine. Notice may be taken of the very heavy stiffness of the bulkhead, and there may be seen, although, perhaps, indistinctly, the expan-sion-joint in the athwartship bulkhead, where the exhaust bend passes through to the condenser-room.

The view, Fig. 183 on Plate XXXI., is taken on the top of the boiler, at No. 2 starboard aft boiler. This indicates the roominess of the platforms, and it may be stated, also, that the temperature is comparatively low. The various pipe connections and the valve from one of the boilers can be seen.

The other illustration on Plate XXXI. is some-

FIG. 178. WASH DECK AND SANITARY PUMPS.

what unique. It is a view taken from the platform over the turbines looking upwards to the skylight. We have already pointed out that the height from the platform level to the top of the skylight is 79 ft.

On Plate XXXII. there is given a view in the main turbine-room looking forward. This, how-ever, conveys but a vague idea either of the extent of the engine-room or of the great size of the tur-bines; indeed, it is impossible to get such a photo-graph. The illustration, however, is instructive. It shows one of the main bearings, and one of the lifting-gear brackets with the two columns for guiding this bracket during the process of lifting either the upper part of the casing or the rotor. The lifting-shaft, which is screwed at its upper end, is also seen. To the left of the engraving are

several of the auxiliary engines, principally pumps, with their steam connections.

Fig. 186, Plate XXXII., gives a view in the pump-room. In the centre is the port inner shaft, which is operated by the low-pressure turbine. The engines for driving the main circulating-pumps are shown on the higher platform to the left of the engraving, while below are the pump inlet-valves. To the right of the engraving are the main air-pumps, and beyond them the longitudinal bulk-head, which divides the pump-room illustrated, from the starboard pump-room, which exactly corresponds.

These photographs, however, as we have already stated, do not convey a clear idea of the magnitude of the equipment, and in our description we have only succeeded in suggesting to the thoughtful reader the reflection that the experience, ingenuity, and thoughtfulness in carrying out the undertaking were equal to the courage and responsibility in-volved in guaranteeing the results. The whole pro-fession will, we are sure, associate themselves with us in congratulating the contractors upon achieving a success worthy of their efforts.

The photographs reproduced in connection with the description of the ship have been taken by Messrs. Bedford, Lemere, and Co., London, Mr. William Parry, of South Shields, and Mr. J. S. Dodds, staff photographer of Messrs. Swan, Hunter, and Wigham Richardson, Limited.

THE AUXILIARY MACHINERY.

Much of the auxiliary machinery fitted is common to both the Lusitania and the Mauretania, and as our issue of August 2, 1907, and the reprint of all the Lusitania articles, are out of print, we have thought it well to reproduce here descriptions and illustrations of such of these auxiliaries as have only been referred to in the preceding pages.

THE PASSENGER HOISTS.

A feature in the arrangement for the comfort of passengers is the complete equipment of lifts for passengers, baggage service, &c., by Messrs. R. Waygood and Co., Limited, London. In all eleven lifts and hoists have been installed by this firm, all worked by electric current supplied by the ship's generating plant at a pressure of 110 to 120 volts.

Of these hoists, we illustrate on pages 39 and 40 (Figs. 187 to 193) the two passenger lifts running within the stair-well, which are probably the most in-

FIG. 187. ELECTRIC DRIVING-GEAR OF PASSENGER-HOIST.

teresting in the ship. These travel through a height of 36 ft. 3 in. between the main and boat-decks, opening on to the splendid vestibules, or halls, on each deck leading to the various public saloons or to the alleyways through the extensive ranges of cabins. The cars are constructed in polished mahogany, and are each guided by two round steel guides attached to the staircase framing. Special safety apparatus on the cars come into operation on the failure of the lifting-ropes. This apparatus has a positive action, and is not dependent on springs. Each car is raised by steel cables, which pass through the double dome roof of the staircase, over top sheaves, and thence horizontally to the winding gear, which is fixed at the boat-deck house level (Fig. 188). The counterbalance weights travel in a trunkway, forming a ventilator, the counterweights being guided by round steel guides attached by suitable brackets to the trunkway (Fig. 188).

The lifting-gear is clearly illustrated by Fig. 187. The cables for each lift are two in number, of best crucible-steel wire, attached to the winding-drum.

Two independent ropes are also attached to the drum and connected to the counterbalance weights already referred to, to ensure a positive drive. The winding-gear is of the worm-and-wheel type, the worm being of steel, cut from the solid, while the wheel has a centre of cast-iron with a phosphor-bronze tooth-ring, into which the teeth are hobbed. The worm and wheel are enclosed in a cast-iron box, forming an oil bath. The worm-shaft is fitted with special adjustable thrust-bearings in order to reduce friction, and the winding drum is securely keyed to the worm-wheel shaft. This winding-drum is turned and grooved with right and left-hand spiral grooves, in which the lifting-cables coil. The brake-gear is of the electric mechanical type, actuated by a magnet, so arranged that the brake is released when current is switched on, and is applied automatically on the current being cut off by the control.

The magnetically-operated controller is worked from the car by means of a special car-switch having an "up," "down," and "stop" position. The main controller consists of a panel, upon which are mounted an "up" and "down" circuit-breaker, each operated by a magnet, and a rheostat actuated by a solenoid, and provided with air-retardation. Each of the two circuit-breakers is fitted with a magnetic blow-out, and the contacts, which are of copper, are so arranged that although the current is interrupted at four points, the actual breaking is performed in the field of this blow-out, thus readily disrupting the arc and preventing destructive arcing. The rheostat cuts out the main resistance (which is in series with the armature at starting) in sixteen steps, and is connected to a resistance frame fixed behind the controller panel, and constructed of fireproof materials. The car-switches are of cylindrical type, with a movable self-centring handle, so that in the event of the attendant releasing the handle for any purpose, it at once flies to the "off" position, cutting off the controller and stopping the lift. The controller is also fitted with a special

type of automatic cut-off switch, positively driven from the drum-shaft of the machine, and arranged so that, should the attendant omit to switch off the current when approaching the top or bottom levels, the corresponding automatic switch will come into action and will stop the lift before any damage is done.

Each car is fitted with Waygood's patent slack-cable switch. In the event of the car or balance-weight, while descending, meeting with any obstruction to cause the ropes to become slack, this switch is immediately opened and cuts off current from the machine by causing the controller to come to its "off" position, simultaneously applying the brake, and, of course, stopping the lift.

In order to afford security against the lift entrance doors being left open, or inadvertently opened, these are all fitted with automatic locks and electric contacts, arranged so that any door can only be opened when the lift-car is opposite it. Nor can the car be moved away until the doors are closed. An electric bell and indicator are provided in each car, with a push at each deck, to enable the car to be called by passengers.

TABLE XV.—*Capacity of Passenger and Baggage Hoists.*

Load.	Speed.	Travel.	Motors.
	ft. per min.		B.H.-P.
Two passenger lifts :			
10 cwt.	150	From main deck to top deck, 36 ft. 3 in.	8
Two baggage-lifts :—			
40 cwt.	100	From orlop-deck to shelter-deck	15
Two service-lifts :—			
10 cwt.	100	From lower deck to shelter-deck	5
Three food-lifts :—			
2 cwt.	60	10 ft. to 11 ft.	1½
Two ash-hoists :—			
2 cwt.	200	About 60 ft.	3¼

The two baggage lifts, fitted in a convenient position to the baggage-holds, are each designed to carry a load of 2 tons, and are arranged as shown on page 41, (Figs. 194 to 196). The winding gear is of the worm-and-wheel type, somewhat similar to that described for the passenger lifts, but the drive is a friction one. The lifting cables are attached at each end at the top of a trunkway, and they pass around sheaves attached to the cage and on the balance-weight, being led to the "V" lifting wheel by suitable diverting sheaves, as shown by Fig. 196. The cars are constructed of steel angle and channel framework, and are guided by steel channels on each side, the counterbalance weights being guided by round steel guides attached to the trunkway. The control of these baggage lifts is very similar to that already described for the passenger lifts, but instead of a car-switch being fitted, sets of "up," "down," and "stop" buttons are fixed in the cars, and also on each deck-level.

There are, further, two 10-cwt. service lifts, illustrated on page 41 (Figs. 197 to 200), the general construction and working being similar to the two baggage lifts. There are also three small service lifts for carrying food, as well as two electric friction hoist-gears for raising ashes from the stokehold.

THE REFRIGERATING MACHINERY.

Two complete and independent installations of refrigerating machinery are fitted on board the ship, one for the preservation of the ship's provisions, and the other for the carriage of perishable cargo. Both have been constructed by the Liverpool Refrigeration Company, Limited, and must be described together. The ship's provision-machine is situate near the forward end of the turbine engine-room on the main-deck level, and the chambers on the lower deck, port and starboard sides at some distance forward of the machine. These chambers have been insulated with granulated cork, in combination with specially-treated damp and rot-proof paper, with linings of white-pine boards. The chambers are divided into compartments for beef, mutton, poultry and game, bacon, milk, fruits and vegetables, and ice, and the wine and

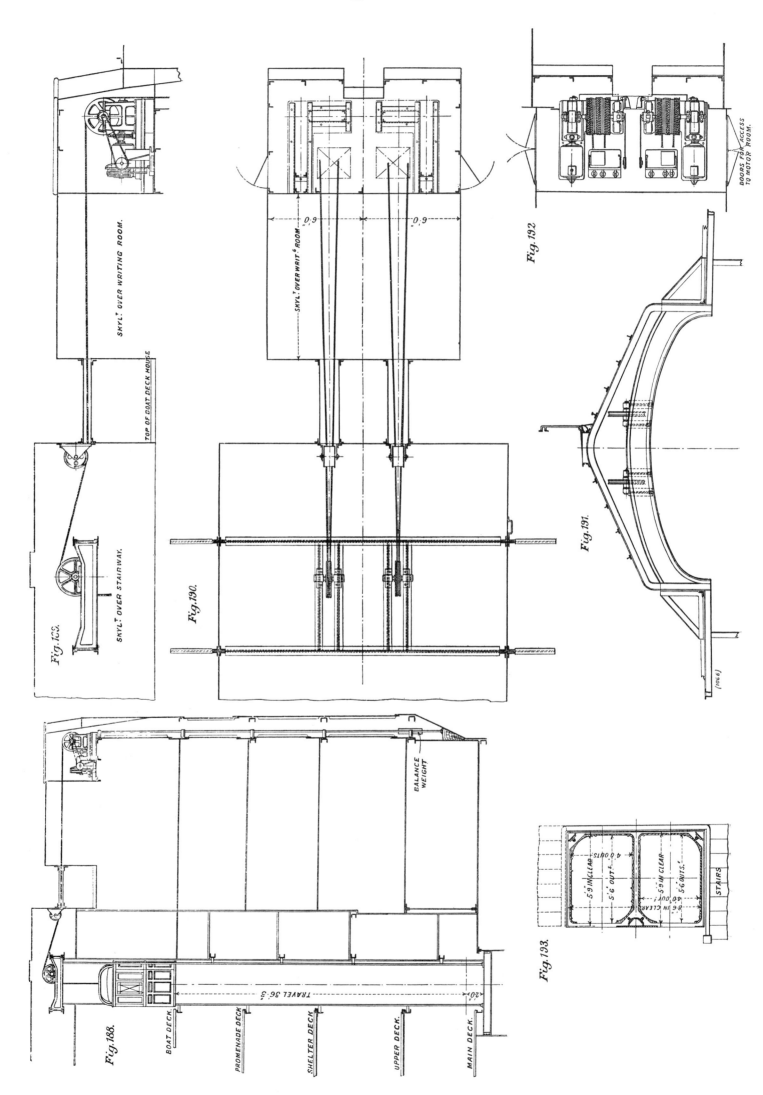

ELECTRIC PASSENGER HOIST.

CONSTRUCTED BY MESSRS. WAYGOOD AND CO., LIMITED, ENGINEERS, LONDON.

Fig. 188.

Fig. 189.

Fig. 190.

Fig. 191.

Fig. 192.

Fig. 193.

BAGGAGE AND SERVICE ELECTRIC HOIST.

CONSTRUCTED BY MESSRS. WAYGOOD AND CO., LIMITED, ENGINEERS, LONDON.

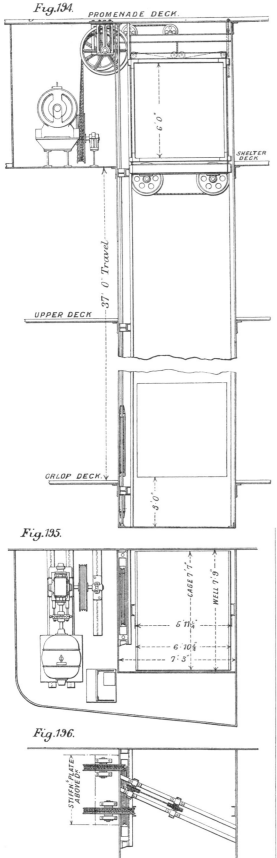

Fig. 194.   PROMENADE DECK.

Fig. 195.

Fig. 196.

Fig. 197.   PROMENADE DECK.

Fig. 198.

Fig. 199.

PLAN OF TOP GEAR

SECTION A. B.

Fig. 200.

SUSPENSION SHEAVES

beer and spirit-chambers are also lightly insulated and cooled to a suitable temperature.

The chambers have a total capacity inside the insulation of about 13,000 cubic feet, and, in addition, there is a large cold larder on the upper deck, besides cold boxes in the first and second-class bars and still-room. There is also an installation for the supply of cooled water for drinking and other purposes. In this connection every possible requirement has been thought out and arranged, not only for the preservation of the perishable provisions in bulk, but also for the convenience of the catering and culinary departments generally.

The installation is of the carbonic-anhydride type, illustrated on pages 42 and 43. It consists of a horizontal compound duplex machine, mounted on a cast-iron box-bed, which is divided by a longitudinal bulkhead into two portions, each of which contains an independent set of gas-condenser coils. These coils are of special soft-iron lapwelded tube, galvanised on the outside. The compound steam-cylinders drive from their tail-rods two horizontal double-acting CO_2 compressors. The crank-shaft runs in four bearings, and is in two portions, coupled in the centre and with a distance-plate between the faces of the coupling. A neat arrangement of steam-valves is fitted, so that the engine can work compound, or independently as two high-pressure engines. By taking out the coupling-bolts and distance-plate each side of the machine can be run quite independently of the other. Cross-connections are provided, so that either compressor can deliver into either or both gas-condensers, and the machine is the full equivalent of two independent machines combined on one base.

The evaporator is of the vertical type, the shell enclosing two independent nests of circular coils, one coupled to each compressor, with cross-connections, the same as for the condensers. Two horizontal duplex brass-fitted brine-pumps circulate the brine, and a third smaller and independent pump is provided for the special duty of pumping the brine supply to the cold larder and refrigerators in the saloon-bars and other places independently of the main pumps. The whole brine distribution forms an entirely closed system. The brine is drawn from the evaporator and delivered into a distributing header, with valves and connections leading to the various pipe sections in the cold rooms. After passing through these the brine returns to a similar collecting-header, and thence back to the evaporator, there being no open brine-tank whatever. All the chambers are cooled with galvanised brine piping, arranged to suit various temperatures required in the several compartments, each of which is regulated independently of any other. The installation is, we believe, the largest and most complete of its kind.

The cargo-refrigeration plant is situate on the shelter-deck, starboard side forward, just abaft the forward funnel hatch. There is an extensive range of cold chambers on the orlop decks forward. There are six chambers in all, the largest being divided by longitudinal central bulkheads. They have all been fitted for the carriage of frozen meats and poultry, cheese, bacon, butter, and fruits, and particularly for the carriage of chilled beef. The compartments are quite independent of each other, and can be supplied with brine for cooling at any temperature suitable to the cargo carried. The brine circulates through galvanised wrought-iron piping, and the chambers are fitted with meat rails and removable hooks for hanging chilled meat, and also with removable side tables for the stowage of forequarters. As the machinery is at a considerable distance from the chambers, a brine distribution-house has been fitted on the shelter-deck near to the chambers, from which the regulation and distribution is controlled.

The machinery in this case also is of the carbonic-anhydride type, and special care has been taken to ensure silent running. The plant is in duplicate throughout, and is electrically driven. There are two horizontal gas-compressors, each direct coupled to a powerful electro-motor, shown in Fig. 205, page 43. These motors have been specially designed and constructed for the purpose by Messrs. Boothroyd, Hyslop, and Co., of Bootle, and are so arranged, by means of shunt regulation, that they can run at any desired speed from 40 to 110 revolutions per minute. The speed can be regulated with absolute ease by the turning of one hand-wheel only, the motor running at the same speed as the compressor, and no gear-wheels whatever are used. The compressors—Webb and others' patents—embody several new features, which it will be of interest to mention. The outer casing,

G

of soft cast steel, encloses and supports a liner of hard close-grained cast iron, which forms the working bore of the cylinder, but is easily withdrawable from either end of the casing. Two forged-steel headers, carrying the valves, are bolted, one to each end of the casing. The one at the front end is fitted with the stuffing-box and gland, and that at the back end with the plug-cover. The piston is fitted with metallic packing-rings of special metal, very accurately turned and finished, and held in place by a patent junk-ring head, which, while doing away with all screws, keys and pins, absolutely secures the rings in place, so that they cannot get adrift as long as the piston is within the cylinder-bore. The gland is also fitted with a particular form of metallic packing, and no leather cups are used. The valves and seats are of special hard steel; the valves lift vertically, are of large area, and have no springs whatever. The compressors are constructed so as to be capable of long continuous runs without stop; the absence of leather cups entirely does away with the necessity for frequent renewals of the packing.

The gas-condensers are independent, are of the vertical type, and consist of soft lap-welded coils of wrought iron, galvanised on the outside, and contained in galvanised wrought-steel shells. The evaporators are similarly constructed to the condensers, ample facilities being provided for easy access to the coils for cleaning.

Two high-lift Gwynne centrifugal pumps circulate the brine. These are direct coupled to variable-speed electro-motors, which are constructed by the same makers as the main motors, and are so arranged that the speed of each pump can be regulated to suit the resistance to be overcome, this resistance varying somewhat, according to the number of chambers in use, and the quantity of brine being circulated. We have already mentioned a large variety of goods that may have to be carried in the chambers, some frozen and others chilled. Frozen goods, of course, require brine at a low temperature for circulation through the cooling-pipes in the chambers, but for chilled beef, for example, brine at a temperature suitable for frozen goods is altogether too cold, and, if circulated, would rapidly freeze the quarters, especially those stowed nearest to the pipes. The temperature must be regulated with great accuracy. The same remark is also applicable to certain fruits and other chilled produce. A brine supply at an accurate and easily regulated temperature is, therefore, of great importance, and in the installation under review special means have been provided so that this can be secured. This warmer brine is circulated by an independent pump, and in the distribution-room mentioned above special duplex headers have been arranged so that either the coldest brine, or the warmer brine, can be supplied to the cooling-pipes in any one or more chambers, according to the cargo carried, whether chilled or frozen.

Webb and others' patent brine attemperator is illustrated in section in Fig. 204, page 42, and consists of a simple three-ported slide-valve, enclosed in a cast-iron casing, and attached to a screwed spindle with a hand-wheel, so that the movement of the valve over the ports can be accurately regulated as required. The valve is kept up to its face by a suitable coach-spring. A branch from the cold-brine supply main is coupled to one end of the valve-casing, and the return warmer-brine main is coupled to the other end, the mixed or attemperated brine escaping through the central port and pipe, which is connected to the warmer-brine pump. An overflow pipe is connected back to the evaporators.

In working the apparatus, the warmer-brine pump draws from the mixing or attempering valve-chamber, delivering to the headers already mentioned, thence through the pipes in the chilled chambers back to the attemperator, there to be mixed with any given proportion of the coldest brine necessary to lower its temperature to the required degree. A suitable and specially-constructed pyrometer indicates the temperature, both the valve-handle and thermometer being carried outside the insulated brine-room. The temperature can be regulated by means of the handle controlling the valve exactly as required, and the control is positive. The brine circulation generally, as in the provision plant, is an entirely closed circuit. There are no brine-tanks, except a small one for mixing brine in the first instance, for charging the machine, or for adding a little from time to time. Any little air or foul gas in the system is automatically disposed of

through a small vent-pipe carried outside from each evaporator. Though there are a large number of independent circuits, no trouble whatever is experienced in regulating each exactly as required. With the closed circuit there is no difficulty with air-locks or aeration of the brine, and the system is surprisingly simple, clean, and easy to work.

In both the cargo and provision installations the cold parts of the plants are not individually lagged, but are placed together in a well-insulated chamber or brine-room, where they are always accessible, without the necessity of removing any lagging. The whole of the machinery, piping, and fitting

out of both plants has been carried out by the Liverpool Refrigeration Company, Limited, Liverpool, the installation being the latest of a large number of refrigerating plants fitted by this company for the Cunard Line.

ELECTRIC TURBO-GENERATORS.

In the electric generating station there are four generating sets, all alike, and each of 375 kilowatts capacity, the voltage being 110 to 120. The prime movers are Parsons turbines. Fig. 207 on page 44

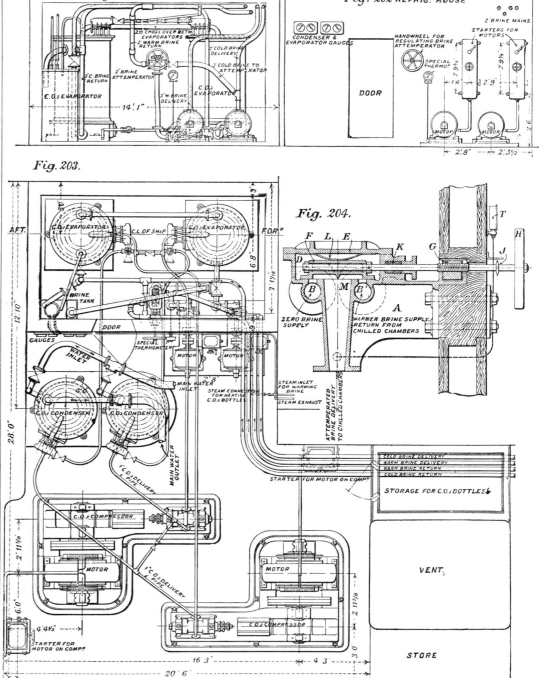

FIGS. 201 TO 204. DETAILS OF REFRIGERATING PLANT.

TABLE XVI.—SUMMARY OF OFFICIAL TRIALS OF TURBO-GENERATORS.

Number of machine ..	1034.			1077.	1078.			1079.
Date of test ..	4/8/06	4/8/06	4/8/06	14/8/06	13/8/06	13/8/06	13/8/06	14/8/06
Load ..	Full	Three-quarter	Half	Full	Full	Three-quarter	Half	Full
Stop-valve pressure ..	167	167	173	166	158	161	160	164
Barometer in inches of mercury .	29.77	29.77	29.77	29.54	29.4	29.4	29.4	29.54
Back pressure in pounds ..	5	5	5	4.95	4.86	5	5	5
Speed—revolutions per minute ..	1200	1200	1200	1200	1200	1200	1200	1200
Voltage ..	111	111.2	113.6	115.2	107	109.8	112.3	114.5
Average kilowatts ..	373.27	288.9	188.42	375.38	371.75	285.28	188.3	373.31
Field volts ..	87.6	88.73	86.06	92.46	87.5	89.6	90.6	92.08
,, amperes ..	33.31	31.15	30.9	30.76	30.8	30.8	30.8	31.5
Average quantity of water per hour in pounds ..	17,831	15,017	11,419	17,301	17,888	15,104	11,649	17,546
Water consumption per kilowatt-hour in pounds ..	47.76	51.97	60.60	46.08	48.14	52.94	61.86	47

REFRIGERATING MACHINES.

CONSTRUCTED BY THE LIVERPOOL REFRIGERATION COMPANY, LIMITED, LIVERPOOL.

FIG. 205. ELECTRICALLY-DRIVEN REFRIGERATING MACHINE.

FIG. 206. STEAM-DRIVEN REFRIGERATING MACHINE.

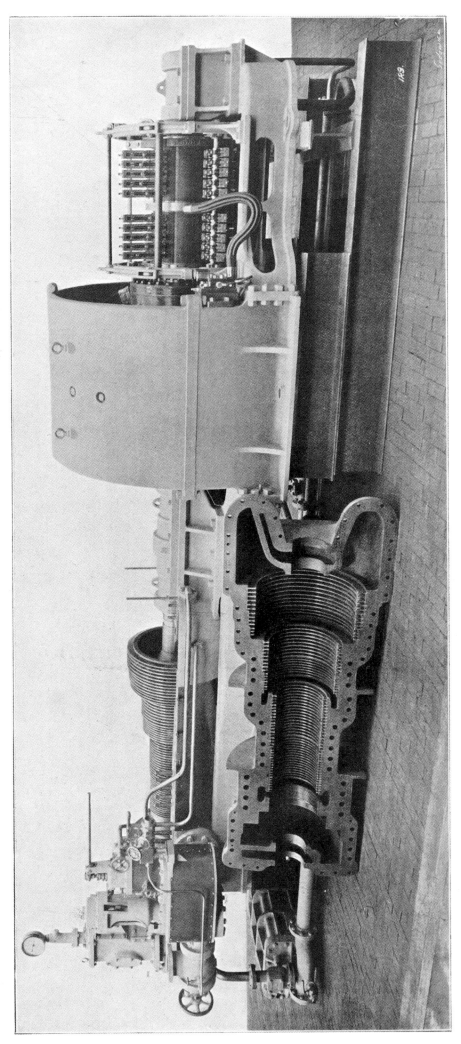

375-KILOWATT TURBO-GENERATOR.

CONSTRUCTED BY MESSRS. C. A. PARSONS AND CO., LIMITED, ENGINEERS, NEWCASTLE-ON-TYNE.

FIG. 207.

is a view of one generating set, with the turbine casing removed, showing the blading in the various expansions, while Figs. 208 and 209 on page 45, and Fig. 210 on the present page, show the general arrangement of a set, and details of fixing. The turbines were designed to give full load when exhausting into a back pressure of 10 lb. They run the dynamos at 1200 revolutions per minute; but an overload of 10 per cent. for two hours is provided for. Each dynamo is shunt wound. The armature is of the surface drum-wound type, with one turn per section. No relative movement between the conductors and commutator bars is possible, but as an additional safeguard, the connections between these are made flexible. Special driving horns in the ends of the core are provided. The insulation of the whole machine was tested with an alternating pressure of 2000 volts between the conductors and the frame, and the insulation resistance after the above test was found to be not less than one-half of a megohm for the whole machine, one megohm for the armature winding, one megohm for the field winding, and one megohm for each of the brush-holders.

Tests were made of the various turbo-generators water consumption was in one case 60.60 lb., and in another 61.86 lb. per kilowatt hour; at three-quarter load the consumption was 52 lb. to 53 lb., and at full load from 46 lb. to 48 lb., the back pressure in each case being about 5 lb. The tests were carried out in the presence of representatives of the Cunard Company.

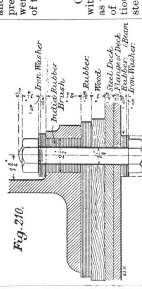

Fig. 210.

THE DISPOSAL OF ASHES.

One of the difficulties which have to be dealt with in vessels burning such a large amount of coal, as will be the case in this instance, is the disposal of the ashes. As a matter of fact, the expeditious disposal of the ashes has a direct effect on the steaming capabilities of any high-powered vessel, as it is impossible for the firemen to give proper attention to the firing when the stokeholds are hampered with ashes. Eight See's ash-ejectors are fitted to the vessels, and with this apparatus all that is necessary is for the fireman to shovel the ashes into a hopper in the stokehold, after which they are dealt with by the apparatus without further manual labour on the part of the firemen, and are discharged twenty or more feet clear of the ship's side. As illustrated on Fig. 211 on page 46, the ejector consists of a hopper W, having a hinged watertight cover, secured, when not in use, by butterfly nuts. At the bottom of the hopper a special form of nozzle is fitted, which discharges up the pipe V. This nozzle forms a loose or removable portion of the ejector cock P, and is combined with an escape-valve, which acts as a relief to any shock on the connecting-pipe from the duplex pump due to the sudden closing of the cock. The cock is in communication, by pipe D, with a suitable duplex pump, which draws water from the sea, and delivers it under pressure to the ejector-cock.

In order to work the ejector, the discharge-valve Z on the ship's side is first opened, and the duplex pump started, so that sea-water is forced through pipe D. When the water-pressure shown by the pressure-gauge M reaches 200 lb., the ejector cock P is *quickly* opened, the water from the pump

375 - KILOWATT TURBO-GENERATOR.

CONSTRUCTED BY MESSRS C. A. PARSONS AND CO., LIMITED, ENGINEERS, NEWCASTLE-ON-TYNE.

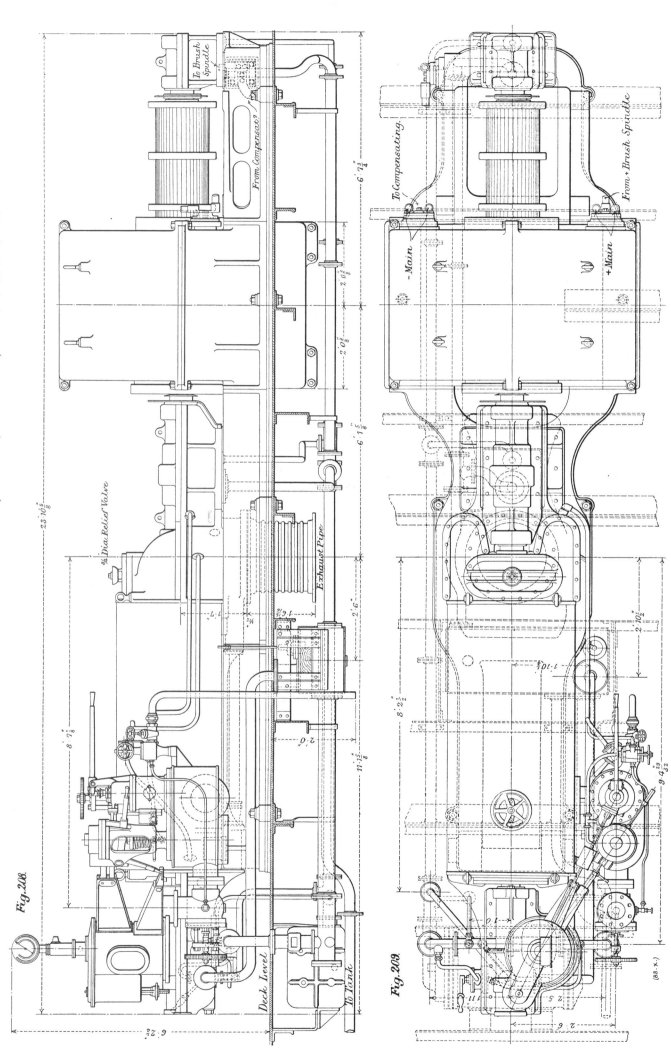

Fig. 268.

Fig. 269.

being then discharged through the nozzle up the discharge-pipe V at a pressure of about 150 lb., and the ejector is now working and ready to receive the ashes. The cock can be opened either with the hopper-lid closed or open; but when closed it must be noticed that the air-inlet T is open. The ashes may now be continuously shovelled into the hopper W, the lid of which remains open during the operation and until the whole of the ashes have been removed. When the ashes enter the hopper they are quickly drawn down towards the water-jet by the rush of air, and on reaching the jet are carried up the discharge-pipe, deflected by means of the bend Y shown at the top, and passing through the clack-valve Z, are discharged well clear of the side of the vessel. The valve Z is kept shut when the ejector is not working, and is opened or shut from the stokehold by means of suitable rods or by a patent automatic hydraulic cylinder.

When the whole of the ashes are discharged the ejector cock P is closed quickly, so that all water that has passed the cock may be discharged overboard, thus leaving the discharge-pipe free of water and ready for further use. The clack-valve Z and the hopper-lid are also now closed until the apparatus is again required. The bend Y is fitted with removable segments X on the top side, which are interchangeable, and easily replaced if worn out by the scour of the ashes. It will be observed that

Co., London. This system, known as the Crompton atmospheric silent ash-hoist, is illustrated on page 46 (Figs. 212 to 215), and the drawings reproduced are largely self-explanatory. In the cylinders or tubes, which are copper-lined throughout, there works a flexible cup piston, to which

the air-evacuator instrument which controls the ash-hoist in all its actions. This evacuator is shown in Fig. 215. S is a 1-in. steam-pipe from the main and donkey boilers which supplies steam, the velocity of which passing through the evacuator creates the vacuum for working the ash-hoist when

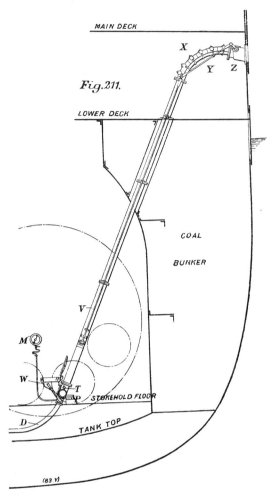

FIG. 211. SEE'S ASH-EJECTOR.

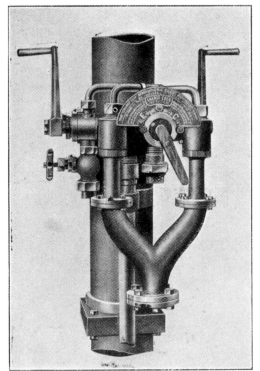

FIG. 215.

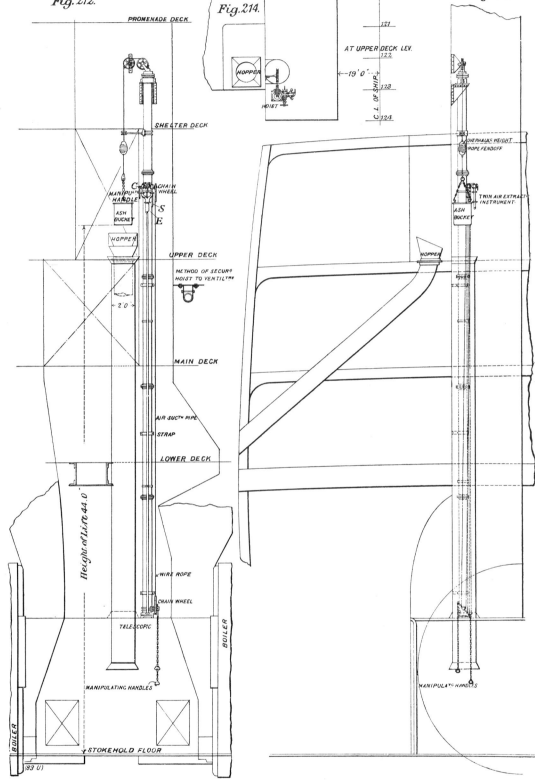

FIGS. 212 TO 215. CROMPTON'S ASH-HOISTS.

there is no loss of fresh water by the use of this apparatus, and the only steam used is for working the pump, the steam passing back to the condenser in the usual way. Ten to fifteen minutes each watch will suffice to clear each stokehold of ashes.

An alternative system of dealing with the ashes, and for disposing of them when in harbour, has been fitted by Messrs. T. Albert Crompton and

is attached at one end a steel wire rope, which passes over the swivel-head fixed at the top of the tubes. A pair of clip-hooks is attached to this rope for connecting to the bucket-ropes of each ventilator as may be required to be worked. Inside the ventilators are fixed spindles and patent roller-bearing pulleys for carrying the bucket-ropes down the ventilators, each rope being provided with patent adjustable thimble-eyes for connecting to the ship's bag-hooks, or ash-bucket slings, in the usual way. At the bottom end of the tubes is a portway chamber, provided with a door for examining or drawing the pistons (shown in Fig. 212), and to this chamber is connected a 1½-in. wrought-iron pipe. At the top end of this pipe is secured

the vessel is in port, E being the exhaust-pipe connection to the funnel or to the auxiliary exhaust-tank. C is the vacuum-pipe connection direct to the condenser of the main engines (vacuum side).

This apparatus is worked as follows:—An eighth of a turn of the operating handle admits steam through the air-evacuator, and at the same time opens up a communication direct to the bottom side of the piston in the tube, thereby creating a vacuum below the piston; and the atmospheric pressure acting on the top side of the piston forces it down the tube, when the ash-bag or bucket will ascend the ventilator, reaching the door as the piston arrives at the bottom of the tube. A quarter of a turn backwards of the operating handle destroys the

CONTROLLING GEAR FOR ELECTRIC FANS FOR FORCED DRAUGHT.

CONSTRUCTED BY MESSRS. W. H. ALLEN, SON, AND CO., LIMITED, ENGINEERS, BEDFORD.

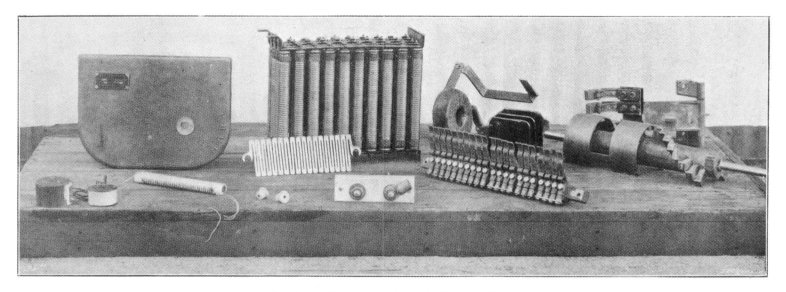

FIG. 216. DETAILS OF ALLEN'S CONTROL-GEAR.

FIG. 217. ALLEN'S CONTROL-GEAR.

vacuum, and the weight of the empty bucket causes the latter to return to the stokehold floor.

When the vessel is at sea the steam is shut off entirely, and the handle of the change-cock (which is shown in Fig. 215) is moved over to C on the name-plate. This change-cock is then in direct communication with the main engine's condenser by the connection marked C in Fig. 215, when the vacuum in the condenser becomes the agent used for working the hoist, the manipulation of the operating handles being exactly the same as before. Whether the hoist is being worked at sea or in port, the operation of moving the change-cock from E to C, or *vice versâ*, is such that it is absolutely impossible for any of the connections to be opened to the atmosphere and the condenser at the same time. Neither is it possible for any steam to pass into the hoist-tubes, irrespective of the position of the operating handles of the air-evacuator—*i.e.*, whether left in after working, or whether any steam passes into the condensers of the main engines when the vessel is in port. The height of lift being a net one, the length of the hoist-tubes is always constructed in proportion thereto, which makes it impossible for any overwinding to occur.

CONTROLLING-GEAR WITH ELECTRIC FAN FOR FORCED DRAUGHT.

In the description of the Mauretania (page 37) we have given sectional drawings of the forced draught fans which were supplied by Messrs. W. H. Allen, Son, and Co., Ltd., of Bedford, and on this page we reproduce views of the controlling-gear for the motors, as these are of much interest. They are arranged to give a large variation in speed rising in equal increments from about 185 to 500 revolutions per minute. The construction is well shown in Fig. 217, while Fig. 216 exhibits some of the internal parts when removed from the casing. The fans are also provided with water-pressure gauges connected to the fan casing, and with tachometers.

FEED-WATER PUMPS AND HEATERS.

To the condensers, four in number, are connected four Weir wet-air pumps, 40 in. in diameter by 24 in. stroke. These are of Messrs. G. and J. Weir's twin type, having two steam cylinders, two pump-barrels, with the pump-rods cross-connected by a beam. Steam is admitted to both cylinders by a single valve of the Weir pattern, designed specially for air-pump duty, but comprising the usual and distinguishing features of the well-known Weir valve. Gun-metal has been adopted for the pump-barrels, the buckets, foot and head valve-seats, which latter are fitted with Kinghorn valves and gun-metal guards. The cylinders are supported on a cast-iron entablature set on angle wrought-iron columns. The piston-rods are of steel, connected by a cross-head with the pump-rods, which are of manganese-bronze, and work in vertical guides.

In addition to these wet-air pumps, which are capable of maintaining the requisite vacuum when the system is reasonably tight, provision is made for unexpected or accidental leakage by fitting four sets of Weir double dry-air pumps, 24 in. in diameter and 7 in. stroke, for dealing with air only. In these the air-pump chambers are situated over the steam cylinders of a double-connected enclosed high-speed engine. These chambers are of gun-metal, and are of the single-acting type. The air passes into the barrel above the buckets through annular openings, and is forced through the head valves on the up stroke of the pump. The compression of the air results in a certain rise of temperature, which is taken care of by a small supply of circulating water, which passes through the chamber and carries off the heat. Steam is admitted to the engine by a piston-valve controlled by a governor fitted on the shaft in the usual manner.

From the air-pumps the feed water passes to the hotwell, from which it is taken by four Weir hotwell pumps, 14½ in. by 30 in., of the firm's light-duty type, fitted with Kinghorn valves, and having gun-metal liners, brackets, and manganese-bronze rods. These pumps are automatically controlled by Weir control-gear fitted in the hotwell, so that the speed of the pumps corresponds to the quantity of water passing into the chamber. The feed-water is discharged by these pumps through two Weir surface feedheaters, where the exhaust steam from all the auxiliaries (with the exception of the turbo-generators) is utilised to heat the feed, and as this steam is impregnated with oil, it flows, after condensation, by gravity through an oil-filter into the hotwell tank. In addition to this feed-heater there are also fitted two Weir direct-contact heaters (Fig. 220 on page 48), into which the exhaust steam from the turbo-generators is led. There is here also control-gear for regulating the speed of the main feed-pumps. These consist of three pairs of Weir standard feed-pumps, 13½ in. in diameter, with a 30-in. stroke, which are supplemented by a duplicate installation of auxiliary feed-pumps of the same size and number. These pumps, illustrated by Fig. 218, page 48, have all gun-metal barrels, with manganese-bronze valves and pump-rods, steel piston-rods, with the requisite suction

AIR-PUMP, FEED-WATER PUMPS, AND HEATERS.

CONSTRUCTED BY MESSRS. G. AND J. WEIR, LIMITED, ENGINEERS, CATHCART.

FIG. 218.   FEED-PUMP.

FIG. 219.   MONOTYPE AIR-PUMP.

and discharge stop-valves for drawing from the feed-heaters and discharging to the boilers.

In addition to these auxiliaries, Messrs. G. and J. Weir, Limited, have also supplied four duplex pumps of special design for ash-ejector and auxiliary feed duty, 10 in. in diameter, with a 14-in. stroke, and three duplex pumps for sanitary and wash-deck purposes, also four single direct-acting bilge-pumps, 10 in. in diameter, with a 21-in. stroke. For the supply of oil to the turbine bearings, six of their special direct-acting lubricating-pumps are fitted. For dealing with the water and air from the auxiliary condensers, they have furnished two of their latest type of single direct-acting air-pumps, known as the "Monotype" pattern, 22 in. in diameter, with a 12-in. stroke. These represent the latest developments in air-pump design, and are illustrated by Fig. 219, above. The installation of Weir auxiliaries, it will be observed, is very complete and representative, and practically handles the feed-water from the time it leaves the condenser until it is returned to the boilers; a responsible duty which calls for most reliable equipment.

FEED-WATER FILTERS.

Two feed-water filters of the well-known Harris type, supplied by the Harris Patent Feed-Water Filter, Limited, are fitted in connection with the hot-well pumps of the main turbines, and filter the water on its passage to the feed-heaters. The filters, which are clearly illustrated on this and the next pages, are each 36 in. in diameter, and of gun-metal throughout, the principal feature in their internal construction being the central sludge out-

FIG. 220.   CONTACT FEED-WATER HEATER.

let—an ingenious arrangement, by which the filtering area is divided into eight separate sections, each of which can be sludged out independently of the rest, the whole force of the reversed current of the water, when cleaning, being concentrated on only one-eighth of the surface, so that the cleaning is most efficient, and can be effected in a few minutes without the necessity of opening up. The filters present a most compact appearance, and everything is well arranged to facilitate their ready manipulation. Two smaller filters, 20 in. in internal diameter, also in gun-metal, are fitted in connection with the auxiliary machinery. These filters are of the same type as the larger ones, but with all valves self-contained.

DISTILLERS AND EVAPORATORS FOR MAKING-UP THE FEED WATER.

The distilling machinery is of Quiggin's well-known type, and was manufactured by the Liverpool Engineering and Condenser Company, Limited, Brunswick Dock, Liverpool. The complete set is illustrated in Figs. 230 to 233 on page 51.

There are two complete sets of plant, and these supply the whole of the distilled water required for all purposes, the total capacities of each plant being, for cooking and drinking purposes, 18,000 gallons per 24 hours; for baths and washing, 15,000 gallons per 24 hours; while the evaporators for feed-make-up purposes for the boilers, when working compound-effect, supply 240 tons per 24 hours, and, when working single high-pressure effect, 350 tons per 24 hours.

Each plant consists of one evaporator for the

FEED-WATER FILTERS.

CONSTRUCTED BY THE HARRIS PATENT FEED-WATER FILTER, LIMITED, ENGINEERS, LONDON.

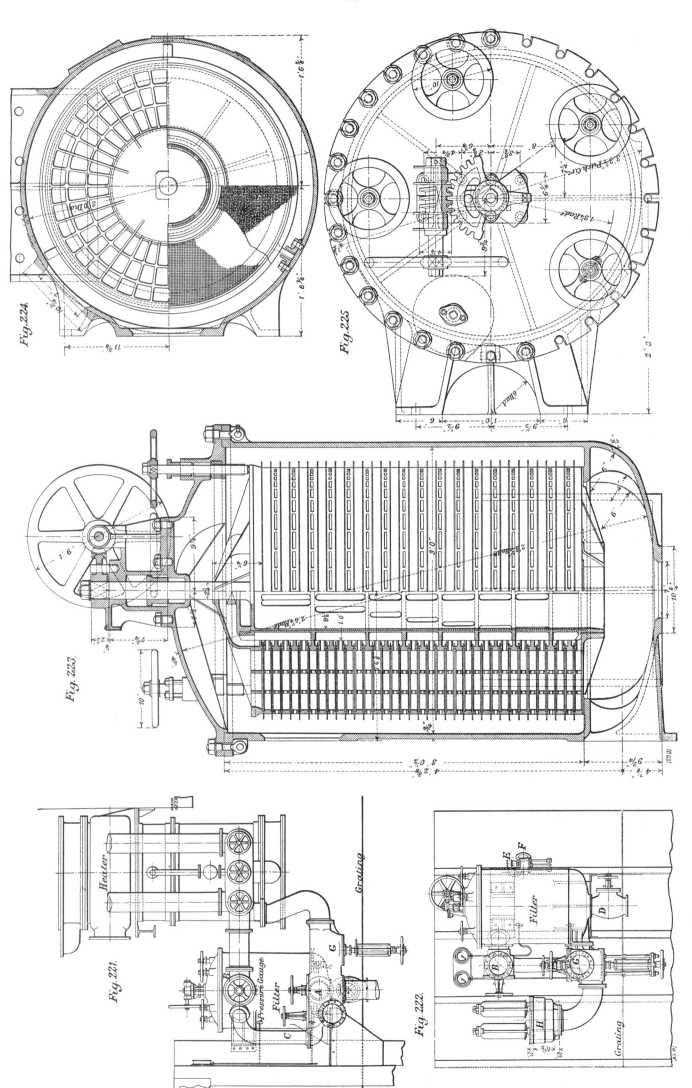

Fig. 224.

Fig. 225.

Fig. 223.

Fig. 221.

Fig. 222.

production of distilled water, and two for feed- | in Fig. 231. All the evaporator shells are made of | gun-metal. The coils are made so that they can | heating surface is provided for each size of evapo- make-up purposes, the two latter being arranged | rolled naval brass, double-riveted. This is for the | be withdrawn bodily, and are all interchangeable, | rator, in order that the coils may be replaced by a to work in series—compound, or separately—single | purpose of reducing the weight as far as possible. | and the coils can be taken out separately for the | clean set, when required, in a few minutes. An effect. The evaporator is shown in section in | The ends of the evaporators, all the mountings, as | purpose of cleaning and for inspection; while in | automatic feed-water regulator, shown in Fig. 232, Fig. 233, page 51, and the condense: in section | well as the frame and doors, are constructed of | order to facilitate this operation a complete spare | is provided for each evaporator, and this maintains

H

DETAILS OF THE HARRIS FEED-WATER FILTERS.

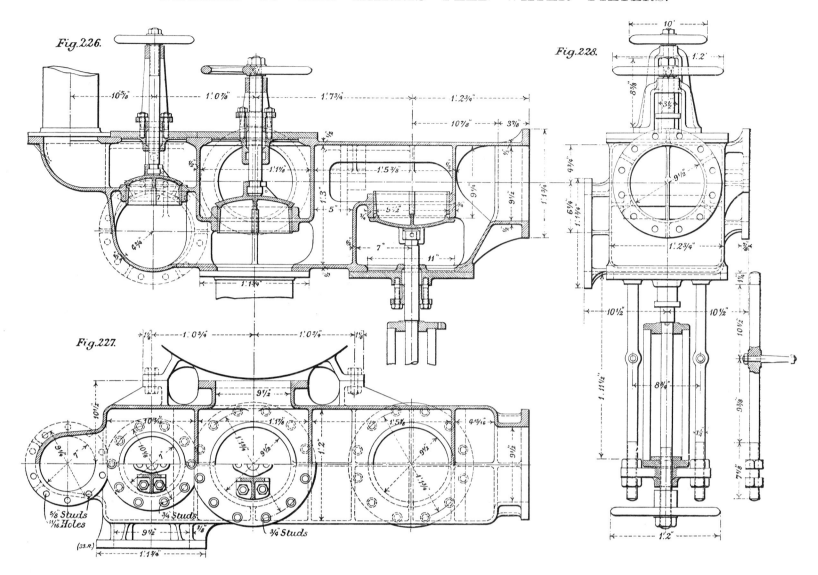

Fig. 226.

Fig. 227.

Fig. 228.

the water-level in the evaporator at a constant height. It acts in the following manner :—The rise and fall of the water acts on the corrugated float F, the motion of which shuts or opens the pilot-valve P, which in turn governs the control-valve C, by allowing the pressure to increase or decrease in the chamber D on the top of the valve C. The pump is always in communication with the chamber D, the valve C fitting loosely in its casing, and allowing a constant leakage past it for this purpose. The water to the condenser passes through the opening shown. Should the valve C wear too slack, the leakage past it to the chamber D may be more than the pilot-valve P can pass, in which case the valve C will not open enough, and the water in the evaporator will fall in consequence. When a new valve is fitted, care must be taken that it does not fit too tight, as the leakage past it would then be insufficient ; the control-valve would remain open too long, and the water would then rise in the evaporator. The evaporator shells are lagged with hair-felt, and sheathed with galvanised sheet steel.

The condensers have coils of solid-drawn copper, and are tinned inside and outside ; the coils can be withdrawn bodily with the cover by simply un-screwing a nut on the spigot end at the bottom connection to the filter. The sectional area of the coils diminishes from top to bottom, but each coil has a parallel surface throughout. The inlet for the steam is of full bore where the steam enters, but is gradually reduced in area to a crescent section, until at the outlet end it is only about one-third of the original sectional area. The volume of the steam is reduced as it condenses, and is kept in contact with the condensing surface, owing to the diminishing area of the coil. It is claimed that in this way the surface is rendered much more effective than it would be if the coils were of the same sectional area throughout. The filter, which is charged with animal charcoal and limestone chips, is in the base of the condenser. As a means of aerating the distilled water there is a pipe fitted, which is

FIG. 229.

tapped from an iron-pipe connection, and there is a door for access to the filter. The circulating water enters and flows, as shown. There are two condensers in each set. The shells of the condensers are of galvanised mild steel.

In each set of apparatus there are three pumps—namely, one vertical duplex circulating pump, one vertical duplex evaporator feed-pump, and one vertical single direct-acting type brine-pump for pumping the brine from the low-pressure evaporator (when working compound effect); after the water has been diluted and cooled with sea-water it is pumped overboard. All these pumps are made with solid gun-metal water ends.

EVAPORATORS AND DISTILLERS FOR MAKING-UP FEED-WATER.

CONSTRUCTED BY THE LIVERPOOL ENGINEERING AND CONDENSER COMPANY, LIMITED, LIVERPOOL.

FIG. 230.

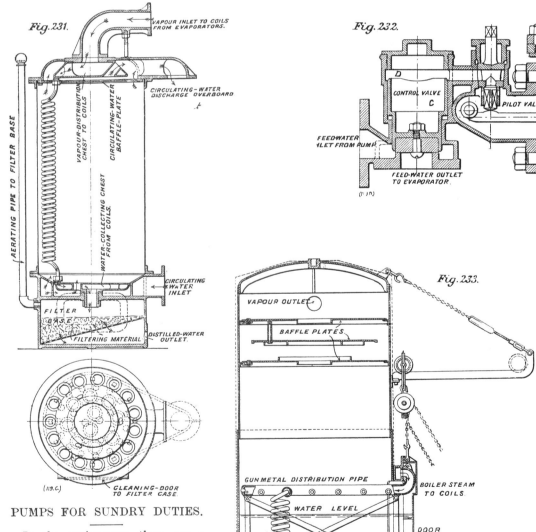

PUMPS FOR SUNDRY DUTIES.

In the engine-room there are a great variety of pumps for sundry duties. Many of these have been supplied by Messrs. J. H. Carruthers and Co., Limited, Polmadie, Glasgow. An illustration of a set of their typical ballast-pumps is given on page 52; the others are of similar design. The arrangement of framing in this type gives very free access to all the moving parts. All the important

joints of the valve gear are adjustable. The water valves are easily examined through the front doors of the pump.

Among the pumps supplied are the following :—

Two for ballast service, with cylinders	... ... 8 in. and 10 in. by 10 in.		
Two for water service, with cylinders	... ...7½ ,, 10 ,, 12 ,,		
Two for washing decks	...6 ,, 6 ,, 6 ,,		
One for sanitary service	...6 ,, 7 ,, 7 ,,		

All of the pumps have gun-metal ends.

VENTILATION OF THE ENGINE-ROOM.

Messrs. Laurence, Scott, and Co., Limited, Norwich, supplied twelve fans of 35 in., two of 30 in., and two of 25 in. diameter, all electrically driven and adapted for the ventilation of the engine-room. The outputs specified were respectively 26,000 and 14,000 cubic feet per minute, with free discharge at 315 and 450 revolutions per minute, the fans being direct driven and carried on an extension of the motor spindle. The company's standard type of semi-enclosed motor was adopted, fitted with gauze grids, the magnets being series wound for the reasons given below. In view of the high temperature of the situations in which some of these fans work, the motors were made large, and the temperature rise in a six hours' run was kept below 50 deg. Fahr. The armature is all built up on a cast-iron quill, and is self-contained and independent of the shaft, on to which it is slipped when completed. Series winding was adopted for the magnets, as this gives better regulation of the load than shunt winding would do. The power required by a centrifugal fan at a constant speed goes up rapidly as the resistance to its free discharge is removed, reaching a maximum when disconnected altogether from its air-trunks. The variation in speed of a series-wound motor tends to correct the effect of variations in the resistance to discharge of the air, and keeps the load on the motor and the volume of air more nearly constant than would be the case if a shunt motor were used. The series winding also gives a simple method of speed-control without the use of resistances. For slow speed all four field coils are arranged in series with each other and the armature. For full speed the field coils are arranged in two parallel circuits, each of two coils in series, these being still in series with the armature. The motor is then running with a lower resistance in series with the armature and with a weaker field, and therefore at a higher speed. The barrel-controller is protected by an overload and no-voltage device. In the event either of an overload or failure of supply, the barrel carrying the contacts flies to the "off" position, even if the operating handle is being held "on." The fans are Messrs Davidson and Co.'s make, of the well-known Sirocco type, and, like the motors, are amply large for the work.

FIG. 234. CARRUTHERS' BALLAST PUMPS.

CARGO APPLIANCES.

We come now to the mechanical appliances for the navigation of the ship and for the handling of the little cargo that is carried.

The cargo appliances are not of first-class importance, for the best of all reasons—that the minimum of cargo will be accepted, since it is not profitable to add to the load transported at a speed of 25 knots, unless it is at very high freight rates. There are, as shown on the plans on the two-page Plate XXXIV., two holds for cargo, the capacity being 17,500 cubic feet. For coping with this cargo Messrs. John H. Wilson and Co., Limited, Sandhills, Liverpool, have fitted two winches, having two 8-in. cylinders adapted to a stroke of 14 in., which drive single-geared four-drum winches, and a winch with a 12-in. cylinder and a 16-in. stroke, operating a double-purchase warping-winch, with extended barrel-shaft and warping-drums. The arrangement and details of Messrs. Wilson's productions are well known and do not call for special description or illustration. These will be used largely in connection with the handling of cargo taken in the refrigerated holds.

There are also holds for stowage of mails, and a mail-room for the sorting of letters, &c., before the arrival of the ship in port. This mail-room is aft on the orlop-deck, and the fittings have been carried out under Government supervision. The postal

clerks' rooms are overhead, with the sorting-room at hand. There are various appliances for dealing with mails, baggage, &c., and these may now be described before we give details of the machinery in connection with the navigation of the ship.

BOAT-HOISTS.

Four electrically-operated boat-hoisting winches have been fitted. These were manufactured by Messrs. Laurence, Scott, and Co., Limited, Norwich, and are illustrated below (Figs. 235 and 236).

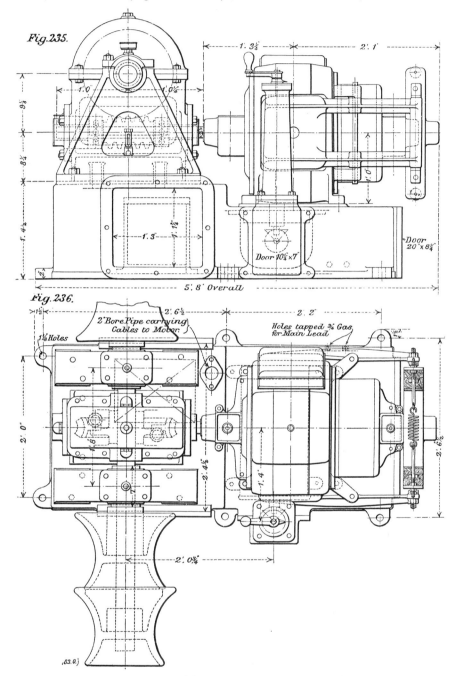

FIGS. 235 AND 236. ELECTRIC BOAT-HOISTS; CONSTRUCTED BY MESSRS. LAURENCE, SCOTT, AND CO., LIMITED, NORWICH.

The duty specified was to lift a total load of 12 cwt. at a speed of 250 ft. per minute. As two warping-drums are provided on each side, this pull can be distributed over four ropes. As will be seen from the drawings reproduced, the slow-speed shaft, with its four warping-drums, is carried on two substantial pedestal bearings, bolted directly to the box bed-plate on each side of the separate gear-case. The gear consists of a cast-iron worm-wheel with machine-cut gun-metal rim, mounted on the slow-speed shaft, and engaging with a worm of forged steel carried by an extension of the motor spindle. Ball-thrusts and gun-metal journals are provided in the gear-case, the lower part of which forms an oil-bath for the worm.

The motor, which is of Messrs. Laurence, Scott, and Co.'s "Crane" type, series-wound and watertight, is rated at 14 brake horse-power when making 600 revolutions and using current of 110 volts pressure. The specification provided that the

temperature rise should not exceed 80 deg. Fahr. after one hour's full-load run. The actual temperature rise of the motor used under these conditions was under 60 deg. Fahr., and no difficulty was experienced in dealing with 100 per cent. overload for short periods. Series winding of the magnets was adopted to enable the motor to adapt its speed to various lifts, excessive speed at light loads being prevented by the Scott patent "flapper" brake with which these machines are provided. These brakes depend for their action on the magnetic field of the motor itself, some of the metal round the root of a pole, on either side of the motor, being cut away, so that most of the flux has to pass through steel plates or "flappers" connected to the brake-blocks by pivoted arms. The "flappers" thus experience a pull (tending to close them on to the side of the motor frame) which varies with the strength of the main field, and therefore with the load. The brakes are arranged to come right off with ordinary work, and to come into action gradually as the load is reduced, just enough to prevent the motor attaining an excessive speed when running light. The commutator end-brackets are circular, and are fitted with sheet steel covers pulled down by eccentrics on to a turned surface, with rubber sealing. The covers are slightly flanged, and fit into a turned groove, so that very little moisture can get even as far as the rubber, the arrangement making a satisfactory job, capable of standing anything but actual immersion under pressure. The armature is built up complete on a

ELECTRIC CRANES AND BAGGAGE-HOISTS.

CONSTRUCTED BY MESSRS. STOTHERT AND PITT, LIMITED, ENGINEERS, BATH.

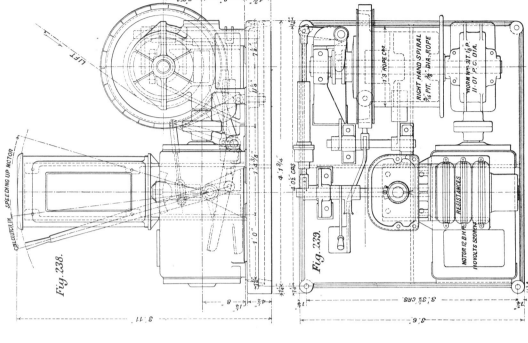

Fig. 238.

Fig. 239.

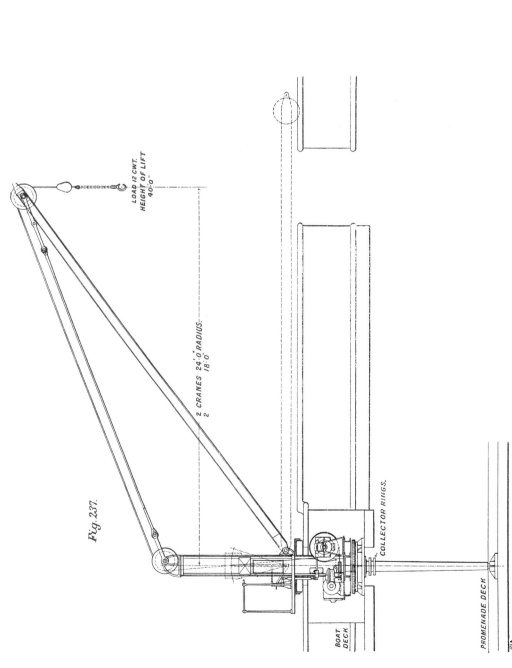

Fig. 237.

CRANES AND BAGGAGE-HOISTS.

There are on the vessel four deck-cranes, as well as the same number of baggage and mail-hoists, all constructed by Messrs. Stothert and Pitt, Limited, of Bath. These are illustrated above (Figs. 237 to 239). The deck-cranes are electrically driven, and are capable of handling loads up to 30 cwt., two at 18-ft. radius and the other two at 26-ft. radius. The superstructure consists of a vertical main frame of plates and angles carrying the lifting and slewing gear, while the jib is formed of a pair of rolled sections braced together. Tie-rods of wire rope are used to enable the jibs to be

lowered conveniently. Separate totally-enclosed series-wound motors, working at 110 volts, are provided for lifting and slewing. The lifting motor is rated at 15 brake horse-power at 500 revolutions, and raises the full load at a speed of 100 ft. per minute. The motor drives through worm-reduction gear, working in an oil bath, the worm being of forged steel, and the wheel provided with phosphor-bronze teeth. Messrs. Stothert and Pitt's "free barrel" system is employed for lifting and lowering. In this the barrel runs loose on the shaft, to which it can be connected by means of a coil-clutch. The lever for operating the coil-clutch is connected with the controller-handle in such a way that the same motion which gives current to the motor causes the engagement of the clutch. A powerful foot-brake is also provided, which is

also interlocked with the controller-handle, so that it is impossible to work one against the other.

The advantage of the free-barrel system is that the load, after having been lifted to any desired height, may be released immediately and lowered under the control of the foot-brake. Thus no time is lost in bringing the armature and gearing to rest before lowering commences, and the motor has only to run in one direction.

Slewing is performed at the rate of 400 ft. per minute by means of a 2½-brake horse-power motor running at 750 revolutions. The speed reduction is effected by means of worm and spur-gearing, driving a pinion engaging with the externally-toothed fixed slewing-ring. The weight of the revolving structure is carried on spherical-faced friction-pads in the foot-step, and the horizontal

cast-iron quill independently of the shaft, on which it is secured by a long feather key. The armature can be withdrawn from the worm shaft, if necessary, without disturbing the gear-case, and the omission of an intermediate coupling, possible with this arrangement, makes a compact design.

The controller is of the tramway type, and is placed horizontally inside the deep box-bed under the motor, being operated through bevel-gear by a handle beside the winch. The resistances consist of cast-iron grids, and are also placed in the bed-plate for protection, and are indicated in the illustrations under the gear-box and one pedestal-bearing. The interior of the box-bed is roomy, and is made accessible by several large watertight doors, while ventilation is provided for in a space under the gear-box, where vent-pipes are so arranged as

to prevent water getting down to the control-gear.

STEAM STEERING-GEAR.

CONSTRUCTED BY MESSRS. BROWN BROTHERS AND CO., LIMITED, EDINBURGH.

Fig. 240.

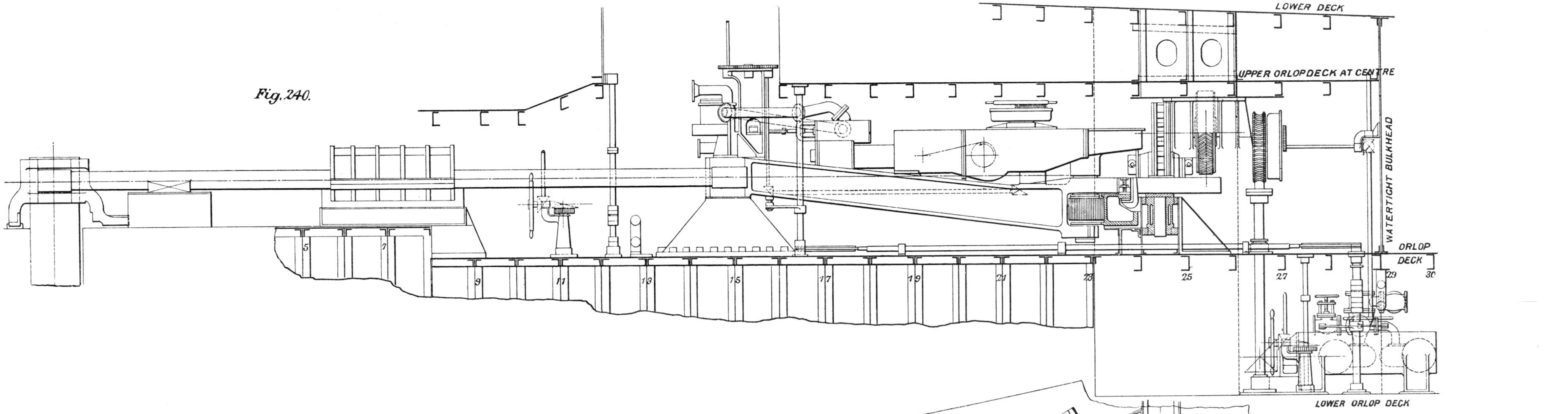

Fig. 241.

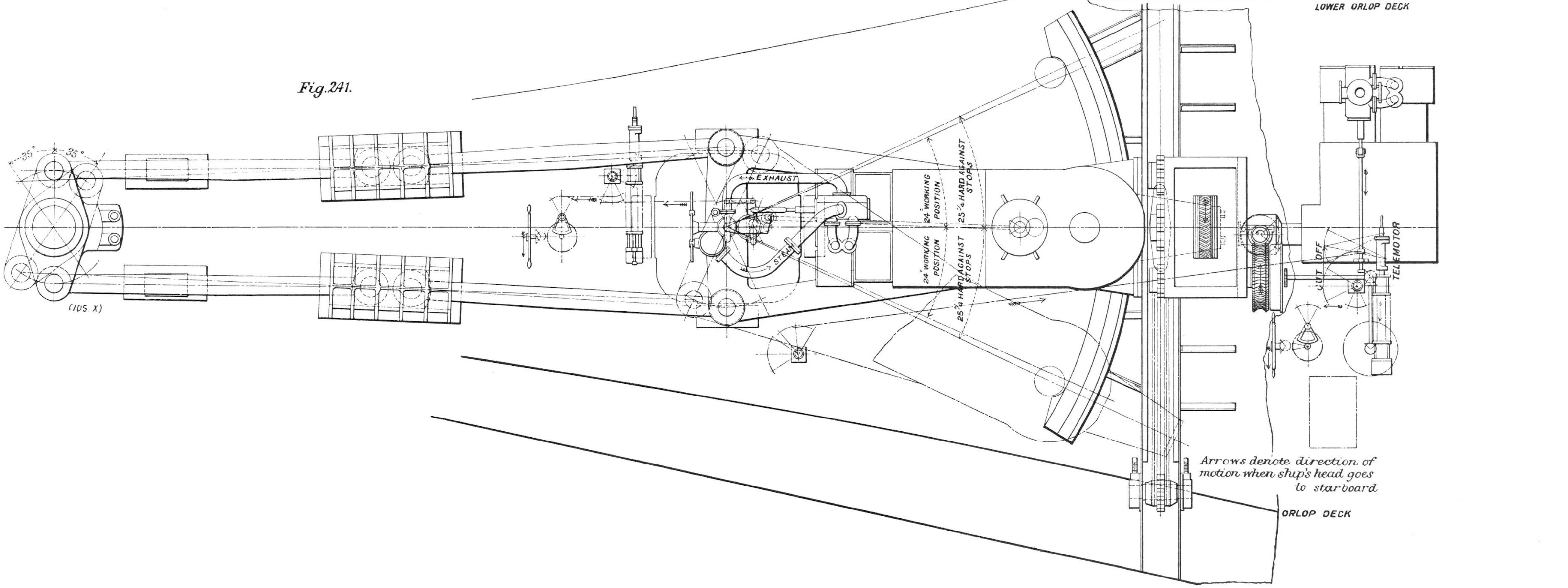

Arrows denote direction of motion when ship's head goes to starboard.

STEAM STEERING-GEAR AND ANCHOR-GEAR.

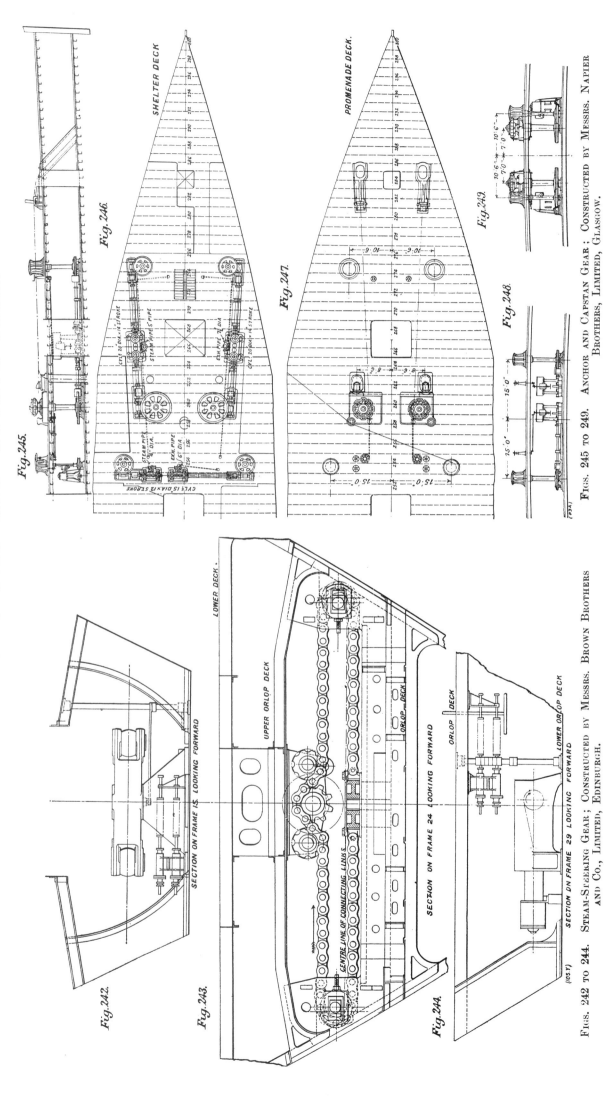

Fig. 245.

Fig. 246.

SHELTER DECK

Fig. 247.

PROMENADE DECK.

Fig. 248.

Fig. 249.

FIGS. 245 TO 249. ANCHOR AND CAPSTAN GEAR; CONSTRUCTED BY MESSRS. NAPIER BROTHERS, LIMITED, GLASGOW.

Fig. 242.

Fig. 243.

LOWER DECK.

UPPER ORLOP DECK

SECTION ON FRAME 29 LOOKING FORWARD

SECTION ON FRAME 15 LOOKING FORWARD

CENTRE LINE OF CONNECTING LINKS

ORLOP DECK

Fig. 244.

SECTION ON FRAME 24 LOOKING FORWARD

ORLOP DECK

LOWER ORLOP DECK

FIGS. 242 TO 244. STEAM-STEERING GEAR; CONSTRUCTED BY MESSRS. BROWN BROTHERS AND CO., LIMITED, EDINBURGH.

load taken by rollers bearing in a path turned in the foundation-casting in the boat-deck.

The baggage and mail-hoists have lifting gear of the same type as that of the cranes, many of the parts being interchangeable.

STEAM STEERING-GEAR.

The steering-gear has been supplied by Messrs. Brown Brothers and Co., Limited, Edinburgh, and, in addition to the gear, there is fitted reserve gear, as illustrated on pages 54 and 55, Figs. 240 to 244. On the rudder-post is a Siemens-Martin cast-steel cross-head, with long press-forged steel connecting-rods in two lengths, with guide-blocks connecting it to the cross-head end of a Siemens-Martin cast-steel tiller. This tiller is supported at its after end by a forged-steel dummy-post fitted into a large cast-iron bracket, which is bolted to the deck. The engines are mounted on the forward end of the tiller, and have cylinders 14 in. in diameter, with a stroke of 14 in. By means of worm-gear, friction-clutch, and spur-gear the engines drive a cast-steel rack, which is made in three pieces, so that when the teeth of the centre part become worn, this part can be replaced independently.

The whole of the moving parts are contained in the engine bed-plate, which has sides cast on it so as to form an oil-tank, in a pocket in the bottom of which a pair of valveless oil-pumps are placed, driven by the eccentric-rods. These throw the oil into a small tank placed above the working-parts, from which it is syphoned by pipes to all the engine bearings. A coil of copper pipe is fitted in the oil-tank for cooling water.

The engine for the reserve Rapson slide-gear is placed forward of the main gear-rack on the lower orlop-deck. It has cylinders 14 in. in diameter, with a 14-in. stroke, and is a duplicate in every way of the engine on the tiller, so far as its working parts are concerned. It is placed so that the crank-shaft lies fore and aft, and the after end of the shaft is prolonged outside the pan, and carries one of a pair of cast-steel mitre-wheels. By means of gearing a sprocket-chain is finally driven.

This chain passes to port and starboard, and is laid round a cast-iron pulley at each side of the ship. The ends are returned where they lay hold of a bridle which slides in a slot on a prolongation on the top jaw of the forward end of the main tiller. The guide-pulleys, round which the chain is laid, are held in place by means of cast-steel brackets, which can, by means of large screws, be made to take up any slack in the chain.

The rudder moves through an angle of 35 deg. on each side of the centre when the stops of the tele-

WINDLASS AND CAPSTAN-GEAR.

CONSTRUCTED BY MESSRS. NAPIER BROTHERS, ENGINEERS, GLASGOW.

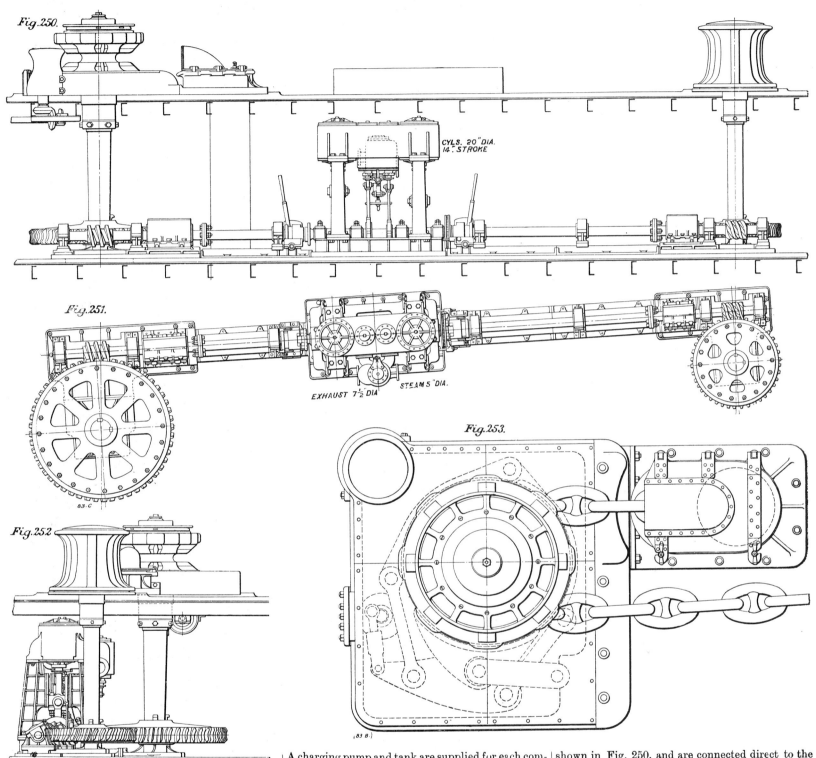

Fig. 250.

CYLS. 20" DIA.
14" STROKE

Fig. 251.

EXHAUST 7½ DIA   STEAM 5 DIA.

83·C

Fig. 252.

63·D

Fig. 253.

(83 B.)

motor are adjusted ; but the whole gear is arranged so that an angle of 37 deg. is obtained before coming on the rubber-stops. Each set of engines is capable of exerting a torsional strain of 1240 foot-tons on the rudder-stock, the steam pressure in the cylinders being 150 lb., and the back pressure 20 lb.

Two complete telemotors are fitted in the wheel-house on the navigating-bridge, and are worked from a central wheel through a horizontal shaft provided with a clutch, so that each telemotor can be used separately. A complete telemotor is also fitted in the steering-station on the boat-deck aft, under the docking-bridge. Each telemotor has its own independent lead of copper pipes to a set of change-cocks on the athwart bulkhead at the end of the tiller-room, and can be operated from each side of the bulkhead.

Three motor cylinders are provided in each steering compartment, and each pair has a separate pair of copper pipes led to the change-cocks. The motor cylinders are so arranged that they can be put in or out of gear from either side of the bulkhead.

A charging pump and tank are supplied for each com-partment, and the motor cylinders are arranged so that those not in use can be charged by themselves.

WINDLASS AND CAPSTAN-GEAR.

The windlasses for working the 3¾-in. stud link-chain cables are placed on the promenade-deck, and are of the well-known Napier type, manufactured by Messrs. Napier Brothers, Limited, of Glasgow. The drawings of the gear are reproduced on pages 55 and 56 (Figs. 245 to 253). There are two cable-holders mounted on vertical spindles, 16 in. in diameter, in the deck bearings, and fitted at their lower parts with powerful Napier patent differential brakes. These are unequalled for their holding power where heavy loads have to be dealt with in a limited space ; they will hold a load, when riding at anchor in heavy weather, of about 250 tons, notwithstanding that the brake is not more than 5 ft. in diameter. All parts of these windlasses are made of cast steel, of massive proportions, with gun-metal liners and bear-ings. The vertical spindles are carried to the shelter-deck, right below the promenade-deck, as

shown in Fig. 250, and are connected direct to the engines by a single worm and worm-wheel gear. There is one engine for each windlass (Fig. 250), of ample proportions, and capable of indicating up to a large horse-power with the full boiler pressure. For warping the ship in harbour there are four vertical capstans. The two capstans forward of the windlasses are each driven from one of the windlass engines, and the two immediately aft of the windlasses are each driven by a separate engine of slightly smaller dimensions. This arrange-ment enables all four capstans to be used simul-taneously, the actual hauling power amounting to over 1000 horses. A similar set of four capstans, exactly the same, are fitted at the after part of the vessel. It may be added that nearly every part of the gear, with framing and base-plates, is made of steel, cast or forged, with the exception of the cylinders and slide-casings, which are of special close-grained cast iron. The object of using steel so exclusively was to provide a maximum of strength with a minimum of weight. Handling-wheels for controlling the different engines, as well as the windlass brakes, are fitted in convenient positions on the promenade-deck.

PRINTED AT THE BEDFORD PRESS, 20 AND 21, BEDFORDBURY, STRAND, LONDON, W.C.

PLATE I.

QUADRUPLE-SCREW TURBINE-DRIVEN CUNARD LINER "MAURETANIA."

Fig. 44. View of Ship in Course of Construction, showing Double-Bottom and Coal-Bunkers; April 18, 1905.

PLATE II.

QUADRUPLE-SCREW TURBINE-DRIVEN CUNARD LINER "MAURETANIA."

FIG. 45. THE SHIP READY FOR LAUNCHING.

PLATE III.

QUADRUPLE-SCREW TURBINE-DRIVEN CUNARD LINER "MAURETANIA."

MAURETANIA

FIG. 46. THE SHIP IMMEDIATELY AFTER THE LAUNCH.

PLATE IV.

QUADRUPLE-SCREW TURBINE-DRIVEN CUNARD LINER "MAURETANIA."

Fig. 47. The Ship in the Fitting-Out Berth at the Wallsend Shipyard.

PLATE V.

QUADRUPLE-SCREW TURBINE-DRIVEN CUNARD LINER "MAURETANIA."

FIG. 48. THE SHIP UNDER EASY STEAM OFF THE TYNE.

B.

PLATE VI.

QUADRUPLE-SCREW TURBINE-DRIVEN CUNARD LINER "MAURETANIA."

FIG. 62.   THE SMOKING-ROOM, LOOKING FORWARD.

FIG. 63.   SMOKING-ROOM.   VIEW FROM SIDE OF FIREPLACE.

FIG. 64.   SMOKING-ROOM.   VIEW OF FIREPLACE.

PLATE VII.

QUADRUPLE-SCREW TURBINE-DRIVEN CUNARD LINER "MAURETANIA."

FIG. 65. LOWER AND UPPER DINING-SALOONS AND DOME.

PLATE VIII.

QUADRUPLE-SCREW TURBINE-DRIVEN CUNARD LINER "MAURETANIA."

Fig. 66.   View in Lower Dining-Saloon.

Fig. 67.   Upper Dining-Saloon, or Restaurant.

PLATE IX.

QUADRUPLE SCREW TURBINE-DRIVEN CUNARD LINER "MAURETANIA."

Fig. 68. The Lounge, or Music-Room, Looking Aft.

PLATE X.

QUADRUPLE-SCREW TURBINE-DRIVEN CUNARD LINER "MAURETANIA."

FIG. 70. THE LOUNGE. VIEW OF STARBOARD SIDE

FIG. 72. THE LOUNGE. VIEW OF THE FIREPLACE.

FIG. 69. THE LOUNGE. VIEW IN ONE OF THE BAYS.

FIG. 71. THE LOUNGE. VIEW OF TAPESTRY PANEL, &C.

PLATE XI.

QUADRUPLE-SCREW TURBINE-DRIVEN CUNARD LINER "MAURETANIA."

FIG. 73.   THE LIBRARY AND WRITING-ROOM.   VIEW LOOKING ATHWART THE SHIP.

FIG. 74.   VIEW FROM LIBRARY, LOOKING TOWARDS GRAND
ENTRANCE AND LOUNGE.

FIG. 75.   FIREPLACE IN LIBRARY, WITH SYCAMORE PANELLING.

PLATE XII.

QUADRUPLE-SCREW TURBINE-DRIVEN CUNARD LINER "MAURETANIA."

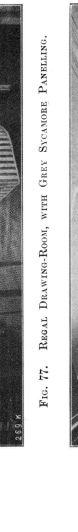

FIG. 77.   REGAL DRAWING-ROOM, WITH GREY SYCAMORE PANELLING.

FIG. 79.   REGAL SUITE.   BEDROOM.

FIG. 76.   REGAL SUITE.   VIEW FROM DRAWING-ROOM INTO DINING-ROOM.

FIG. 78.   REGAL SUITE   BEDROOM IN WHITE, WITH CARVED MOULDINGS AND MAHOGANY FURNITURE.

PLATE XIII.

QUADRUPLE-SCREW TURBINE-DRIVEN CUNARD LINER "MAURETANIA."

FIG. 82. THE SMOKING-SALOON FOR SECOND-CLASS PASSENGERS.

FIG. 83. THE DRAWING-ROOM FOR SECOND-CLASS PASSENGERS

PLATE XIV.

QUADRUPLE-SCREW TURBINE-DRIVEN CUNARD LINER "MAURETANIA."

Fig. 84.   State-Room for First-Class Passengers.

Fig. 85.   State-Room for Second-Class Passengers.

PLATE XV.

THE WORKS OF THE CONSTRUCTORS OF THE MACHINERY.

THE WALLSEND SLIPWAY AND ENGINEERING COMPANY, LIMITED, WALLSEND-ON-TYNE.

Fig. 110. Safe for Storing Drawings, &c.

Fig. 112. The Tracers' Room.

Fig. 109. Photographic-Room for Printing from Tracings.

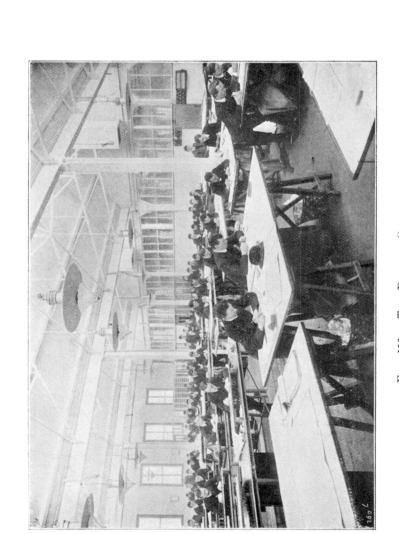

Fig. 111. The Drawing-Office.

PLATE XVI.

THE WORKS OF THE CONSTRUCTORS OF THE MACHINERY.

THE WALLSEND SLIPWAY AND ENGINEERING COMPANY, LIMITED, WALLSEND-ON-TYNE.

FIG. 114.   THE BOILER MACHINE-SHOP.

FIG. 115.   THE BOILER-FLANGING SHOP.

PLATE XVII.

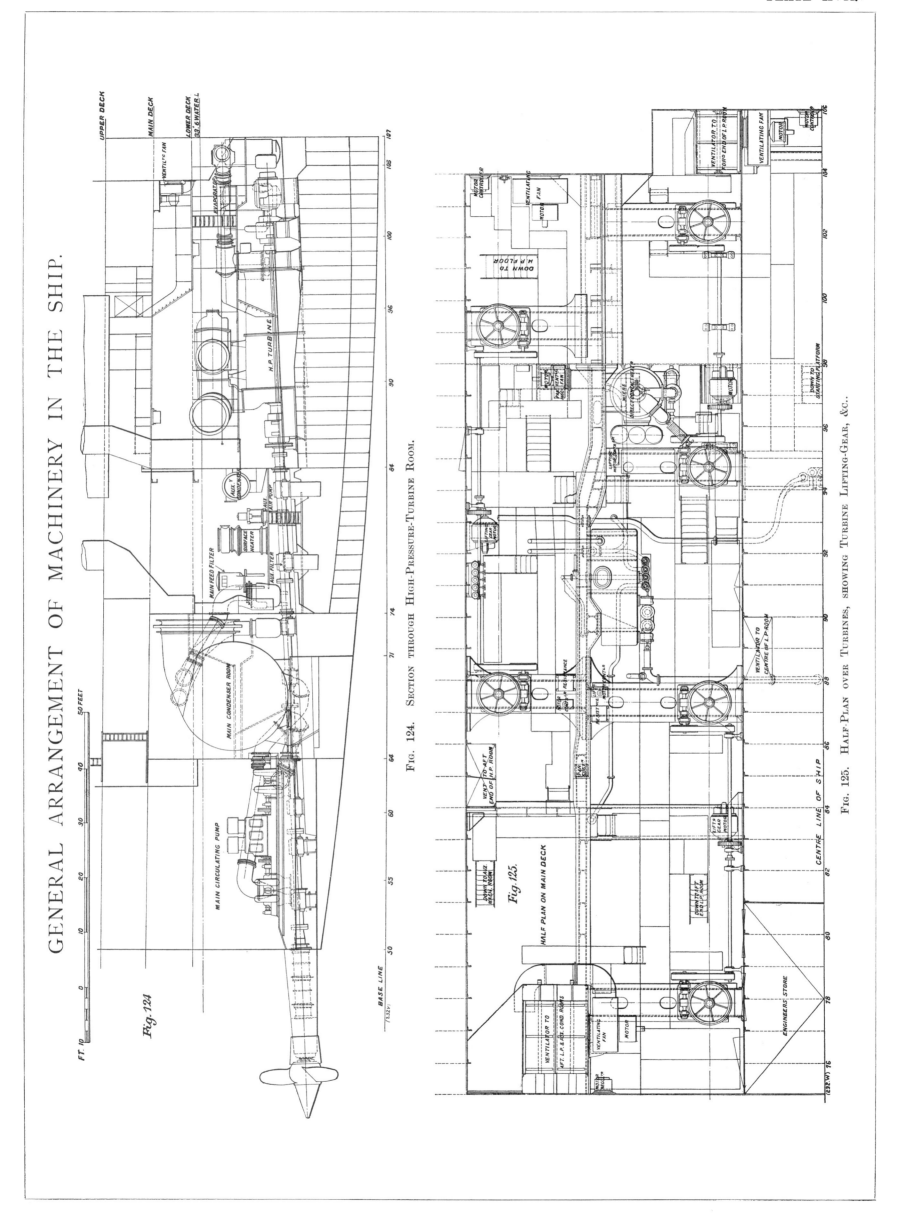

GENERAL ARRANGEMENT OF MACHINERY IN THE SHIP.

Fig. 124

FIG. 124. SECTION THROUGH HIGH-PRESSURE-TURBINE ROOM.

FIG. 125. HALF-PLAN OVER TURBINES, SHOWING TURBINE LIFTING-GEAR, &c..

PLATE XVIII.

THE TURBINE MACHINERY OF THE SHIP.

FIG. 128. ONE ASTERN, ONE LOW-PRESSURE AHEAD, AND ONE HIGH-PRESSURE AHEAD TURBINE IN THE ERECTING-SHOP AT THE WALLSEND WORKS.

PLATE XIX.

THE TURBINE MACHINERY OF THE SHIP.

FIG. 130. LOW PRESSURE TURBINE AND ROTOR, WITH TOP HALF OF TURBINE-CASING RAISED.

FIG. 131. AFTER PORTION OF LOW-PRESSURE TURBINE-CASING.

PLATE XX.

THE TURBINE MACHINERY OF THE SHIP.

FIG. 132. LOW-PRESSURE DRUM OF FLUID-PRESSED STEEL; SIR W. G. ARMSTRONG, WHITWORTH, AND CO., LTD., MANCHESTER.

FIG. 133. LOW-PRESSURE ROTOR IN LATHE AT WALLSEND WORKS.

PLATE XXI.

THE TURBINE MACHINERY OF THE SHIP.

FIG. 134. ROTOR AND THRUST-SHAFT OF HIGH-PRESSURE TURBINE.

FIG. 135. BOTTOM HALF OF CASING OF LOW-PRESSURE TURBINE.

PLATE XXII.

THE TURBINE MACHINERY OF THE SHIP.

Fig. 140.   Part of Turbine-Casing in Circular Planing-Machine at the Wallsend Works.

Fig. 141.   Turbine-Blading at the Wallsend Works.

PLATE XXIII

THE TURBINE MACHINERY OF THE SHIP.

FIG. 142.   SEGMENTS OF LOW-PRESSURE ROTOR-BLADING.

FIG. 143.   COMPLETE RING OF LOW-PRESSURE ROTOR-BLADING.

PLATE XXIV.

THE TURBINE MACHINERY OF THE SHIP.

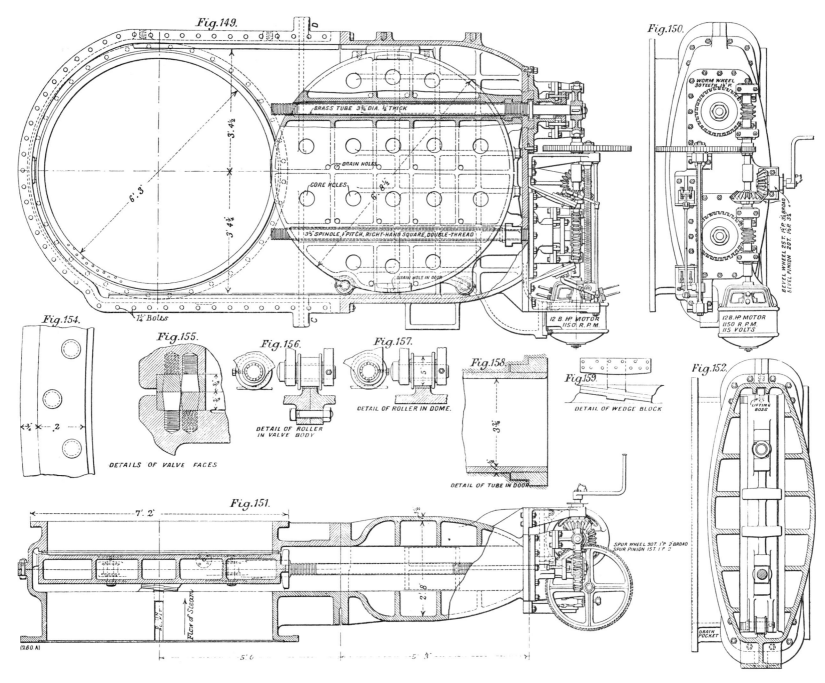

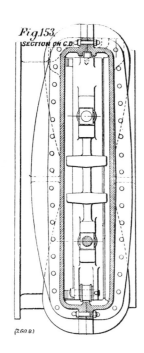

FIG. 160.

FIGS. 149 TO 160. 75-IN. SLUICE-VALVE, WITH OPERATING-GEAR.

PLATE XXV.

THE TURBINE MACHINERY OF THE SHIP.

Fig. 163. Exhaust-Bends of Low-Pressure Turbines.

Fig. 164. After-End of Top Half of Low-Pressure Turbine-Casing in Vertical and Horizontal Planer at the Wallsend Works.

PLATE XXVI.

THE TURBINE MACHINERY OF THE SHIP.

FIG. 166. END VIEW OF CONDENSER COMPLETED.

FIG. 165. CONDENSER SHELL, BUILT OF BOILER-PLATES AND ANGLE-BARS.

PLATE XXVII.

DETAILS OF BOILERS.

FIG. 171. REAR VIEW OF FIRE-BOXES, FURNACES, AND BOILER FRONT.

FIG. 170. VIEW SHOWING BOILER FRONT, WITH FURNACES.

PLATE XXVIII.

FUNNELS AND BOILERS.

FIG. 174. FUNNELS IN ERECTING-YARD AT THE WALLSEND WORKS.

FIG. 175. VIEW IN STOKEHOLD No. 3.

PLATE XXIX.

THE MACHINERY IN THE SHIP.

FIG. 180. SHAFT ALLEYWAY.

FIG. 179. STARTING-PLATFORM, LOOKING TOWARDS THE PORT SIDE.

PLATE XXX.

THE MACHINERY IN THE SHIP.

FIG. 181. VIEW IN THE TURBO GENERATOR ROOM.

FIG. 182. AFTER-END OF LOW-PRESSURE-TURBINE ROOM, LOOKING ATHWART THE SHIP.

PLATE XXXI.

THE MACHINERY IN THE SHIP.

FIG 183. VIEW AT TOP OF BOILERS.

FIG. 184. VIEW LOOKING UP THE ENGINE-ROOM HATCH.

PLATE XXXII.

THE MACHINERY IN THE SHIP.

FIG. 185. VIEW IN THE MAIN TURBINE-ROOM, LOOKING FORWARD.

FIG. 186. VIEW IN THE PUMPING-ENGINE ROOM.

QUADRUPLE-SCREW TURBINE-DRIVEN CUNARD LINER "MAURETANIA."

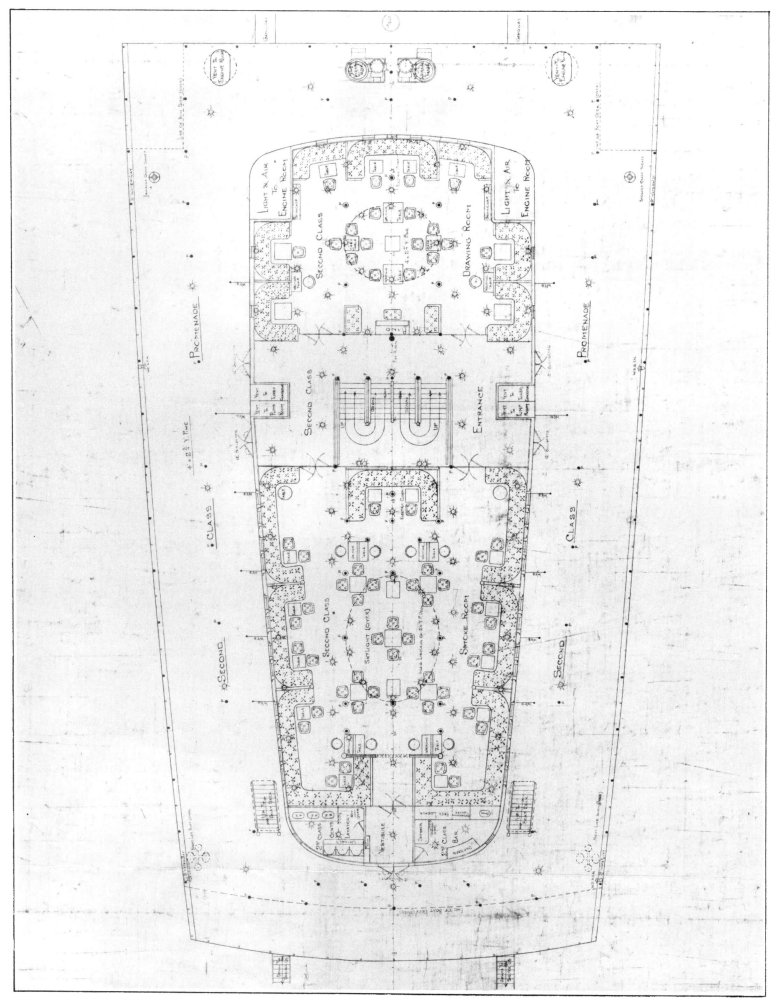

PLAN OF SECOND-CLASS SMOKE ROOM AND DRAWING ROOM
ON THE PROMENADE DECK

Fig. 13. General View of th

Fig. 14. Shipbuilding Berth, showing Construction of Double Bottom of the "Mauretania," looking Forward; November 26, 1904.

PLATE XXXIII.

S OF THE "MAURETANIA."

ARDSON, LIMITED, WALLSEND-ON-TYNE.

DING WORKS FROM THE RIVER TYNE.

FIG. 15. SHIPBUILDING BERTH, WITH THE "MAURETANIA" IN FRAME; FEBRUARY 23, 1905.

PLATE XXXIV.

THE QUADRUPLE-SCREW TURBINE-DRIVEN CUNARD LINER "MAURETANIA": ELEVATION AND DECK PLANS.

CONSTRUCTED BY MESSRS. SWAN, HUNTER, AND WIGHAM RICHARDSON, LTD., WALLSEND-ON-TYNE; ENGINED BY THE WALLSEND SLIPWAY AND ENGINEERING CO., LTD.

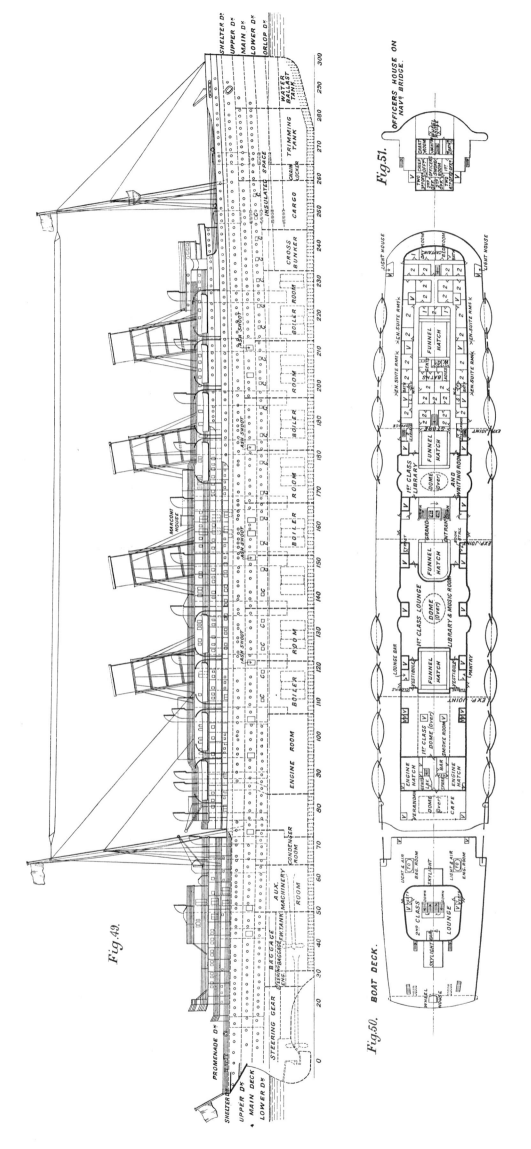

Fig. 49.

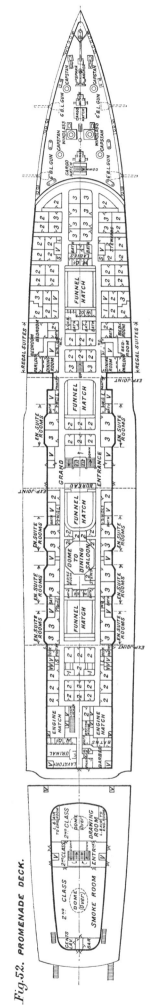

Fig. 50. BOAT DECK.

Fig. 51. OFFICERS' HOUSE ON NAVE BRIDGE.

Fig. 52. PROMENADE DECK.

Fig. 54. UPPER DECK.

Fig. 55. MAIN DECK.

Fig. 56. LOWER DECK.

Fig. 57. ORLOP DECK.

(233.c)

FIG. 106. GENERAL VIEW

FIG. 107. THE BOILERS OF THE "MAURETANIA" IN THE BOILER-ERECTING SHOP.

PLATE XXXV.

HE MACHINERY OF THE "MAURETANIA."

COMPANY, LIMITED, WALLSEND-ON-TYNE.

WORKS FROM THE RIVER TYNE.

FIG. 108. THE TURBINE-SHOP.

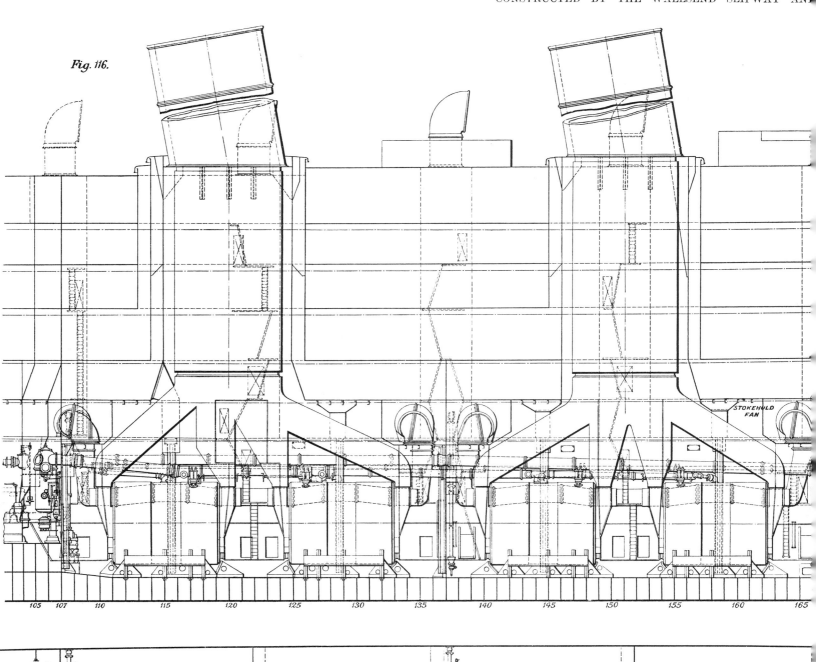

Fig. 116.

STOKEHOLD FAN

105 107 110 115 120 125 130 135 140 145 150 155 160 165

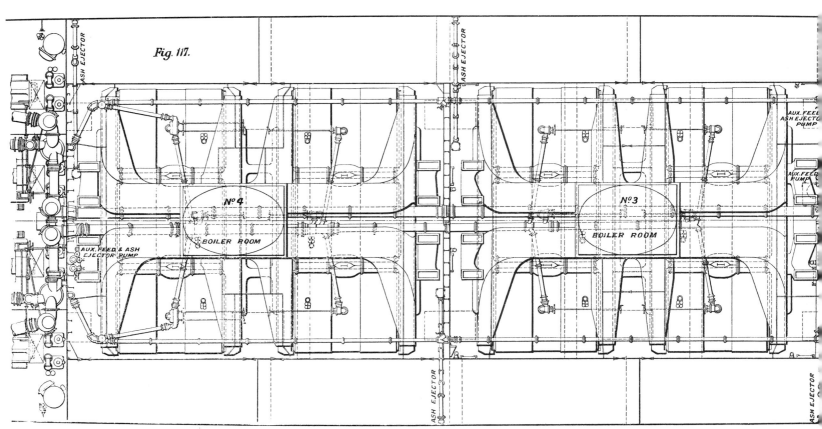

Fig. 117.

ASH EJECTOR

AUX. FEED
ASH EJECTOR
PUMP

AUX. FEED & ASH
EJECTOR PUMP

AUX. FEED &
ASH EJECTOR PUMP

N° 4
BOILER ROOM

N° 3
BOILER ROOM

ASH EJECTOR

ASH EJECTOR

ASH EJECTOR

PLATE XXXVI.

OILERS OF THE "MAURETANIA."

EERING COMPANY, LIMITED, WALLSEND-ON-TYNE.

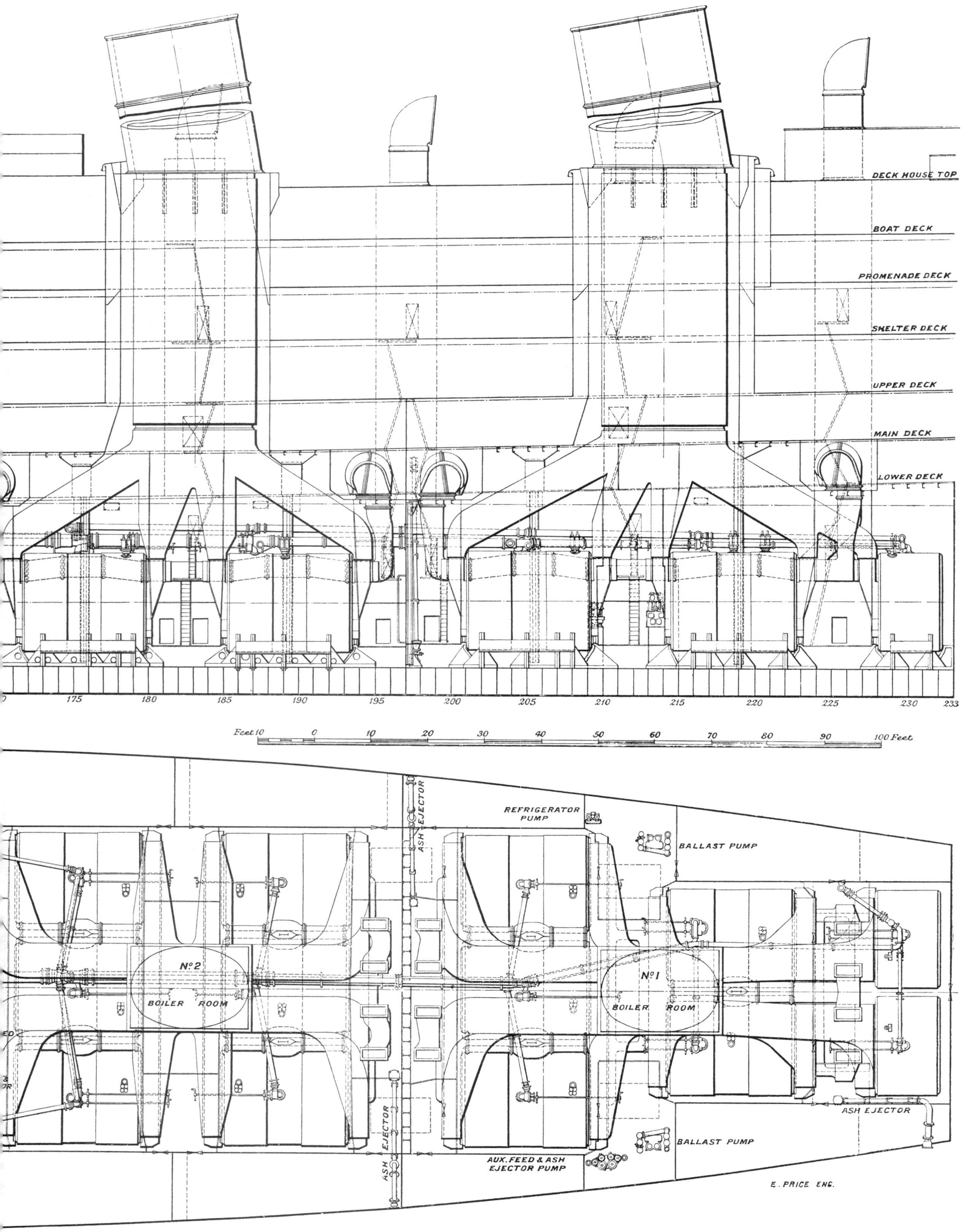

DECK HOUSE TOP

BOAT DECK

PROMENADE DECK

SHELTER DECK

UPPER DECK

MAIN DECK

LOWER DECK

175   180   185   190   195   200   205   210   215   220   225   230   233

Feet 10   0   10   20   30   40   50   60   70   80   90   100 Feet

REFRIGERATOR PUMP

BALLAST PUMP

ASH EJECTOR

N°2 BOILER ROOM

N°1 BOILER ROOM

ASH EJECTOR

AUX. FEED & ASH EJECTOR PUMP

BALLAST PUMP

ASH EJECTOR

E. PRICE ENG.

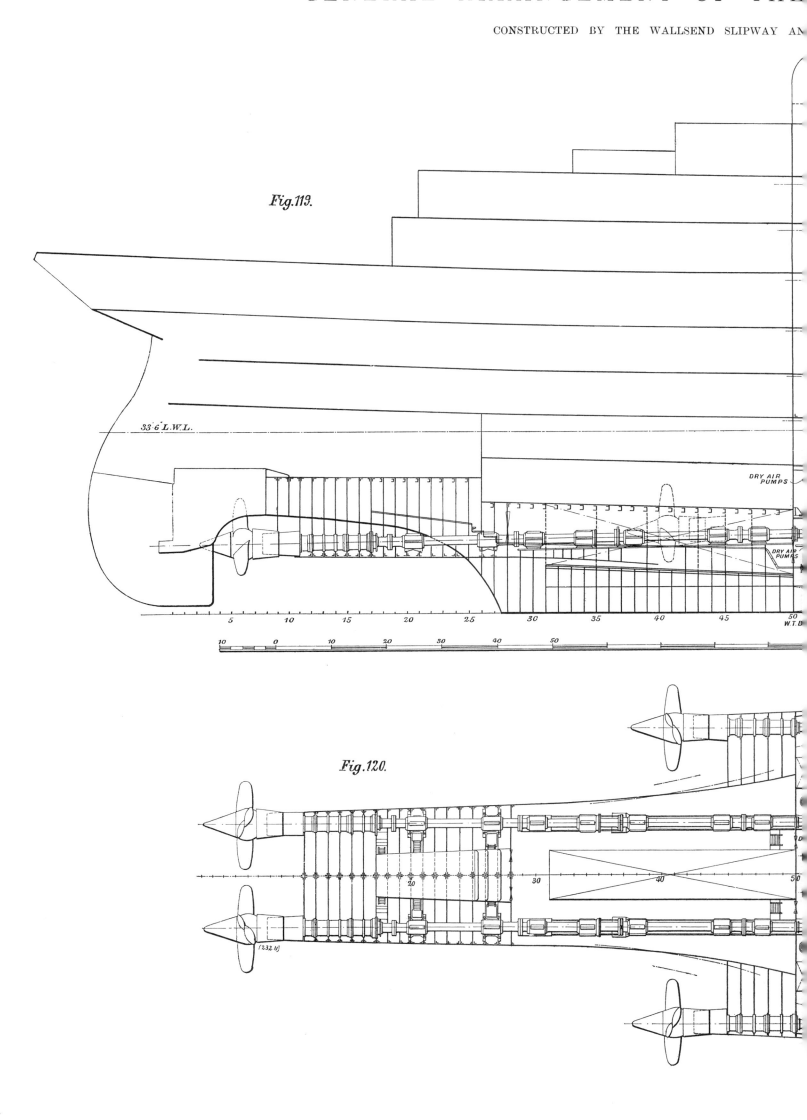

Fig.113.

33'6 L.W.L.

DRY AIR
PUMPS

DRY AIR
PUMPS

5   10   15   20   25   30   35   40   45   50
W.T.B

10   0   10   20   30   40   50

Fig.120.

[232.0]

PLATE XXXVII.

ACHINERY OF THE "MAURETANIA."

EERING COMPANY, LIMITED, WALLSEND-ON-TYNE.

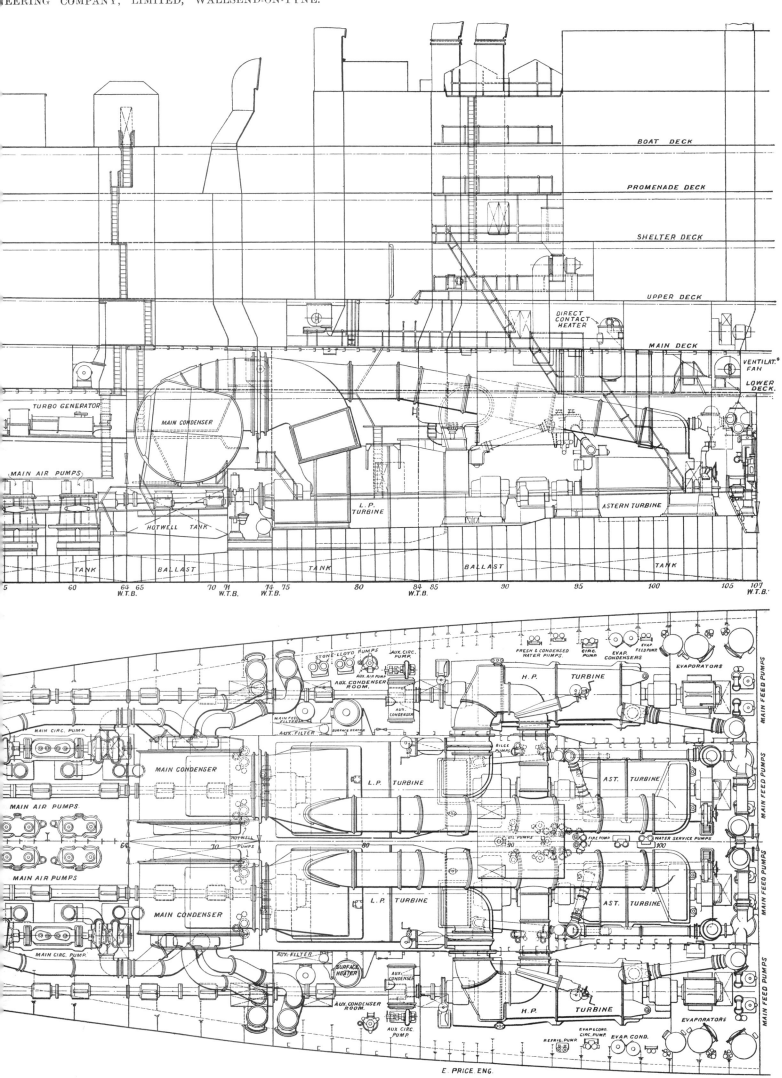

BOAT DECK

PROMENADE DECK

SHELTER DECK

UPPER DECK

DIRECT CONTACT HEATER

MAIN DECK

VENTILAT.G FAN

LOWER DECK.

TURBO GENERATOR

MAIN CONDENSER

MAIN AIR PUMPS

L. P. TURBINE

ASTERN TURBINE

HOTWELL TANK

TANK

BALLAST

TANK

BALLAST

TANK

5   60   64 65   70 71   74 75   80   84 85   90   95   100   105 107
       W.T.B.   W.T.B. W.T.B.   W.T.B.   W.T.B.

STONE-LLOYD PUMPS

AUX. CIRC. PUMP.

AUX. AIR PUMP

AUX. CONDENSER ROOM.

AUX. CONDENSER

FRESH & CONDENSED WATER PUMPS

CIRC. PUMP

EVAP. CONDENSERS

EVAP. FEED PUMP

EVAPORATORS

MAIN FEED PUMPS

H. P.   TURBINE

MAIN FEED FILTERS

MAIN CIRC. PUMP

AUX. FILTER

SURFACE HEATER

MAIN CONDENSER

BILGE PUMPS

MAIN FEED PUMPS

MAIN AIR PUMPS

L. P. TURBINE

AST. TURBINE

HOTWELL PUMPS

64   70   80   OIL PUMPS 90   FIRE PUMP WATER SERVICE PUMPS 100

MAIN FEED PUMPS

MAIN AIR PUMPS

L. P. TURBINE

AST. TURBINE

MAIN CIRC. PUMP

MAIN CONDENSER

AUX. FILTER

SURFACE HEATER

AUX. CONDENSER

AUX. CONDENSER ROOM.

AUX. CIRC. PUMP.

MAIN FEED PUMPS

H. P.   TURBINE

REFRIG. PUMP

EVAP.& COND. CIRC. PUMP.   EVAP. COND.

EVAPORATORS

E. PRICE ENG.

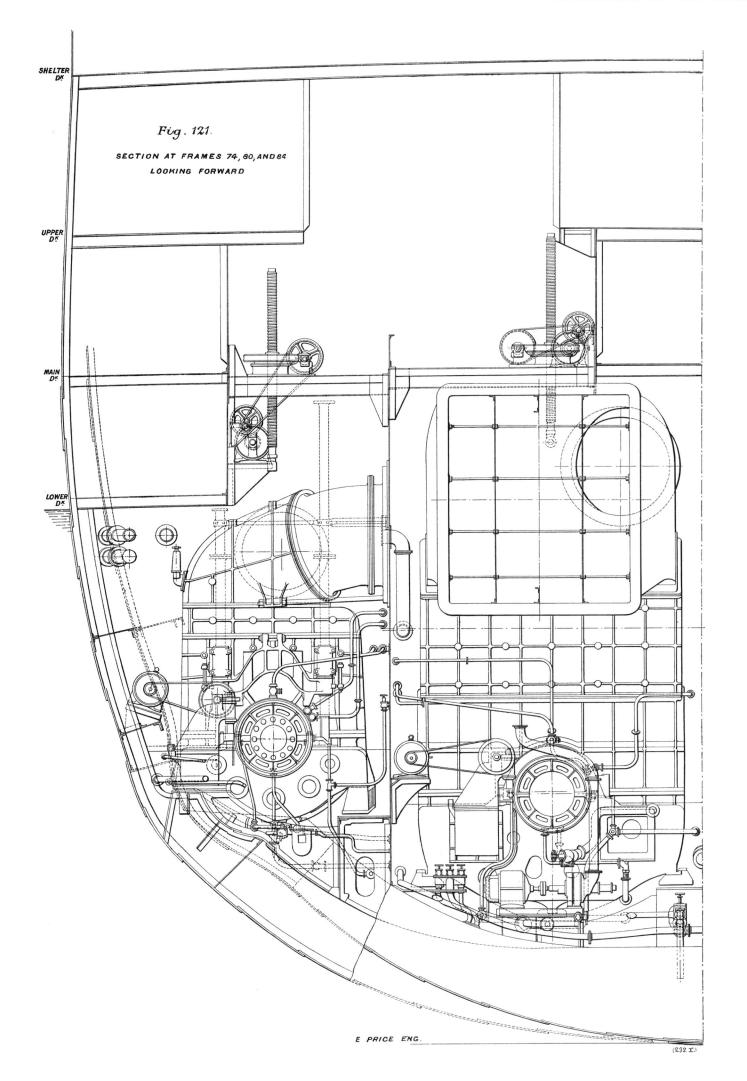

SHELTER Dᵏ

Fig. 121.

SECTION AT FRAMES 74, 80, AND 84
LOOKING FORWARD

UPPER Dᵏ

MAIN Dᵏ

LOWER Dᵏ

E PRICE ENG.

(292.X.)   (292.Y.)

PLATE XXXVIII.

CHINERY OF THE "MAURETANIA."

EERING COMPANY, LIMITED, WALLSEND-ON-TYNE.

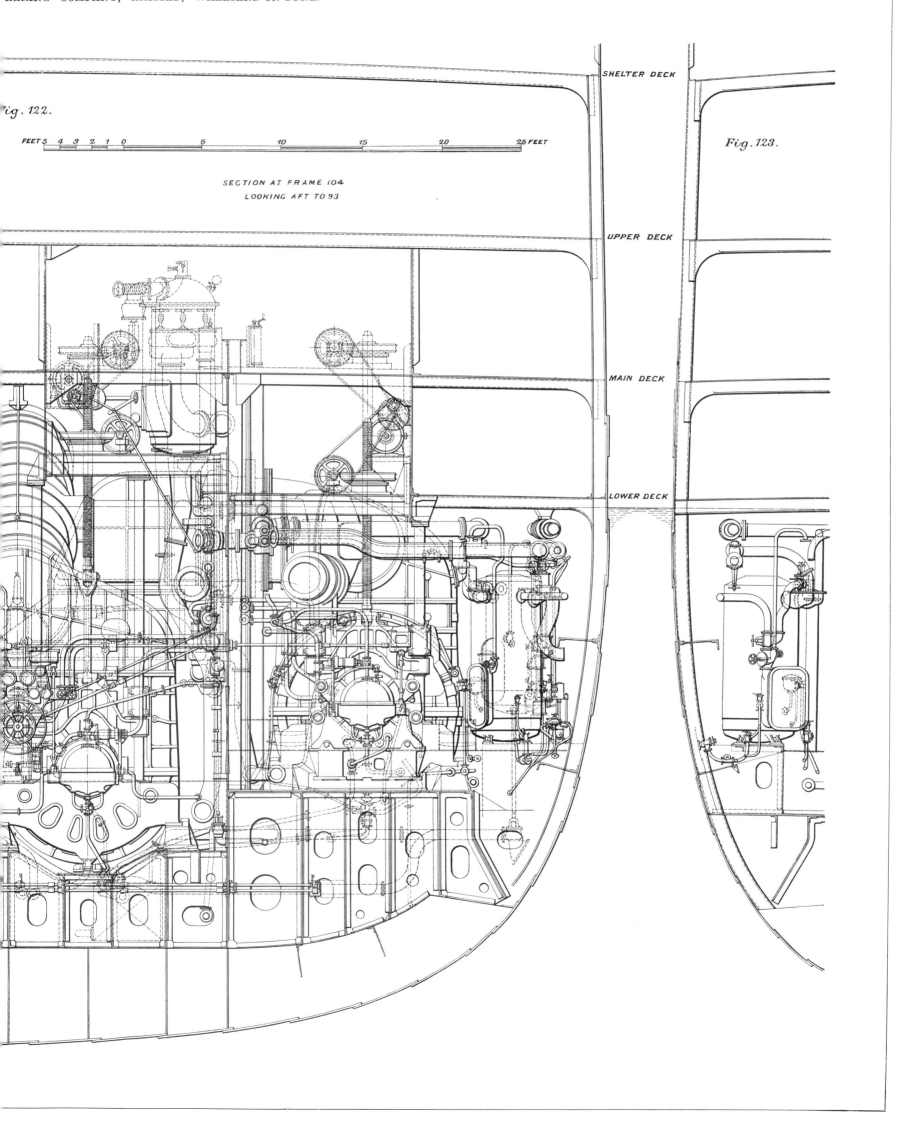

Fig. 122.

FEET 5 4 3 2 1 0   5   10   15   20   25 FEET

SECTION AT FRAME 104
LOOKING AFT TO 93

Fig. 123.

SHELTER DECK

UPPER DECK

MAIN DECK

LOWER DECK

PLATE XXXIX.

QUADRUPLE-SCREW TURBINE-DRIVEN CUNARD LINER "MAURETANIA."

FIG. 254. NAVIGATING HOUSE ON BRIDGE.

FIG. 255. BUREAU, PROMENADE DECK.

PLATE XXXX.

QUADRUPLE-SCREW TURBINE-DRIVEN CUNARD LINER "MAURETANIA."

FIG. 256. FIRST-CLASS LIFT, BOAT DECK.

FIG. 257. ENTRANCE HALL, BOAT DECK.

PLATE XXXXI.

QUADRUPLE-SCREW TURBINE-DRIVEN CUNARD LINER "MAURETANIA."

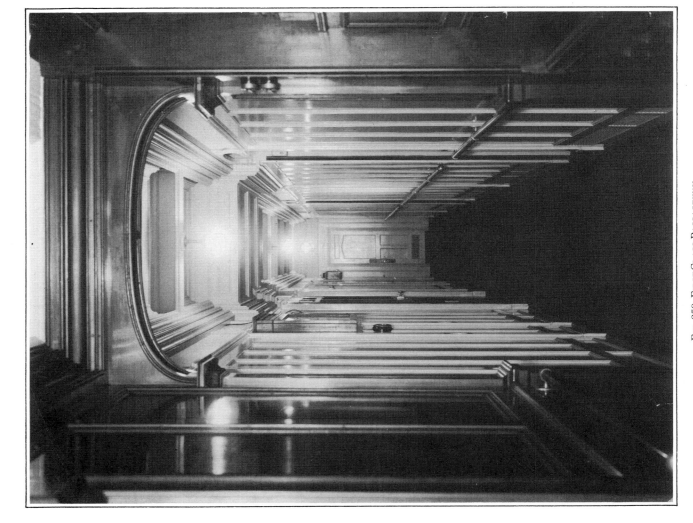

FIG. 259. FIRST-CLASS PASSAGEWAY.

FIG. 258. FIRST-CLASS PASSAGEWAY, BOAT DECK.

PLATE XXXXII.

QUADRUPLE-SCREW TURBINE-DRIVEN CUNARD LINER "MAURETANIA."

FIG. 261. THE LIBRARY AND WRITING-ROOM, LOOKING AFT, PORT SIDE.

FIG. 260. THE LOUNGE, OR MUSIC ROOM, LOOKING FORWARD, PORT SIDE.

PLATE XXXXIII.

QUADRUPLE-SCREW TURBINE-DRIVEN CUNARD LINER "MAURETANIA."

Fig. 262. The Lounge, or Music-Room Entrance, Looking Forward, Starboard Side.

View from Inside the Lounge.

PLATE XXXXIV.

QUADRUPLE-SCREW TURBINE-DRIVEN CUNARD LINER "MAURETANIA."

FIG. 263. THE LOUNGE, OR MUSIC ROOM, LOOKING FORWARD.

PLATE XXXXV.

QUADRUPLE-SCREW TURBINE-DRIVEN CUNARD LINER "MAURETANIA."

FIG. 264. THE LIBRARY AND WRITING-ROOM ENTRANCE, LOOKING AFT, PORT SIDE.

VIEW FROM INSIDE THE LIBRARY.

PLATE XXXXVI.

QUADRUPLE-SCREW TURBINE-DRIVEN CUNARD LINER "MAURETANIA."

FIG. 265. FIRST-CLASS LIBRARY AND WRITING-ROOM BOOKCASE.

FIG. 266. FIRST-CLASS LIBRARY AND WRITING-ROOM FIREPLACE.

PLATE XXXXVII.

QUADRUPLE-SCREW TURBINE-DRIVEN CUNARD LINER "MAURETANIA."

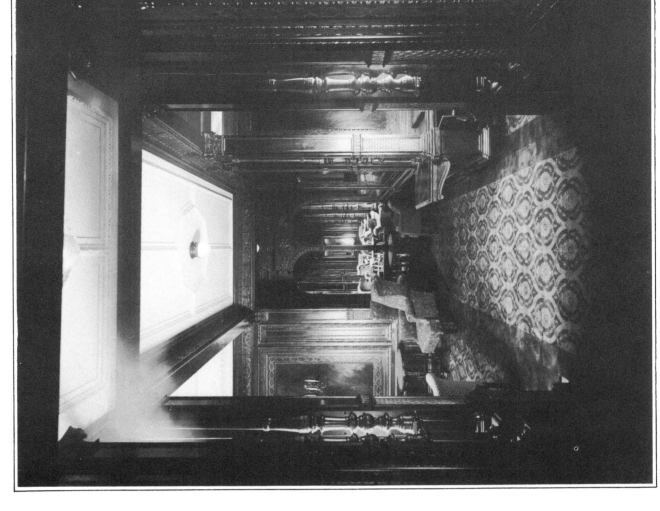

FIG. 268. FIRST-CLASS SMOKING-ROOM, PORT SIDE, LOOKING AFT.

FIG. 267. FIRST-CLASS SMOKING-ROOM FIREPLACE, FORWARD SECTION,

LOOKING FORWARD.

PLATE XXXXVIII.

QUADRUPLE-SCREW TURBINE-DRIVEN CUNARD LINER "MAURETANIA."

FIGS. 269. AND 270. FIRST-CLASS SMOKING-ROOM SITTING RECESSES.

PLATE XXXXIX.

QUADRUPLE-SCREW TURBINE-DRIVEN CUNARD LINER "MAURETANIA."

FIG. 271. REGAL SUITE PARLOUR ROOM, PORT SIDE.

FIG. 272. REGAL SUITE PARLOUR AND DINING ROOM, PORT SIDE.

PLATE L.

QUADRUPLE-SCREW TURBINE-DRIVEN CUNARD LINER "MAURETANIA."

Fig. 273. Parlour of *En Suite* Room, Promenade Deck.

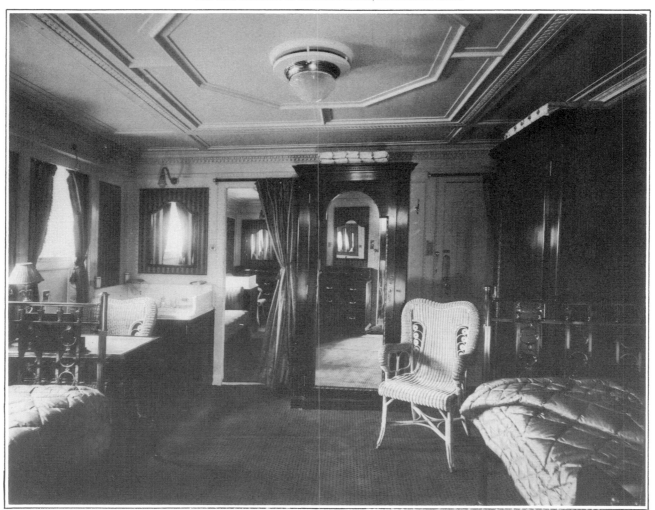

Fig. 274. Regal Suite Bedrooms, Starboard Side, Looking Aft.

PLATE LI.

QUADRUPLE-SCREW TURBINE-DRIVEN CUNARD LINER "MAURETANIA."

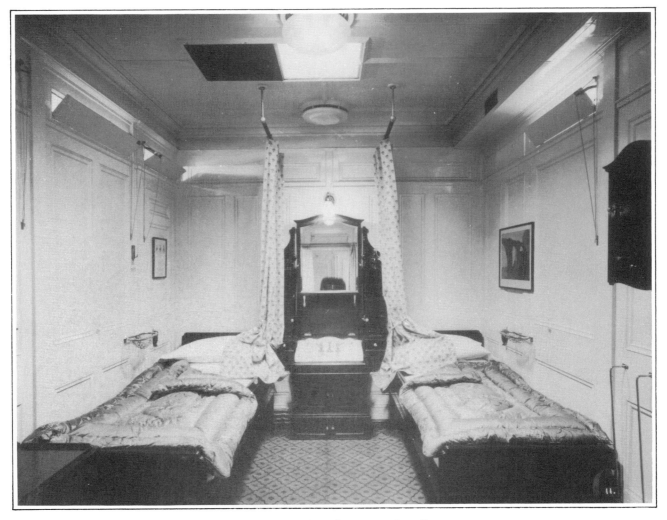

Fig. 275. First-Class Stateroom, Boat Deck.

Fig. 276. Regal Suite Bedroom, Port Side, Looking Aft.

PLATE LII

QUADRUPLE-SCREW TURBINE-DRIVEN CUNARD LINER "MAURETANIA."

FIGS. 277. AND 278. FIRST-CLASS SPECIAL STATEROOMS.

PLATE LIII.

QUADRUPLE-SCREW TURBINE-DRIVEN CUNARD LINER "MAURETANIA."

FIG. 279. *EN SUITE* STATEROOM, BOAT DECK.

PLATE LIV.

QUADRUPLE-SCREW TURBINE-DRIVEN CUNARD LINER "MAURETANIA."

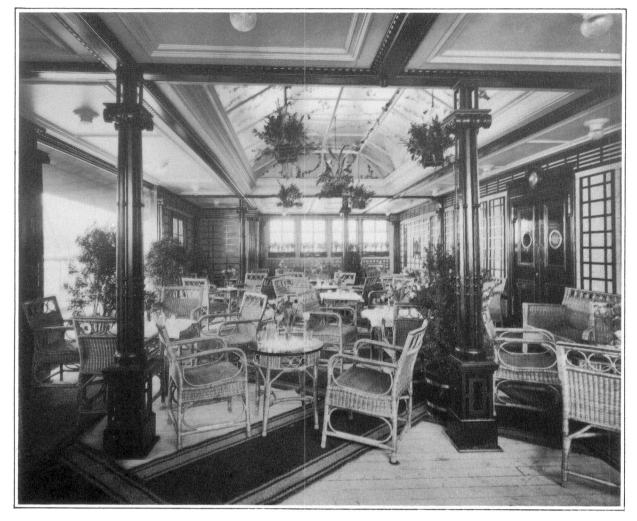

FIG. 280. VERANDAH CAFÉ.

FIG. 281. *EN SUITE* STATEROOM, BOAT DECK.

PLATE LV.

QUADRUPLE-SCREW TURBINE-DRIVEN CUNARD LINER "MAURETANIA."

FIG. 282. LOWER FIRST-CLASS DINING SALOON BUFFET WALL, UPPER DECK.

FIG. 283. LOWER FIRST-CLASS DINING SALOON WALL, UPPER DECK.

PLATE LVI.

QUADRUPLE-SCREW TURBINE-DRIVEN CUNARD LINER "MAURETANIA."

Fig. 284. One of the First-Class Pantries.

Fig. 285. First-Class Kitchen.

PLATE LVII

QUADRUPLE-SCREW TURBINE-DRIVEN CUNARD LINER "MAURETANIA."

FIG. 286. FIRST-CLASS CHILDREN'S ROOM.

FIG. 287. SECOND-CLASS LOUNGE.

PLATE LVIII.

QUADRUPLE-SCREW TURBINE-DRIVEN CUNARD LINER "MAURETANIA."

FIG. 288. SECOND-CLASS DINING SALOON.

FIG. 289. THIRD-CLASS DINING SALOON.

PLATE LIX.

TELEGRAPHIC ADDRESS:
"WHEELRACE, LONDON."

TELEPHONE 2823 GERRARD,
AND 696 WESTMINSTER.

· ALBEMARLE · ST.
· LONDON · W ·

S.S. MAURETANIA

LOUNGE AND LIBRARY

DECORATED AND FURNISHED

BY

MELLIER.

PLATE LX.

S.S. "MAURETANIA"
Decoration and Furniture
BY
W. Turner LORD & Co..
MOUNT STREET,
LONDON, W.

Telephone: 5273 GERRARD.

Telegrams: "LORDOSIS, LONDON."

SMOKING ROOM.

DINING SALOON.   RESTAURANT.

GRAND ENTRANCES.   STAIRCASE AND GRILLE.

2 REGAL SUITES.   52 STATE ROOMS.

PLATE LXI.

QUADRUPLE-SCREW TURBINE-DRIVEN CUNARD LINER "MAURETANIA."

FIG. 290. UNDER FULL STEAM ON HER TRIALS.